10.17

D1237048

The Triumph of Patience

Pacientia, engraving by Hans Sebald Beham (1540). Courtesy of the
Rosenwald Collection, National Gallery of Art, Washington.

The Triumph of Patience

Medieval and Renaissance Studies

edited by

GERALD J. SCHIFFHORST

A Florida Technological University Book

University Presses of Florida

Orlando / 1978

University Presses of Florida is the
scholarly publishing agency for the State
University System of Florida.

Library of Congress Cataloging in Publication Data
Main entry under title:

The Triumph of Patience.

"A Florida Technological University book."
Bibliography: p.
1. Patience—Addresses, essays, lectures.
2. Patience in literature—Addresses, essays, lectures.
3. Patience (Middle English poem)—Addresses, essays,
lectures. I. Schiffhorst, Gerald J.
BJ1533.P3T74   241'.4   77-12732
ISBN O-8130-0590-6

To my mother
and the memory of my father

Love is patient. . . . There is no
limit to love's forbearance, to its
trust, its hope, its power to
endure.

I Corinthians 13:4. 7

Acknowledgments

As many parts of this volume attest, I am inestimably indebted both to William S. Heckscher, who has very generously aided my investigation of patience, and to one of his former graduate students at Duke University, Priscilla Tate. I am also grateful to John M. Steadman of the Henry E. Huntington Library, Siegfried Wenzel of the University of Pennsylvania, and Lawrence J. Ross of Washington University for numerous suggestions and insights. To those who first introduced me to Renaissance studies at St. Louis University—Walter J. Ong, S.J., William C. McAvoy, and Clarence H. Miller—I shall always be indebted.

A National Endowment for the Humanities fellowship, administered by the Southeastern Institute of Medieval and Renaissance Studies, and two research grants from Florida Technological University made much of my research possible. I have benefited from the library resources of Duke University, the University of North Carolina at Chapel Hill, the University of South Florida, the Newberry Library, the Folger Shakespeare Library, the New York Public Library, and the Henry E. Huntington Library, where Noelle Jackson and Stanford E. Bergstrom provided special courtesies. At the Florida Technological University Library, the assistance of Laurie S. Hodge and her associates in the reference department has been invaluable. My colleagues Roland A. Browne, Richard S. Grove, and Stuart

E. Omans have been supportive in numerous ways. Finally, and most importantly, my collaborators made possible the Modern Language Association comparative literature seminar which resulted in this collection of essays—the product of their imagination, industry, and patience.

Gerald J. Schiffhorst

Preface

This book represents an initial step in assembling materials for the study of patience as it relates to medieval and Renaissance thought and expression. Though various scholars have cited the importance of patience in the work of Langland, Shakespeare, Milton, and others, this virtue has rarely, if ever, been isolated for study; and little has been done to collect those sources which, from Cicero onward, have played a major role in the conception of the virtues of resistance and endurance, of passivity and activity, in both visual and literary works. Because of its link with secular virtues such as fortitude, patience through the ages has psychological and sociological overtones as well as a fundamental philosophical bearing on the epic, tragedy, poetic imagery, and iconography (among others) which demand the attention of scholars in various disciplines. The vastness of the topic and its interdisciplinary nature are represented in the divergent approaches represented here.

Each of the essays helps to define patience in terms of one of its varied manifestations in medieval and Renaissance times. Collectively, the essays not only reveal the pervasiveness of the virtue among English writers as well as artists in the age of mannerism, but also indicate the long, distinguished, and multifarious tradition of patience discussions among thinkers in various literatures. The contributors indicate how this virtue signified a more positive and complex response to life than the mere endurance of afflictions with the meek, passive submission branded as "womanish" by Cassius in *Julius Caesar* (I.iii.84). Because of its inseparability from hope, constancy, and temperance, its supernatural meaning as heroic, redemptive suffering, and its implied meanings of calm expectation and self-assured maturity, patience is seen as the ideally balanced emotional and spiritual strength of those who can profit from afflictions and can thus be affirmatively reconciled to the personal, social, moral, or religious values of perseverance. To accept suffering and loss, we see in *King Lear*, implies the fundamental capacity to grow in self-knowledge; understanding how to endure pain is an essential part of being human. These manifold implications of patience for Tudor-Stuart literature alone are extensive and important, especially when seen in the context of medieval and Renaissance expression as a whole. *The Triumph of Patience* is an attempt to discuss some of these implications.

The volume had its genesis at Duke University, where, as a postdoctoral fellow, I began to study emblematic and doctrinal renderings of patience with William S. Hecksher. He later suggested that a symposium, bringing together interrelated literary, theological, and iconographic approaches to the topic, would make a valuable contribution to humanistic studies. Such a seminar was held as part of the national Modern Language Association Convention in San Francisco on December 28, 1975. Abbreviated versions of several of the essays here were part of that seminar. These include the essay by Ralph Hanna III of the University of California at Riverside, whose important discussion of medieval theological definitions of patience reveals, among other things, the nature of patient action and the distinction between patience and endurance. Elizabeth D. Kirk of Brown University, concerned with the transformations which the idea of patience undergoes in the B-text of *Piers Plowman* and in the Middle English poem *Patience*, demonstrates how the two medieval poets build a cumulative definition of the term into the structure of their works. Albert C. Labriola of Duquesne University uses biblical typology to show how patience as suffering indicates the centrality of Christ's role in *Paradise Lost*. Priscilla L. Tate of Columbia University, in her study of the allegorical engravings which provide the title for this volume, affirms that, for Renaissance man, patience was the virtue which enabled princes to endure nobly: it is dominant in the art and literature of the time because it closely links political and theological ideas.

I am grateful to these scholars for allowing my initial undertaking—a brief study in Renaissance attributes—to become a fuller excursion into cultural history and a more properly inclusive examination of the major features of patience, which is, as Professor Hanna aptly says, a virtue for all occasions. Though the book constitutes the first such interdisciplinary study of the subject, it is necessarily limited and selective. The relationship between patience and fortune and the notion of patience in classical thought are but two areas which require further elaboration. But it is hoped that our varied, discrete approaches to the subject may suggest directions for other studies. If so, this collection will have served a valuable purpose.

Since a full discussion of the virtue of patience in English Renaissance literature—even if limited to Elizabethan religious works—would require a separate book, I have for the most part confined my investigation to those major works likely to be available in England during the Tudor and Stuart periods, roughly from 1480 to 1680. One result is my selectively annotated inventory of sources, too incomplete to be called a critical bibliography; it is hoped that additions can be made in future works and by others. I have provided annotation only where I thought it appropriate, focusing on the representative works and avoiding the repetition of issues cited in the initial essay.

My introductory essay is intended to offer some typical Renaissance definitions of patience and thereby to suggest the direction for further examinations of Shakespearean and other related loci. This survey of emblematic renderings of patience as well as certain homiletic and doctrinal works on the subject in English demonstrates, as does the work of my collaborators, that patience was variously and extensively treated in medieval and Renaissance times as a virtue of singular importance. From such a seemingly limited perspective on the culture of the past, it is possible to discern a rich, revealing cross-section of that culture and its intellectual background.

Gerald J. Schiffhorst

Illustrations

Contents

Yield not thy neck
To Fortune's yoke, but let thy dauntless mind
Still ride in triumph over all mischance.

Shakespeare, *III Henry VI*, III.iii.16–18

Some Prolegomena for the Study of Patience, 1480 — 1680

GERALD J. SCHIFFHORST

 principal aim of literary scholarship is to provide sufficient background on the controlling ideas of an earlier period so that its students can properly understand the assumptions which an artist might presuppose his audience to have shared. One such key idea which enjoyed prominence in the Renaissance is the importance of patience as an essential virtue in the scheme of Christian salvation. This notion had long been treated by writers, theologians, and artists, but the humanists' interest in reinterpreting Seneca, Cicero, and other Stoic writers brought it to new attention. Its full meaning, however—in the work of Shakespeare, Spenser, or Milton, for example—is often lost on the twentieth-century reader unaware of the specific religious force which the word once had. For instance, behind Milton's definition of "patience as the truest fortitude" (*Samson Agonistes*, line 654), there lies a rich tradition of iconography, theology, and religious commentary which is seldom studied.[1] Yet, since our understanding of man's tragic fate in *King Lear* or of *Hamlet* as a revenge tragedy depends in large measure on conventional notions of patience, and since Milton's *Paradise Lost* defines Adam's accep-

1

tance of evil in terms of patience, it would seem obvious that this virtue should be defined and examined as it was understood in the Tudor and Stuart periods.

This essay is a step toward that end. It is not an investigation of sources for poetic imagery, though many illuminating analogues will be apparent. It is, rather, a brief examination of certain emblematic conceptions of patience, generally current in England between 1480 and 1680, and a survey of representative definitions of the virtue provided by selected English homiletic and other religious tracts.

I

The concept of Christian patience, as it was understood in the Renaissance, had its origins in biblical, classical, patristic, and medieval writings, only a few of which can be mentioned here. Along with its closely related virtues—especially constancy, hope, and fortitude—it is a homiletic theme and iconographic attribute, used so widely by artists, poets, and theologians as to be commonplace. The definitions cited in the *Oxford English Dictionary* (VII:555) conveniently summarize some of the most common meanings of the virtue, then as now: "The suffering or enduring (of pain, trouble, or evil) with calmness and composure . . . forbearance, long-suffering, longanimity under provocation of any kind; the calm abiding of the issue of time, processes, etc.; quiet and self-possessed waiting for something; constancy in labor, exertion, or effort; the fact or capacity of enduring." Moreover, it came to mean something other than Stoic fortitude or passive endurance; it was seen as an active virtue and a positive response to God's will in time of suffering.

Though not one of the traditional seven cardinal virtues, patience is often singled out as a principal virtue for man or is implicitly included as an aspect of fortitude.[2] An example of the importance of patience is Peter Brueghel the Elder's use of it as the transitional allegory separating his drawings of the Seven Deadly Sins from those of the Seven Virtues.[3] And Patience leads a triumph of seven other personifications of the virtue in Maarten van Heemskerck's elaborate series of engravings (by Coornhert), *Patientiae Triumphus* (c. 1555); see Figure 5. This is an interesting variation on the theme of Patience led by Job, which had much earlier become part of the concept of the triumph of virtue.[4]

An early definition of Christian patience frequently encountered in subsequent centuries is provided by Cyprian of Antioch's sermon *De Bono Patientiae* (A.D. 356), which had some influence on Augustine's later treatise.[5] Like Tertullian before him, Cyprian first distinguishes the virtue from the pagan concept of patience—true Christian patience is God-like because it follows the example of Christ—and he urges his readers to practice it throughout their lives. He emphasizes the universality of this virtue, upon which every other virtue relies; charity without patience, he says, will not last. Patience is thus central to Cyprian's concept of Christianity.[6] Its origin and greatness are in God, whose patience is essential to His perfection. After citing the heroic patience of Isaac, Jacob, Moses, and David, among others, he asserts that we need patience to bear the assaults of the devil and to persevere in our faith. Job and Tobias show us that true patience is a mark of the just, whereas Adam, Cain, and Esau are examples of *Ira*, that rash, impatient anger of the vengeful man who slanders the just will of God.

The conflict between Patience and Wrath is dramatized in the *Psychomachia* of Prudentius, who was influential in the allegorization of the virtues and vices as well as in the traditional personification of most virtues as females. His late-fourth-century Christian poem developed Roman tendencies to personify abstract ideas and, more significantly, influenced the medieval allegories of virtues and vices in art and literature.[7] His treatment of the war between *Patientia* and *Ira* (lines 109–47), as translated by Thomson, depicts "mild Long-Suffering" with "staid countenance unmoved in her struggle with Wrath." She "abides undisturbed, bravely facing all the hail of weapons and keeping a front that none can pierce."[8] No virtue enters this struggle without the aid of Patience, Prudentius tells us, for her strength upholds every other virtue.[9]

Such early Christian writers, of course, like their medieval and Renaissance successors, would have found countless references to forbearance, long-suffering, endurance, hope, and patience itself in the scriptures as well as in the Latin poets.[10] In Matt. 10:22 we read, "He that endureth to the end shall be saved," and Luke 21:19 is often quoted: "By your patience you shall possess your souls." The admonition to wait with hope is found in Job 14:14 and Psalms 69:3, among many others. "I waited patiently for the Lord," states Psalms 40:1; and Lam. 3:26 says that a man should both hope and quietly wait. That patience has a sacrificial power to transform evil is often apparent in the Old Testament, even when the word itself does not appear in the text. In Exod. 34:6 and Num. 14:18, patience becomes much more than the long-suffering trials of Job: it is God's own character which, in turn, is the source of human patience. The term implies not only physical and spiritual endurance but an expectation for someone to help or for something to happen.[11]

A similarly wide range of meaning is evident in the New Testament, where the Greek υπομονη (Heb. 12:1) can be variously translated.[12] Patience occurs more frequently in the New Testament, almost always in connection with the Second Coming. In the Apocalypse (especially 1:9, 2:3, 2:19, 3:10), the word is often repeated, and John advises that the churches have patiently suffered, as Christ had suffered, because of His coming again. In Rom. 15:5 the patience of God is cited along with the idea that human endurance is more than expectation: it is part of a fabric of virtues which leads to faith in the love of God. Therefore, Patience's central role in the allegorical portrayals of virtues in works by Brueghel, van Heemskerck, and others should not be too surprising. For the latter artist, the triumph of Patience leads to a fulfillment in Christ (see I Thess. 3:5). So, too, Christian patience may be seen in the scriptural, hagiographic, and patristic traditions familiar to Renaissance artists as more than passive acquiescence in the face of temporal evils. It is, rather, a lively, active, energetic power of faith (Rev. 12:12) perfected in Christ and is thus constantly merging into hope and faith in the Son of God at the end of time. The entire Epistle of James concerns the theme of endurance, with 5:7–11 specifically concerned with patience. Here we read that the farmer (often cited by emblematists) as well as Job and the prophets (as in van Heemskerck) should be models for our patient expectation of the Lord.

As for medieval treatments of patience, a separate treatise would have to be written, comparable in scope to Siegfried Wenzel's study of sloth.[13] It should suffice here to note only the most famous of Middle English poems on the subject, *Patience*, by the *Pearl* poet (fl. 1360–90).[14] Instead of employing the more obvious story of Job, the poet has imaginatively used the Jonah story (translated from the Vulgate with some additions) as a negative exemplum and image of patience under adversity. The conclusion asserts that man should be steadfast and patient in both pain and joy, for complaining only intensifies, never relieves, pain. Yet Jonah himself seems chiefly conceived as an embodiment of humility, of which patience and poverty are constituent parts. The homiletic narrator of this alliterative poem links the first and last of the Beatitudes: patience and poverty, he asserts, are of one nature (prologue, line 4). It is clear from the early part of the poem that patience is regarded, as it was generally in the Middle Ages, to be a chief virtue for the poor. Patience ("suffraunce"), says the narrator, also assuages those who have been scorned, quells evils, and quenches malice; it cannot remove the ills of the world, but it can allow man to endure them—indeed, endurance is the most he can hope for. The poem's opening asserts:

Patience has its good points, though not often pleasant.
When heavy hearts are hurt by something hateful
long-suffering may cure them and cool them off,
for she quells every evil and quenches malice. (lines 1–4)

In commenting on the poem, Margaret Williams observes that *patience* in a medieval context meant more than sitting still and waiting. "It was cognate with 'passion,' the act of suffering, undergoing, submitting as patient to agent, being passive under action. It involved humility and obedience, an acceptance of the right order of things, especially the right order between creature and creator. . . ."[15]

Especially apposite to the study of patience in the Renaissance are works such as Domenico Nani Mirabellio's *Polyanthea*, an exhaustive sixteenth-century index of abstract concepts, which suggests the wealth of material on patience inherited from the Middle Ages and the classical past.[16] After some definitions, an etymology, biblical quotations, citations from the Fathers, Latin poets, Boethius, and many others, there is a hieroglyphic reference, quoted from Valeriano,[17] followed by a cross-reference to *fortitudo* and *perseverentia*, under which headings we are led to *tolerantia, fiducia, spes*, and *constantia*, among others.[18] It is evident here, as elsewhere, that patience is easily associated with, and often indistinguishable from, its sister virtues and can thereby be enriched as a source for writers and artists. Moreover, the Renaissance concern with mythography evident in such an encyclopedic lexicon suggests that emblems, impresas, allegorical prints, and hieroglyphs were seen by Renaissance commentators as containing a kind of knowledge which could not be found in discourse.[19] Before considering some of these visual images of patience, however, we should first examine certain definitions of the virtue (as found in representative Tudor-Stuart writings) and its attainment of new prominence in the sixteenth century.

II

As we have seen, patience means (among other things) to bear trouble bravely and calmly, without perturbation, for God's sake. John Florio's *A Worlde of Wordes . . .* , an Italian-English dictionary (1598), provides some useful Renaissance definitions of patience: "suffrance, endurance, 'forbearing, constancie in abiding evil, aptness to suffer or abide." He also cites subjection and obedience and says that the patient man is "one that can suffer, endure, abide, sustaine, tollerate or beare"

(p. 262).[20] For Renaissance man, Priscilla Tate says, it could also signify that virtue which enables princes to endure nobly.[21] As Shakespeare's *Henry IV* plays reveal, the true prince must learn to forbear, trust, and wait, achieving his identity by learning to curb the self and the appetites. Patience is thus associated both with expectation and with temperance, which also has as its antithesis impatient wrath and grief. Along with tranquillity and other Stoic virtues, patience is a dominant theme in sixteenth- and seventeenth-century art and literature because it so closely links political and theological ideals.

If we focus on certain typical homilies, exegetical tracts, and other religious treatises in the Tudor-Stuart period, we will see some important variations on the meaning of patience. It is not surprising for that era of religious turmoil to find patience often discussed and defined, specifically as the chief virtue enabling man to maintain faith in God's goodness and obedience to His law of love. Thomas Wilson's *Christian Dictionary* (1612) provides the following definition: "it is that gift of God, which enableth the Christian soule to endure crosses, quietly, and with ready submission to the will of God, because it is his pleasure to have it so, for our tryall, or chastisement; and for the manifestation of his own power and goodnesse, to the praise of his glory; and finally, for a testimony against those that do trouble and vex his children" (pp. 352–53). William Jeffray, in *The Picture of Patience* (1629), tells us that, for Augustine, patience is a religious man's grateful undergoing of all troubles and labors for the love of God and for the much-desired reward of eternal bliss. For Gregory the Great, it is to endure mischief from other men and not to be moved to anger. Finally, patience is a virtue which enables one to bear all infirmity and adversity that can betide him with an undaunted and constant resolution for God's sake; this last definition, says Jeffray, is the best (p. 8).

According to Miles Coverdale, whose "A Spiritual and Most Precious Pearl" (1550) is representative of Elizabethan treatises on patience, this virtue ("the most necessary of all the virtues" [p. 169]) represents faith withstanding the apparent contradictions of reality; it is charity withstanding the temptations of both affliction and prosperity; it is the will holding on through faith to a belief that life has meaning in spite of appearances. For the Elizabethan, patience clearly denoted what one displays when he submits himself to God's will amid the fortunes and (especially) the misfortunes of life. Many Elizabethan theologians assert that, though the will of God is the primary cause of all human events, man is nevertheless responsible for working out his own salvation. And the virtue most capable of meeting this responsibility is patience. Even the Boethian tradition reminds man to concentrate on that virtue which Fortune and mutability cannot impair. The faithful Christian achieves such virtue by remembering that he is not governed by Fortune but Providence and by maintaining that faith in God which allows him to remain in patience. Coverdale says that "to bear and forbear" earthly and spiritual fruits is a token of wisdom and is profitable in the lengthening of one's life.[22] For Nicholas Breton, it is the means of dramatizing the qualities of the Christian soldier and servant.[23]

As the Book of Common Prayer and other works reveal, the Christian should always hope for a happy resolution of his afflictions. Such a viewpoint is in sharp contrast to that of the Stoics, who nevertheless have an important bearing on our understanding of Christian patience. Stoic patience, which humanists in the sixteenth century saw as a valuable supplement to Christian precepts, is generally defined as a controlled, unemotional indifference to the adversities of life, with a contempt for worldly goods (but not for virtue). It is a state of perpetual calm and wise passivity.[24] The Stoic ideal of fortitude in adversity gained popularity in the Renaissance, as numerous treatises on the subject indicate; the pagan capability for virtue is admired along with a regret that Christians are often less capable. But, together with the mildness and gentleness advocated by Marcus Aurelius, Seneca, and others, Christian patience emphasizes charity, forgiveness, meekness, and humility—a quality which, in contrast to the pagan view, recognizes the weakness of the human reason and will when unsupported by divine strength.[25] Precise distinctions between Christian and Stoic teachings, however, were largely unsuccessful among philosophers as well as poets of the time. Though Justus Lipsius saw that Stoic indifference precludes Christian hope, he and Erasmus, Elyot, Du Vair, and others were generally unclear in drawing distinctions between the cold, proud, defiant patience of the ancients and the humble, ardent, submissive Christian virtue. One reason may have been the influence of a third factor: the Aristotelian concept of honor, by which one is not subject to passions but which might include anger as a justifiable part of active virtue (in Spenser, for example). Thus the Christian concept of patience could be set aside by a civil or social law which assumed that might makes right.

Peter de la Primaudaye's definition of true patience as "a voluntary and continual suffering for the love of honesty and virtue"[26] implies an awareness of false patience, which does not allow for cheerful suffering, lowliness of mind, or voluntary endurance of hardship because of the pride associated with Stoic virtue. The variety of terms and the liberties taken in defining virtues closely associated with patience among Renaissance humanists

can be seen by comparing De la Primaudaye's concept of perseverance as a
"perpetual constancie . . . undertaken with consideration following
reason" with definitions of sufferance and continuance by Thomas Wilson
in *The Arte of Rhetorique*.[27] It is not surprising that Shakespeare, for
example, does not follow a consistently "orthodox" doctrine of patience.
From Shylock's "patient shrug" and "suff'rance" (*The Merchant of Venice*,
I.iii.106–7) to *Hamlet*'s "patient as a female dove" (V.i.286), where the
word signifies calm dispassion rather than quiet perseverance, to the
redemptive long-suffering of later (characteristically female) characters
(including Cordelia, Desdemona, and Marina), we find various degrees of
Stoic virtue, Christian fortitude, and heroic honor. When Shakespeare's
Queen Elizabeth speaks of enduring with hope, overcoming despair, and
"bearing with mildness . . . misfortune's cross" (*III Henry VI*, IV.iv.
19–20), she refers to bridling "passion" in such a way as to suggest both
patience and temperance. That these two virtues also are naturally linked
can be seen in Spenser's concept of self-mastery (*The Faerie Queene*, Book
II) in terms which clearly associate temperance with patience as virtues
capable of overturning wrath.[28]

Though patience has an important bearing on a number of Shakespeare's plays, especially *King Lear* and *Hamlet*, his patient Pericles is so
clearly characterized by it that some discussion of this imperfectly realized
though richly suggestive tragicomedy seems apposite here. Though the
pre-Christian story of *Pericles* precludes an explicitly Christian expression
of patience, it is a modification of this virtue, in keeping with the source
(the Appollonius story), which we see the prince of Tyre most consistently
displaying. Though his deprivation is profound there is no despair, but
rather an acceptance of a divine will which is both beneficient and inescap-
able. This necessity is made acceptable by his recognizing the natural cycle
of life, as suggested by the sea, the source of both life and death. As Thaisa's
sea burial implies (III.i.56–69), man is fashioned from the elements,
exposed to them, saved by them, and will revert to them, all under the
guidance of a Providential power. For Pericles, the gradual acceptance of
this cycle requires an education in patience. And, though the hero is more
acted upon than active, the Providential assumptions of the play do not
contravene the hero's human providence or choice or understanding,
limited though these may be. Though he is often dependent on others for
help and is the passive recipient of misfortune as well as happy coinci-
dence, Pericles is not, therefore, incapable of that choice and decisive action
which typify a hero who embodies much that is implied by patience. His
resourcefulness and active faith in the gods (and himself) are continually

manifest. His speeches often reveal an introspective hero capable of resolution, of a courageous acceptance of adversity and, significantly, of choosing what response he will make to the challenges and difficulties he faces. Doubt and grief alternate with patient resignation at the "death" of his wife at the hands of the gods. Though questioning the cruel dictates of these gods, Pericles accepts the nurse Lychorida's urgings to be patient and asserts that he has "Courage enough; I do not fear the flaw" (III.i.139). Concerned more about his newborn daughter than his own suffering, Shakespeare's most overtly patient hero orders the ship toward Tharsus; then, instead of impatiently despairing in the face of loss, loneliness, and old age,

> He bears
> A tempest, which his mortal vessel tears,
> And yet he rides it out. (IV.iv.29–31)

It is clear, in the climactic fifth act, that the hero's trials have been purposeful and that his happiness is not an illusion, not a joy to be snatched away arbitrarily, but a real and just reward for faithful endurance. Providence has replaced evil with order in a sublime double restoration. Significantly, Pericles has been acted upon by Providence throughout the drama; yet he has been free to choose how to respond—to choose an attitude, whether it be rebellion, indifference, sour submission, or cheerful acceptance. Such a freedom to accept seems effortless and spontaneous, but is a manifestation of the hero's patient response to adversity.

Patience, as several other Elizabethan writers more formally defined it, is willingly to "suffer undeserved punishment after the example of Christ, which prayed for them that persecuted and most cruelly tormented him."[29] We read in the tenth Henrician sermon of 1547 that submission is everyone's duty, a precept reinforced by Christ's patience and suffering without any thought of resistance.[30] Obviously, the centrality of Christ distinguishes the Renaissance notion of patience from its pagan prototype.[31] In his second sermon, "Oppression, Affliction and Patience," Roger Hutchinson asserts that Christian patience is different from that of Socrates and Anaxagoras because of the example of Christ (p. 320). We must bear the sins of others as Christ bore ours, he continues. Not every suffering is beneficent, but only in suffering for Christ can patience truly reveal itself. That affliction is the remedy for evil is made abundantly clear through the Son of God. The *Patientiae Triumphus* engravings discussed herein by Tate reveal that, just as Christ suffered yet remained virtuous, so man should patiently endure earthly life. As Christ triumphed over death and Fortune, so shall the victorious man have everlasting life. Christ, as leader of the triumphal procession conceived by van Heemskerck, most perfectly exemplifies patience, since He is the unique hope of mankind, obedient to the Father, even to dying on the cross.

The impatient man complains against God, whereas true Christian patience, in contrast to what Coverdale and others call "heathenish" virtue, comes from God, who "not only commands patience but also is himself patience and long-suffering" (p. 169). The unfaithful ascribe their prosperity to their own wisdom and their adversity to blind Fortune, continues Coverdale, as if she "had a certain power to work of herself, without the working of God" (p. 147). Fortune with her broken wheel, captive behind the car of *Patientia* in van Heemskerck's engraving, captures the idea of the Christian virtue as triumphant over her pagan counterpart.[32]

There was scarcely a minister of the Word in Elizabethan-Jacobean England, Catholic or Protestant, who was not to some degree concerned with an aspect of patience. Of the virtually countless works in English on the subject, a few others may be singled out here. In his "Exhortation to Patience, the eighth Beatitude," Daniel Featley (*Ancilla Pietatis* [1626], p. 287) asserts that all true Christians "must valiantly and cheerfully endure troubles for the Gospell" in respect for God's will and power, Christ's love and example, and the practice of the saints. Through patience, he says, we receive trial, joy, assurance of God's love, righteousness, holiness and perfection, life, protection, honor before God, and inestimable rewards in this life and in the life to come. Jeremy Taylor, writing in the mid-seventeenth century, says that being patient is to rejoice when we are persecuted in a righteous cause, for love is the soul of Christianity and suffering is the soul of love ("The Faith and Patience of the Saints," p. 449). In Isaac Barrow's 1685 sermon "Of Patience," the word signifies, first, a disposition to bear anger and injuries with charitable meekness, and second, the pious sustaining of the adversities disposed to us by Providence. Patience is best understood, he says, by the chief acts it produces (pp. 195–238):

1. a persuasion that nothing befalls us by fate or chance but from God;
2. a firm belief that all occurrences are consistent with divine justice, wisdom and goodness;
3. a full satisfaction of mind that all tends toward our good;
4. an entire submission and resignation of our wills to God;

5. bearing adversities calmly, cheerfully, and courageously so as not to become angry;
6. hopeful confidence in God for removal or easement of our afflictions;
7. a willingness to continue in affliction without weariness;
8. a lowly frame of mind;
9. restraining our tongues from complaints;
10. blessing and praising God in the manner of Job;
11. abstaining from any removal of our crosses but abiding quietly under their pressure;
12. a fair behavior toward instruments of our affliction;
13. particularly regarding those who provoke us, patience teaches:
    a. that we avoid anger,
    b. that we do not harbor ill-will,
    c. that we abstain from revenge;
14. patience includes and produces a gentle meekness and kindness of affection toward all men.

Special mention must also be made of English Recusant Literature, which is, of course, replete with comforting words to Catholics faced with persecution in Elizabethan England. The very titles by such Jesuit writers as Southwell, Parsons, Arias, and others are revealing: "An Epistle of Comfort," "The Palme of Christian Fortitude," "Triumphs over Death," etc. In this last work Southwell commends the virtues of resignation and compliance with the will of God. In a spirit that is almost more Stoic than Christian, Southwell asserts that, if affliction is faced squarely, it will lose its sting.[33] His *Short Rule of the Good Life* reveals the Jesuit ideal of self-control in the face of tribulation, as does the *Epistle to his Father,* wherein he states that God's patience "is only to lend us respite to repent, not any way to enlarge our leisure to sin" (p. 45). *The Epistle of Comfort,* combining Christian resignation with consolations from ancient philosophy, advises tempering grief with reason and piety in order to keep a proper balance of mind and soul. His title and tone remind us of Thomas More's *Dialogue of Comfort against Tribulation.*[34]

Even more representative of such works is the 1630 translation of Francis Arias' *A Treatise of Patience,*[35] prominently featuring the words already cited from Luke: "In your patience you shall possess your souls." The contents of Arias' treatise are familiar: Christ gave us a true example of patience, the saints show us how great the fruit of tribulation is, patience is pleasing to God, and He rewards those who suffer in patience.

Of the many Continental works of this period, special mention may be made of Lipsius' *Monita et exempla politica* (1625), which lists great people who endured with patience; pointing to Christ on the cross, the author says, "That is patience" (p. 208). A remarkably rich and learned treatise on the subject is the Jesuit Jeremias Drexel's *Gymnasium Patientiae* (twice translated into English in 1640), which sees the "school of patience" as a place which people choose to enter for philosophical discussion and moral testing. The "school" is not seen merely as a point of departure for pious consolatory maxims. Combining curious *sententiae* with his extensive spiritual and patristic background, Drexel's work may be seen as something of a "Summa Patientiae" and is thus outlined in the appendix.

Allowing no doubt about the importance of patience, William Cowper asserts that she is the "Lady and Queene of virtues" (*The Praise of Patience*, p. 278) and that he who has patience is invincible. The example of God the Father Himself teaches us patience, Cowper says, for He has zeal without spite and anger without perturbation. Patience will make us perfect, Jeffray enthusiastically asserts, for she fortifies faith, governs peace, assists love, instructs humility, expects repentance, rules the flesh, preserves the spirit, refrains the tongue, expels scandals, comforts the poor, sustains the sick, protects the strong, and delights the faithful, among other things (p. 14). Especially significant is Cowper's almost iconographic procession of virtues. In the Prudentius tradition, Cowper says that, just as the vices are linked together, so are the virtues, and patience is never alone. Truth and Fear of the Lord appear first in his scheme (pp. 275–78), followed by Charity, Holiness, Humility with Meekness, and Patience, followed by Experience. Hope, Fortitude, and Perseverance come last, we discover, because when Patience is troubled, she leans on the pillar of Hope; and, with Experience and Hope, she begets Fortitude. Patience is the armor by which one defends his soul, and it is the laurel immune to storms (p. 270). Such motifs outlined in this 1616 treatise can help clarify the various, often complex representations of the virtue in the visual arts as well as suggest the inexhaustible wealth of definitions and ingenious applications of patience in the Renaissance.[36]

Jeffray's *Picture of Patience* is also interesting in this respect, because, as the title suggests, his 1629 homiletic work combines extensive, traditional exhortations on the nature, value, and functions of patience with such vivid descriptions, borrowed from Prudentius and Tertullian, that some pages almost seem to be intended for emblematists and other artists or to be derived from them. In vigorous and graphic imagery, Jeffray tells us that

Patience turns "the Gall of bitternesse" to sweetness and divides the troubling waters of affliction (p. 7). There is no doubt that his personified virtue is female, for he quotes James 1:4 as the theme for his seventy-eight-page treatise: "Let patience have her perfect work that you may be perfect and entire, wanting nothing." Patience is described (p. 10) as having a most quiet and pleasant appearance, a pure forehead without the wrinkles of care, eyes which are downcast in humility, a mouth sealed with the honor of silence; her complexion is "such as Security and Integritie are wont to have," and her white clothes are tight-fitting to show that she is not puffed up. She is the remedy for misery, the nurse of valor and Christian resolution, the mother of true constancy. She sleeps easily on a bed of nettles and rises with comfort from the couch of care (p. 12). Patience weeps tears of comfort and finds content in the midst of discontent. Golden she is and thus pure for the fire; wheat she is and thus "cleane for the Fanne" (p. 13). As we shall see, a number of such motifs cited by Jeffray are used by emblem writers in their varied depictions of patience.

III

The significant relation between Renaissance literature and the representation of attributes and abstractions in the visual arts has often been recognized.[37] The work of Lawrence J. Ross, John Doebler, and John M. Steadman reminds us how the Elizabethan world picture was expressed as much visually as verbally and how the resulting iconic imagery, especially in drama, is crucial to our understanding of the intended meaning or stage picture. Rosemary Freeman says, "The extent to which the imagery of seventeenth century poetry is visual and clearly outlined yet at the same time rich with meaning is proof of the fruitful way in which it penetrated contemporary habits of thought."[38] Emblem books, which will be our chief concern here, are especially indicative of the Renaissance tendency, still half-medieval, to move quickly from abstractions to particular examples. The resulting vivid language of the time, Freeman reminds us, expresses ideas in concrete and general terms, yet the wealth of concrete references enables a writer to move naturally from general to particular, from abstract idea to specific image.[39] Jean H. Hagstrum, who (among others) has documented the interrelation between poetry and painting in the Renaissance,[40] notes how the emblem, a true "speaking picture," unites the verbal and the visual arts in a singular way. The cult of emblem books, following the Continental lead of Alciati[41] and others, was hardly a novel or surprising development of Horace's *Ut pictura poesis*, a dictum echoed by Petrarch (*Trionfo della Fama*), Alberti (*Della pittura*), Leonardo (*Treatise on Painting*, ed. McMahon), and Giovio (*Dialogo dell'Imprese Militari et Amorese*, which Daniel translated into English in 1585). Heckscher notes that Ripa's 1603 emblem book, *Iconologia*, was seen as "a depository of traditional forms which had the approval of time and use."[42]

Among the representations of Patience in European emblem books which may have influenced Elizabethan and Jacobean writers is the typically saint-like figure found in Achille Bocchi (lib. II, symb. XLIX), whose standing *Patientia* is manacled from above. Head bowed, she holds a staff; featured are a bucranium and a helmet (the attribute of Patience in Prudentius). The scene is rocky and barren, and one assumes that the withered, sawed-off tree nearby may well bloom again if the lady remains resolute. The bare tree with branches green only on top is frequently emblematic of hope with a connotation of patient endurance. Shakespeare's patient Pericles, for example, bears a motto of a "withered branch, that's only green at top" (II.ii.43), and its visual counterpart is seen in Rollenhagen (*Victrix Patientia Duri* [I, no. 28]) and in Peacham's *Minerva Britanna* (*Nitor in Adversum* [II, no. 167]), where the poet tells us that, according to Pliny, "the more with weight oppressed, the more the branch will upward shoot."[43] Wither's *Constante Fiducia* (II, no. 19, identical to Rollenhagen, I, no. 69) is also a standing lady, fully garbed and crowned like a saint, holding sorrow's "bitter cup" and the cross of trust (see Figure 4). She stands, significantly, on a squared stone, which, Wither tells us, will always stand flat. Such a stone, a common attribute of virtues associated with endurance, signifies both physical and spiritual solidity: *terra firma* (in contrast to *Tempestas*) and the man guided by virtue who is the *homo quadratus*.[44] By contrast, unstable Fortune is often shown standing on a rolling sphere, as on the title page of Robert Recorde's *The Castle of Knowledge* (1556). More typical of the emblematic representations of Patience[45] are those by Ripa (1603; see Figure 1) and the equally famous engraving by Brueghel (*Patientia*, 1554), which show her seated on a rock,[46] her hands folded prayerfully in the pose conventionally associated with both Hope and Patience.[47]

That Shakespeare often conceived of Patience as a seated, female, statue-like figure is not only clear from the two enigmatic "smiling" Patience similes (*Pericles*, V.i.134–39, and *Twelfth Night*, II.iv.109–14), which Heckscher has illuminated for us,[48] but also from less conspicuous lines, some of which may have commonplace emblematic analogues. "With what strict patience have I sat," says Berowne in *Love's Labour's Lost* (IV.iii.163). She is a "virtue fix'd" in *Troilus and Cressida* (I.ii.5) and is typically described as "unmov'd" (*Comedy of Errors*, II.i.32). She is also personified as "brave," "gentle," "mild," even "tongue-tied" (Sonnet CXL). The reference to patient Grissel (*Taming of the Shrew*, II.i.295) conveys the traditional concept of the long-suffering folk heroine (cf. Chaucer's *Clerk's Tale*) with her saintly attributes.[49] Like the emblematists, Shakespeare links patience with constancy, temperance, endurance, and with devotion and fortitude (see, e.g., *Macbeth*, IV.iii.94). Edgar's phrase "Ripeness is all" (*King Lear*, V.ii.11), like Hamlet's "The readiness is all" (V.ii.231), suggests patience as expectation, as the kind of mature endurance capable of producing the affection and compassion of Cordelia. Such phrases may have a visual analogue in fields of ripened grain, as in Wither's harvest emblem on hope (I, no. 44), which comes close to connecting patience with ripeness. The basis of this emblem is no doubt the association of Ceres and Constancy and the combination of wheat with the anchor of hope, as cited in note 62. Patient expectation is clearly the proper solution to the mad, impatient grief of Lear, who had (falsely) claimed, "I will be the pattern of all patience" (III.ii.37). His next line, "I will say nothing," suggests patience as silence; but, more importantly, his lines recall the frequent Shakespearean relation between patience and grief,[50] in terms analogous to the sorrowful depiction of the virtue by Ripa and by Joris Hoefnaghel's *Patience and Hope Personified*. Such works are no doubt descended from Albrecht Dürer's celebrated *Melencolia I* (1514), as is Hans Sebald Beham's engraving *Pacientia* (1540),[51] which appears as the frontispiece to this volume.

Such artists depict a sad or at least sober Patience, perhaps reflecting, by a kind of obversion, one of the virtue's chief opposites, *Tristitia*, the vice which reveals lack of faith in the mercy in God. Patience is a remedy for every grief, an English proverb reminds us.[52] The most common antithesis to *Patientia*, however, is *Ira*, the wrathful anger by which a desperate man distrusts the will of God, on whom he should depend. Impatience is the mother of all evil, William Cowper says with some homiletic hyperbole.[53] "Patience over wrath" appears in a woodcut border in Richard Day's *A Book of Christian Prayers* (1579).[54] And the emblem *Laesa Patientia Fit Furor*, recalling the proverb "Patience provoked turns to fury,"[55] appears in numerous collections, often in the form of a peasant walking through thistles (cf. Ripa's thorns of suffering), his finger pointing heavenward in a gesture of hope, though his eyes are on the ground. In the distance we see Saint Christopher, whose sweet but heavy burden reinforces the theme of enduring afflictions bravely. This emblem appears in Simeoni (p. 37) and Rollenhagen (II, no. 74) and is repeated in Wither (IV, no. 24), whose motto reads, "Hee that enjoyes a patient Minde, / Can

FIGURE 1. *Patienza*, woodcut, in Cesare Ripa, *Nova Iconologia* (Padua, 1618).

FIGURE 2. *Patientia and Fortitudo*, engraving by Hendrik Goltzius (1584). Courtesy of the Rijksmuseum, Amsterdam.

FIGURE 3. *Victrix Patientia Duri*, in George Wither, *A Collection of Emblemes, Ancient and Moderne* (London, 1635), I, no. 28.

FIGURE 4. *Constante Fiducia*, in George Wither, *A Collection of Emblemes, Ancient and Moderne* (London, 1635), II, no. 19.

Pleasure in Afflictions finde."[56] In Sambucus (p. 271) and Wither (IV, no. 44—"Who, Patience tempts, beyond her strength, / Will make it Fury, at the length"), a boy is attacked by a normally docile but unduly provoked lamb.[57] An original, though crudely executed, variation is Peacham's *Patientia laesa furorem* (p. 71) wherein a hand (divine Patience?) from a cloud holds captured Wrath in a large net. And Georgette de Montenay's *Patere* emblem (no. 92) shows a patient man with a bellows tempering the wrath of an armed warrior about to strike him (cf. the "cool patience" suggested for the "heat and flame" of Hamlet's "distemper," *Hamlet*, III.iv.124–25).

Despite the legendary patience of Job, Tobias, and other biblical figures, Patience in the arts is most often personified as a woman.[58] An engraving of *Patientia and Fortitudo* (see Figure 2) by Hendrik Goltzius (Bartsch, III:27, pars. 114–17) shows two reclining nude females: Fortitude with her column, Patience with a press, seemingly containing a human heart. *Patientia*'s love (the burning heart) endures suffering and hardship, we can conclude; yet, like the anvil, it remains steadfast. Cornelis Metsijs' *Patientia* (Bartsch, IX:iii, par. 42) is seated, handcuffed, and chained to a wall; there is a burning city in the background, proving her invulnerability to wrath, though the burning city may also be seen as analogous to the chaotic sea of troubles surrounding Patience in Brueghel's engraving.

There are many non-human attributes and symbols also worthy of mention (some already cited) which recur in emblem literature. For example, the importance of the lamb[59] as emblematic of the gentleness and purity of Christian Patience is captured in Oraeus' superb concatenation of symbols, appropriately titled *Patientia vincit omnia* (XXXII:64). It depicts the Lamb of God atop an altar, above which appears the world, an hourglass, the bucranium, and the sword and scales of those virtues—fortitude and justice—which make patience possible.

In a less elaborate emblem, Wither's *Virtus Inexpugnabilis* (III, no. 37) shows a diamond being hammered on an anvil.[60] This conception of the adamantine strength and precious nature of invulnerable constancy is found in Pierio Valeriano's *Fortitudo (De adamante)* and is commonly associated with patience as the spiritual aspect of fortitude.[61] Like the stone already mentioned, the column is frequently an attribute of Christian Constancy-Fortitude because of its association with the Flagellation of Christ (hence the sacrificial implications in Christian iconography of the stone and column, as well as the altar). The bucranium—the skull of an ox or bull, frequently ornamented (as in Oraeus, no. 32) with twigs, wheat,[62] or a yoke (as in Alciati, Bocchi, and Paradin)—is a patience attribute stemming from the *Hypnerotomachia Poliphili* (1499) and can suggest labor as well as the value of enduring hardship: *Victoria ex labore honesta, et utilis* (Bocchi, p. 11). *Patience relishes hardships* (de Montenay, no. 58) is conveyed in terms of a weighted basket[63] atop an acanthus plant. The Latin verse tells us that a strong spirit becomes more lustrous through adversities; weigh in your mind, says the poet, how the acanthus thus oppressed arises from the soil.[64] This is analogous to the weighted palm tree emblems which are so numerous (see Figure 3).

An elaborate bed filled only with the thorns of suffering, upon which Patience supposedly sleeps (as Jeffray describes it in *The Picture of Patience*, p. 10), appears under the motto *Patientia vincit omnia* as the final emblem in Georgette de Montenay's collection (no. 100). In addition to penitence, the sacrificial-redemptive power of patience is illustrated in Peacham's *Minerva Britanna* (*Deus ultimum refugiam* [I, no. 65]); the poet says,

The case is every Christian's in distresse
Who to the Lord, himselfe should recommend,
As who can best the wrongful cause redresse
And patiently t'abide, what he shall send. . . .

The sea, so prominent in depictions of Hope as well as Patience, suggests the contrast between tempest and tranquillity, both of which have maritime connotations in iconography and both of which were long recognized as essential for a virtuous and rational life.[65] Representations of steadfastness (for example, Simeoni, p. 118, and Whitney, p. 129) are replete with raging seas. Peacham's *Nec igne, nec unda* (II, no. 158) is concerned with "manlie constancie of mind" and depicts ships on a raging sea. The *Eikon Basilike* of James I (1649) includes a title piece with a raging sea and an unmoved rock rising from its midst as it withstands winds and waves; hence the lines concerning triumph "in sad affliction's Darksom night."[66] An important emblem (de Montenay, no. 60) depicts Virtue, a female figure with denuded breasts (like Patience) on a rock, holding a column (like Constancy), and, with the other hand, a banner whose inscription reads, "For virtue no path is impossible." She stands on a cliff amid a typical sea of troubles, yet the Latin verse beneath the woodcut indicates that the wrathful warrior vainly hacking at the rock is the main character; he says: "Lofty virtue somehow manages to stand on a broken summit, which spot caused from all sides the sea's foaming waters; my strength nevertheless allows [me] to defeat the rocks and onrushing floods of the virtue whom love on high attracts."

A graphic example of the power of Christian Patience over Fortune is found in *Frangor Patientia* (de Montenay, no. 31), in which Fortune's wheel is broken by the hand of Patience. De Montenay writes, "I am being broken, yet Patience elevates me under adverse circumstances, and hope places me in a solid place. Surely, Provident God, the creator, does not allow me to be oppressed by the inequities of fortune, nor to be delivered unto evil."

The frequent concatenation of attributes and concepts, of tradition and contemporaneity, is captured in a German emblem of *Spes et Patientia* (Cramer, p. 109), in which a man dressed in seventeenth-century attire calmly plays the lute while his feet are locked in a *pedica* (analogous to the yoke or chains of Patience) with the anchor of Hope nearby. The persistent association of fortitude with patience appears in the frontispiece to the 1640 English translation by "R. S." of Drexel's *Gymnasium Patientia*. Patience, on the left, stands holding a column (inscribed *Melior est patiens*) topped with a lamb; beneath her we see Job, while Samson appears beneath the parallel figure of Fortitude, whose column is topped with a lion.

Oxen are also featured among the emblematic representations of patient endurance. Wither (III, no. 39) notes that the ox may be slow but, by plodding on, may travel far. So, too, Erasmus defends the ox as sure, placid, and assiduous, rather than dumb; it works with strength, he says, not heedless rush.[67] *Pas à Pas* is a recurring emblem motto emphasizing the ox's attributes among qualities associated with patience.[68] Giovanni Ferro's collection, important as a catalog of other emblematists, cites oxen for their steady endurance (II, no. 143). The ox is not only a symbol of Perseverance (as on the south door of Chartres) but—since it bears a yoke just as the patient bear misfortunes—often represents Patience, who appears with an ox and yoke in the Cathedral of Amiens and with an ox on the central porch facade of Notre Dame in Paris. In a different variation, Schoonhovius (no. LXII) depicts a trapped starling hanging steadfastly over a field plowed by oxen. Its Latin motto advises "bearing patiently what is necessary." Preceding his quotations from Seneca, Ovid, Virgil, and others, Schoonhovius admonishes the reader: *Perfer et obdura*—"Patience eases many things to correct naturally human corrupt tendencies." The scene is also rural, featuring a farmer with an ox plow, in Gomberville (II, no. 2), who advises, "The Fool Always Complains of his Condition."[69]

A few pages later Gomberville shows us a Job-like old man, seated in the pensive pose suggestive of Patience-Constancy, while his wife pours water on him. This ironic, realistic reversal of the long-suffering wife motif bears the moral "He that suffers much, gains much." Gomberville explains that the old man represents that "glorious conquest which alone remains for us to gain over our last and strongest enemies, anger and impatience" (II, no. 11, p. 147).[70]

Typotius' imaginative collection of royal impresas (1601) includes a traditional rendering of both eternity and perseverance—the serpent eating its own tail—with the clasped hands of love and trust in the circle's center; above it is the motto *Cum Patientia* (III, no. 5). The "sweetness" of patience is conceived in terms of a large rock which a saw cannot penetrate, and atop the rock there appear a triumphant cross and a rose (I, no. 114). The combination of emblematic attributes appears here in the anchor of Hope tied to the column of Constancy (*Confirmata est super nos* [II, no. 20]), in the column upon the sea (*In Fide et Justicia Fortitudo* [III, no. 44]), in a dog[71] tied to a tree stump (*Fide et Patientia* [III, no. 146]), and in the significant relation between silence[72] and courageous hope, portrayed in terms of a shipwreck (*In silentio et spe Fortitudo mea* [II, no. 159]).

The flower prominent in several patience-related emblems (Rollenhagen, nos. 28 and 100, for example) is often the violet, which, Hawkins tells us, represents "lowlie humilitie mixt with solicitude."[73] It may also be the heliotrope (also the marigold or sunflower—see Wither, no. 109), which Jeremias Drexel, in a separate work on the subject,[74] described as that flower which, turning on its stalk in accordance with the movement of the sun, is an image of faithfulness since it behaves toward the sun as man should toward God. More important among symbols drawn from natural history is the palm tree as emblematic of endurance, as in Schoonhovius (no. 74), Simeoni (nos. 76, 78), Le Moyne (p. 71), and, especially, Hawkins (pp. 153–54), who hails this invincible champion of trees as one which can bear "injuries and oppressions without shrinking." According to Chew, "no other emblem was more popular and ubiquitous than that of the weighted palm tree," to which we have referred above.[75]

By way of summary, we can see that, from an iconographical standpoint, Patience in the sixteenth century had accumulated attributes which conveyed her ability to endure suffering. She is shown with her hands bound, her feet fettered, accompanied by sacrificial animals such as the ox and lamb. She suffers physical discomfort in silence, either by bearing a yoke or by awaiting imminent destruction by fire, in either case typically seated with folded hands and downcast eyes on a stone with her bare feet on thorns. When not personified, the virtue is represented by some of these attributes alone or by various symbols of endurance, constancy, or hope. In short, patience was extensively and variously treated in visual arts of the Renaissance as a virtue of major importance.

My intention has been primarily to examine some of the many visual representations of this virtue and its attributes—as well as representations of other closely associated and interrelated virtues—in order to determine how extensive the treatment of patience was in the period from 1480 to 1680. I have limited my focus chiefly to emblems because of their widespread and well-recognized influences on other arts. While examining emblem books likely to be available in England during much of the Tudor and Stuart periods, I also surveyed some of the major theological works on patience published in England during this era in order to provide some intellectual background for considering ways in which the virtue was generally conceived.

It has not been my purpose to speculate on questions of iconographic inspiration, tantalizing though it may be to investigate probable sources in the visual arts for specific poetic images (and vice versa). Rather, it is hoped that this survey, and especially the Inventory, will be helpful to those students who may wish to gain a fuller understanding of the pervasive presence of a virtue such as patience in Renaissance expression. The influence of emblematic and homiletic material on Renaissance English drama has been fruitfully explored by numerous scholars. In these traditional materials, patience has so important a bearing on Shakespearean tragedy and the meaning of Elizabethan revenge, as well as on Spenserian allegory and Renaissance poetic imagery, that its further study is manifestly justified, as this essay has endeavored to show.

NOTES

1. William S. Heckscher observes this in his seminal article, "Shakespeare in his Relationship to the Visual Arts: A Study in Paradox," *Research Opportunities in Renaissance Drama* XIII–XIV (1970–71):5–6 and passim. Patience is treated briefly by Samuel C. Chew, *The Pilgrimage of Life* (New Haven, 1962), pp. 116–22, and by Rosemond Tuve, *Allegorical Imagery* (Princeton, 1966), p. 59 et seq. There are suggestive remarks in William O. Harris, "Despair and 'Patience as the Truest Fortitude' in *Samson Agonistes*," in *Critical Essays on Milton from ELH* (Baltimore, 1969), pp. 277–90, and in Eleanor Prosser, *Hamlet and Revenge* (Stanford, 1967). A useful unpublished study is the dissertation by Ruth Levitsky, "Shakespeare's Treatment of the Virtue of Patience" (University of Missouri, 1959). The studies of emblems by Rosemary Freeman and Mario Praz contain no specific mention of patience, but two unpublished studies I have been privileged to consult do: Lawrence J. Ross, "The Speaking Picture," and Priscilla Tate, "The Triumph of Patience" (Master's thesis, Duke University, 1974). I am much indebted to the latter, which is the source of my Tate references.

2. See my notes on Lorens d'Orleans, *The Book of Virtues and Vices*, as outlined in the Inventory. Adolf Katzenellenbogen (*Allegories of the Virtues and Vices in Medieval Art* [New York, 1964], pp. 80-81) notes that Hugh of St. Victor does not specifically include patience in his "official" cycle of the twelve virtues and vices; but perseverance (like *Fortitudo* in Thomas Aquinas) is so closely related to patience that it may be seen as an equivalent. Henry Hawkins states in his *Parthenia Sacra* (Rouen, 1633), p. 155: "the Vertues of Fortitude and Patience may seeme as two but are easily reduced to one, that is, to a stout Patience, or patient Fortitude." Heckscher summarizes: Fortitude was, from Cicero onward, considered to consist of several parts, "enduring Patience" being among them from the very beginning ("Shakespeare," p. 41). Moreover, the tree of virtues (*arbor bona*, Ghent, Bibliothèque de l'Université de la Ville) includes Patience, who also appears among the other virtues in two eleventh-century Cologne shrines (Katzenellenbogen, p. 47). She also appears with the three theological virtues in frescoes of the two chapels at Bawit (fifth century). The seven virtues produced by the Holy Spirit (*Sapientia, Intellectus, Consilium, Fortitudo, Scientia, Pietas, Timor* [Isa. 11:2, Vulgate]) as depicted in the Book of Job (Floreffe Bible [c. 1155], British Museum, London) include *Patientia* along with *Humilitas, Benignitas, Providentia, Temperantia, Prudentia,* and *Obedientia* (Katzenellenbogen, Fig. 39). Saint Bernard of Clairvaux's sermon on the Passion relates *Patientia, Humilitas, Caritas, Obedientia, Misericordia,* and *Sapientia* with the cross (J. P. Migne, *Patrologia Latina*, 221 vols. (Paris, 1844-90), CLXXX-III:263 ff.). Trust in the cross in the face of adversity is included in many of the representations of Patience discussed below. Commentary on the mingling of Patience and Fortitude is found in Tuve, *Allegorical Imagery*, p. 96 et seq., and appendix, p. 443. Tuve comments: *Patientia* (by the mid-twelfth century), "with its scriptural uses and eminence as Christ's special form of Fortitude, we call sufferance, in lists of the cardinal virtues and their parts; it also became famous in another series of quite other virtues, wherein Patience became the most frequently appearing opposer of *Ira*, especially in art" (p. 60).

3. Reproduced in H. Arthur Klein, *Graphic Worlds of Peter Brueghel the Elder* (New York, 1963), p. 213.

4. Katzenellenbogen, Fig. 14.

5. *The De Bono Perseverantiae of St. Augustine*, ed. and trans. Sister M. Alphonsine Lesonsky (Washington, D.C., 1956). Augustine defines patience: "The patience of man... is that by which we tolerate evil things with an even mind, that we may not with a mind uneven desert good things," quoted in Philip Schaff, ed., *A Select Library of the Nicene and Post-Nicene Fathers of the Christian Church* (New York, 1888), III:527. Cf. also Lactantius (*Divine Institutes*) in *The Ante-Nicene Christian Library*, ed. Alexander Roberts and James Donaldson (Edinburgh, 1867-72), XXI:347, 401-2: Patience is the greatest of all virtues; it is "The bearing with equanimity of the evils which are either inflicted or happen to fall on us." The virtue, he continues, causes no evil to happen, for it calms the mind and restores a man to himself. See Hanna, note 36, in this volume.

6. *De Bono Patientiae*, ed. and trans. Sister M. George Conway (Washington, D.C., 1957), p. 12.

7. Prudentius, "The Fight for Mansoul," lines 109-77, in *Prudentius*, trans. H. J. Thomson (Cambridge, Mass., 1949), I:274-343. See Katzenellenbogen; M. W. Bloomfield, *The Seven Deadly Sins* (East Lansing, Mich., 1952), pp. 63-81; Emile Mâle, *Religious Art from the Twelfth to the Eighteenth Century* (New York, 1958). Elizabethan versions of the *Psychomachia* include Abraham Fleming, *A Monomachia of Motives...* (London, 1582). As to other early representations of the virtue, Tate (p. 5) cites *Patientia* and *Ira* from an eleventh-century manuscript of Moissac (Paris, Bibliothèque Nationale), MS 2077, fol. 168 r.—a miniature sequence of the thirteenth-century *Figurae Bibliorum* (Eton College), MS 177, fols. 34-7v.—in which patience corresponds to Christ bearing the cross, Saint Hildegard of Bingen's *Liber Scivias* (c. 1175) featuring Patience leaning toward God, and other medieval visual renderings.

8. Page 289.

9. Page 291.

10. Cicero is (imprecisely) quoted in the *Fior di Virtu of 1491*, trans. Nicholas Fersin (Washington, D.C., 1953), as stating that "man must be brave in battle and patient in adversity" (p. 75). The idea is, however, implicit in the *De officiis* and the *De inventione*.

11. W. Meikle, "The Vocabulary of 'Patience' in the Old Testament," and "The Vocabulary of 'Patience' in the New Testament," *Expositor* XIX (1920):219-25, 304-13. See Gal. 5:22-23 for the twelve Fruits of the Spirit: *caritas, gaudium, pax, patientia, benignitas, bonitas, longanimitas, mansuetudo, fides, modestia, continentia, castitas.*

12. Tate notes that there were two Greek words used for the virtue, υπομονη and μαχροθυμια (p. 3). The first has to do with circumstances: the man who exercises υπομονη is the one who, under a great siege of trials, bears up and does not lose heart or courage. He endures. This includes also a spiritual readiness to suffer, because of hope and faith in deliverance. The second term has to do with persons, especially in the sense of the man who does not suffer himself to be provoked or blaze up in anger. Thus, in his patient long-suffering, he manifests spiritual fortitude. The second of the two words is related to meekness, humility, and is generally closer to the current English usage of "patience" connoting passive resignation. See R. C. Trench, *Synonyms of the New Testament* (Cambridge, 1880).

13. *The Sin of Sloth: Acedia in Medieval Thought and Literature* (Chapel Hill, 1967). Wenzel, in his paper "Vices, Virtues and Medieval Preaching" (delivered at Duke University, July 25, 1974), notes that Langland's concept of patience in *Piers Plowman* is in keeping with his respect for poverty: "Poure pacient is parfitest lif of alle" (passus xiv, line 99, C text). Poverty as a proof of patience is clear from Psalms 9:19: "The poor man shall not be forgotten in the end; the patience of the poor will never perish." It is also important to recall M. W. Bloomfield's observation in *The Seven Deadly Sins* that the vices are more commonly depicted in medieval literature than the virtues, which are more prominent in the visual arts.

14. *Patience, An Alliterative Version of Jonah by the Poet of Pearl*, Select Early English Poems, vol. I (London, 1913). See *The Complete Works of the Pearl Poet*, ed. Margaret Williams, R.S.C.J. (New York, 1970).

15. *Complete Works*, ed. Margaret Williams, p. 32. See Kirk's valuable commentary in this volume.

16. *Polyanthea* (Venice, 1509); this first edition is much less valuable than the Venice 1630 edition cited. *Patientia* (pp. 992-96) here includes "Sententiae Patrum" (Saints Ambrose, Gregory, John Chrysostom, et al.) and "Sententiae Poeticae" (Virgil, Terence, Menander, Ovid, Horace, et al.). Also quoted are Aristotle, Cicero, Caesar, and Boethius ("Quidam simpliciis inexpugnabiles exemplum caeteris praetulerunt, invictam nalis esse virtutem," *Consol. Phil.* IV.vi.145-74). See also "Apothegmata" (Democritus, Diogenes, Xenophen, et al.), "Similitudines" (Seneca, Martial, Ambrose, Paul, et al.), and "Exempla Profana" (Heraclitus, Diogenes, et al.). Similar *florilegii* (which I have not consulted), as cited by William O. Harris, *Skelton's Magnyfycence and the Cardinal Virtue Tradition* (Chapel Hill, N.C., 1965) are: Joseph Lang, *Florilegii Magni* (London, 1559); Octavianus Mirandula, *Illustrum poetarum flores* (Venice, 1565); Simon Harward, *Enchiridion Morale* (London, 1596).

17. Nani Mirabellio, p. 996: "Sunt qui jugum, significatio patientiae, praeferant," quoted from Pierio Valeriano, *Hieroglyphica* . . . (Basel, 1575), lib. XLVIII.

18. The extensive *Divisio* under *fortitudo* (pp. 484-93) conventionally cites *fiducia, magnificentia, patientia,* and *perseverantia* as key attributes.

19. Liselotte Dieckmann, "Renaissance Hieroglyphics," *Comparative Literature* IX (1957):308-21.

20. Full documentation for such quotations may be found in the Patience Inventory.

21. Page 19. She also notes that patience became prominent in heraldic mottos and royal devices during the time of Charles V.

22. *Writings and Translations of Myles Coverdale* . . . ed. George Pearson (Cambridge,

1844), p. 189. Earlier Coverdale says, "Trouble and afflictions do prove, try, instruct, confirm and strengthen the faith, provoke and stir up prayer, drive and force us to amendment of life, to the fear of God, to meekness, to patience, to constancy . . . and to all manner of virtues . . ." (p. 116). An outline of Coverdale's opening chapter (closely paraphrased) is indicative of his argument: All afflictions come from God; troubles come as a punishment for our sins; troubles are higher than our sins; all such afflictions come from a merciful Father; only God for Christ's sake corrects and punishes us; God chastens us with true love and mercy; afflictions strengthen us and lead to patience; we learn about ourselves and God through adversity; we learn to repent for our sins; troubles help strengthen our faith; afflictions help us to pray and praise God; they lead us to virtue; they lead us to fear and love of God; they teach us pity and patience toward others; patience makes men strong, sober, and temperate; patience helps men defy the world and be fervent in virtue.

23. "The Praise of Patience" (1605), in *The Works in verse and prose of Nicholas Breton* . . . ed. A. B. Grosart (Edinburgh, 1879), I:15.

24. Marcus Aurelius, *The Thoughts of Marcus Aurelius*, trans. John Jackson (New York, 1951), p. 159.

25. Levitsky, pp. 32–33. See also p. 37 ff. for a discussion of which Shakespearean characters exemplify Stoic patience and which reject it as inferior to honor and valor.

26. *The French Academy* (London, 1618), p. 110.

27. Ed. G. H. Mair (Oxford, 1919), pp. 34–35. Wilson defines *sufferance* as "a willing and long bearing of trouble and taking of pains: for the maintenance of vertue, and the welth of his country," reflecting the view that patience is often seen as a necessary virtue for the nobleman. *Continuance* is defined as "a steadfast and constant abiding in a purposed and well advised matter, and yeelding to any man in quarell of the right."

28. Little attention has been paid to the bridle of temperance in Book II, which immediately recalls such commonplace visual renderings as Dürer's engraving *Nemesis* (c. 1520), in Adam von Bartsch, *Le Peintre Graveur*, 21 vols. (Vienna, 1803–1921), VII:77; Brueghel's *Temperance* (1559); and Marcantonio's engraving of the virtue (Bartsch, XIV:295, par. 390), among others. A. D. S. Fowler very briefly mentions the emblematic bridle of temperance in Spenser, but does not relate the virtue to patience, in *RES*, n.s. 2 (1960):143. Not only does Guyon's horse (named Brigador, or "golden bridle") have "gorgeous barbes" (II.ii.11) but, in canto iv, we hear the squire Phedon tell Guyon and the Palmer how, in mad pursuit of his lady Pryene, he was met by Furor, who pursued and scourged him. Overcome by wrath because of the deception of Philomel, Phedon fell into "mischiefe through intemperance" or self-defeating irascibility. After Guyon advises the desperate squire that temperance will cure his wrath, the Palmer speaks of patience ("suff'rance") and the bridle of temperance:

> Most wretched man,
> That to affections does the bridle lend;
> In their beginning they are weak and wan,
> But soon through suff'rance grow to fearfull end. . . (iv.34)

He goes on to cite the "strong warres" which the vices opposed to patience and temperance make against reason. So, too, in v.16, Guyon admonishes Pyrochles to give up the "outrageous anger" and "direfull impatience" which war within the self. Arthur subdues the rash Pyrochles "with patience and sufferaunce sly" (viii.47); for rage, we learn, cannot be overcome by rage. And when the knight of temperance enters the Bower of Bliss, he looks straight ahead, "Bridling his will, and maistering his might" (xii.53): we see again that the bridle as an emblem of temperance is a significant and revealing image in Book II which deserves more attention than Fowler and others have given it. There are, moreover, significant references elsewhere in *The Faerie Queene* (see III.i.50) to the bridle of self-control. In Book VI, the Hermit tells Serena,

Abstaine from pleasure, and restraine your will
Subdue desire, and bridle loose delight. (vi.14)

It is clear from such passages not only that Spenser has in mind the conventional battle
between the vices and virtues, but also that temperance and patience are very closely associated; for their common enemies are wrath and grief, which, in their excess, produce despair.
Moreover, in the opening stanza of II.v, Spenser defines the great enemy of temperance as
stubborn perturbation, the extreme agitation and confusion which overthrow the goodly
peace of "stayed mindes." The roots of such agitation are *Ira* and *Tristitia*, those unbridled
emotions, antithetical to patient endurance, which temperance must control.

29. Thomas Becon, "The Demands of Holy Scripture," in *Prayers and other pieces of
Thomas Becon*, ed. John Ayre (Cambridge, 1844), p. 621.

30. Helen C. White, *Social Criticism in the Popular Religious Literature of the Sixteenth
Century* (Madison, 1943), p. 140.

31. In the 1614 edition of William Peraldus' *Summae virtutem ac vitiorum* (Cologne), the
first of nine chief aspects of patience cited in the opening summary (p. xviii) is that the virtue
is modeled on Christ. See I Tim. 1:16 for Christ as the model of all patience.

32. A verbal analogue of the triumph of virtue over Fortune is King Lewis' advice to
Margaret in Shakespeare's *III Henry VI*: "Yield not thy neck / To fortune's yoke, but let thy
dauntless mind/Still ride in triumph over all mischance" (III.iii.16–18).

33. Robert Southwell, *Triumphs over Death* (1591), ed. J. W. Trotman (London, 1914),
p. 129. Cf. Seneca, *Ad Marciam Consolatio*, in *Opera Philosophica* (Paris, 1827), II:130.

34. Ed. Miles Leland (Bloomington, Ind., 1966). More makes it clear that pagan comfort
against tribulation is insufficient, for it does not account for the fact that "by the pacient
sufferance of their tribulation, men shall attain unto his [God's] favoure, and for theyre payne,
reward at his hands in heaven" (p. 130). Also, John Downame in *Consolations for the
Afflicted* (London, 1622), book II, chap. 1, asserts that true patience did not exist among the
pagans.

35. Trans. 1630, English Recusant Literature, vol. XXI (Menston, 1970).

36. Since allegorists do not always distinguish between faith in and hope of God's mercy
and Mercy herself, she too is often interchangeable with Patience, who comforts the Pilgrim
in Breton's *The Pilgrimage to Paradise* (London, 1592). And the antithesis of Mercy, as of
Patience, is the often dramatized vice of Despair, as seen in numerous English morality plays
(Skelton's *Magnyfycence*, Wapull's *The Tyde Tarryeth No Man*, etc.) which antedate Una's
rescue of the Redcross Knight from Despair (*The Faerie Queene*, I.ix). These and other
Spenserian analogues are cited in Chew, *The Virtues Reconciled* (Toronto, 1947), pp. 110–18.

37. As William O. Harris aptly comments, the pervasiveness of patience "through centuries of European thought can be more easily gauged by noticing its reflection in icono-
graphic and emblematic works": "Despair and 'Patience as the Truest Fortitude,' " p. 281.
(See Chew, *Pilgrimage of Life*, pp. 116–22.) John Doebler's *Shakespeare's Speaking Pictures*
(Albuquerque, 1974) does not cite patience itself but has some suggestive remarks about fortitude (pp. 122, 149) and other abstractions which become visualized stage symbols. See also
Mario Praz, *Studies in Seventeenth Century Imagery*, 2d ed. (Rome, 1964); Rosemary Freeman,
English Emblem Books (London, 1948); R. J. Clements, *Picta Poesis* (Rome, 1960); Erwin
Panofsky, *Studies in Iconology* (New York, 1939); and the works by Tuve, Heckscher, Wind,
and van Marle cited in these notes. More extensive references to the various emblem books
cited are found in the Inventory.

38. Page 31.

39. Page 62. A good example is her observation (p. 147) that Donne's supposedly startling
compass conceit in "A Valediction Forbidding Mourning" is based on an accepted emblem of
constancy as reproduced, e.g., in George Wither, *A Collection of Emblemes, Ancient and
Moderne . . .* (London, 1635), III, no. 9.

40. *The Sister Arts* (Chicago, 1958), pp. 57–92.

41. The precursors of Alciati include epigrams, mottoes, and hieroglyphic woodcuts by Francesco Colonna; see *The Dream of Poliphilus, facsimiles of 168 woodcuts in the Hypnerotomachia Poliphili, 1499*, ed. J. W. Appel (London, 1889).

42. "Shakespeare," p. 56.

43. Wither, IV, no. 9. Scipione Bargagli's impresas (*Dell'Imprese* [Venice, 1594], pp. 335, 489) feature a bare trunk with new branches growing atop a roped-off marker. See also the impresas designed by Camilli for Claudio Paci (*Imprese Illustri di diversi, coi discorsi . . .* [Venice, 1586], I, no. 31), of a dead tree trunk with a blooming branch, and for Eustachio Simoni (I, no. 52) of two trees atop a mountain peak (*Ardua virtutem*). The latter is nearly identical to the "herbal" emblem by Camerarius, *Ardua virtutem*, with its twin-topped mountain crowned with palm and laurel trees (*Symbolorum et emblematum ex re Herberia Desumtorum* [Nuremberg, 1590], no. 5). For a brief discussion of the weighted palm (and cypress) trees, see Chew, *Pilgrimage of Life*, p. 118.

44. Heckscher, "Sturm und Drang," *Simiolus* I (1966–67):94–105. Note also that the cube is emblematic of quiet—Otto van Veen, *Emblemata sive Symbola* (Brussels, 1624), no. 146. Chew (*Pilgrimage of Life*, pp. 66–67) notes the pervasive cube of constancy.

45. The most common attributes of Patience as reflected in emblem literature are the lamb, the rock, the yoke, the *pedica*, the bucranium, and thorns. The ox, cedar, cypress, palm, chalice, sword, column, etc., are easily associated with Patience because of her association with Fortitude, Hope, Constancy, etc. Wither's emblem of *Labor and Hope* (III, no. 16), a woman with denuded breasts holding an anchor and shovel, is typical of the assimilation of attributes, just as *perseverance, constancy, hope, endurance*, and *sufferance* are often interchangeable terms for *patience*.

46. Similar to the stone cube but also symbolic of the hardships which Patience must endure. See the rock of constancy in Bargagli (no. 75) and Borja, *Emblemata Moralia* (Berlin, 1697), no. 17. George Richardson, *Iconology* (London, 1779) shows a woman with her feet on thorns, seated on a rock and bearing a yoke (Fig. 321). She represents "The power of supporting the evils of this world with a becoming fortitude" (p. 84).

47. Patience, with her hands folded across her breasts, her head down in the posture of humility, appears in Ruscelli's impresa for Ercole d'Este in *Le Imprese illustri* (Venice, 1584), p. 156. In Typotius (*Symbola Divina et Humana . . .* [Frankfurt, 1652], II, no. 47), we find Patience chained to a rock, her folded arms scarcely covering her naked breasts. In an early Renaissance bronze medallion (Raimond van Marle, *Iconographie de l'art profane . . .* [The Hague, 1931], I, Fig. 66), Patience is seated with a lamb, but her arms are prayerfully extended. As Heckscher has observed ("Shakespeare," Figs. XXI and XXII), the tightly folded arms are an appropriate motif of personified Patience. In *The Last Judgment* (Sistine Chapel), Mary's pose, with folded arms and downcast eyes, is similar to that of *Patienza* in Ripa's *Iconologia* (Rome, 1603), p. 381. One of the four female attributes in the large engraving *Sine Fine* (Ruscelli, pp. 108–9) surely must be Patience since she stands under the Motto of the Golden Fleece. She looks upward in the pose of Hope; yet her hands, again, are prayerfully folded, and the lamb suggests the sacrificial nature of Christian patience. Her companions are Religion-Faith, Charity, and Fortitude-Constancy. Sicciolante's painting *Pazienza* (reproduced in Heckscher, "Shakespeare," Fig. 22) personifies the virtue with her hands clasped around her waist under naked breasts; her head is turned away from the beholder, and her forward stride is checked by the iron and chain around her ankle (Tate, p. 128; Guy de Tervarent, *Attributs et symboles . . .* [Geneva, 1958–59], I:173).

48. "Shakespeare," pp. 35–56.

49. H. B. Wheasley, ed., *The History of Patient Grissel* (London, 1855). Homer's Penelope, who may be seen as the literary ancestor of long-suffering wives, stands between Patience and Perseverance in a Hardwick Hall tapestry (cited by Chew, *Pilgrimage of Life*, p. 267). "Mourning Penelope" in a red-figured Attic vase from Chiusi (after Roscher) sits holding her head; see R. and M. Alain-Peyrefitte, *Le Mythe de Pénélope* (Paris, 1949).

50. *Richard II*, V.ii.33; *King Lear*, IV.iii.18; *Cymbeline*, IV.ii.57; *Pericles*, I.ii.65; *Hamlet*,

IV.v.68. Constancy (patient fortitude) in the Stoic sense is a recurring word in *Julius Caesar*, as Portia, especially, reveals in II.i.237–302. And Cassius mocks the "Yoke and Suff'rance" of patience as "womanish" (I.iii.84). Also in this play, anger is readily associated with impatience (I.iii.61). Doebler discusses Shakespeare's definition of fortitude, as emphasized by Christian Stoicism of the Renaissance, in his chapter on *Macbeth* (p. 122).

51. All of these works are reproduced in Heckscher, "Shakespeare," Figs. XVII, XX, XXI, XXIV.

52. Morris P. Tilley, *A Dictionary of the Proverbs in England* . . . (Ann Arbor, 1950), P 108. Note also P 103: "He that has no patience has nothing."

53. *The Praise of Patience* (London, 1616), p. 271.

54. Reproduced in Lawrence J. Ross, ed., *The Tragedy of Othello the Moor of Venice* (Indianapolis, 1974), p. x: "Patience overcometh all things; wrath devours itself." A related vice is *Desperatio*, despairing, impatient rage (see, e.g., *King Lear*, V.iii.222–24), which patience should overcome.

55. Tilley, P 113; see also Breton, *Pray Be Not Angry* (1624) in *Works*, ed. A. B. Grosart (Edinburgh, 1879), II:4.

56. The same theme is depicted in an elaborate mythological woodcut in Boissard, *Emblematum liber* . . . (Frankfurt, 1593), XXX:60–61.

57. See the same theme in an engraving after Raphael by the "Master of Dice," 1532 (Bartsch, XV:205, 29). Of the lamb's various attributes, the primary one is that of patience (Tervarent, I:2). Note also Saint Paul's description of Christ as meek and gentle (II Cor. 10:1), one of many references to the Redeemer as the *Agnus Dei* (John 1:29). The lamb in Biliverti's *An Allegory of Gentleness* (Ferrarese school, sixteenth century) suggests that the painting may depict Patience. Note also that Spenser's Una, a multi-foliate symbol of truth and innocence (*The Faerie Queene*, I.i.4–6 ff.) who sits on a "lonely Asse" (humility), leads a "milke white lambe," which may recall the rescue of the king's daughter, marked for sacrifice, by Saint George in the *Golden Legend* (Caxton's fifteenth-century translation of Jacobus de Voragine's *Legenda Aurea*).

58. As in the *Psychomachia* of Prudentius; however, Spenser's Patience is masculine (*The Faerie Queene*, I.x.23–24) and Nicola Pisano's "Fortitude" (Pisa, Baptistry) is depicted as a nude male (reproduced in Kenneth Clark, *The Nude* [New York, 1956], Fig. 37).

59. An early instance in which *Patientia* appears with a lamb is in the choir window of the Auxerre Cathedral (c. 1230). *Patientia* holds a picture of a lamb. Eight virtues are represented enthroned in the sectors formed by the eight radii of the rose. The virtues are near the centre, while the vices are placed close to the circumference. *Patientia* is triumphant over *Desperatio* (i.e., *Ira*), who pierces herself with a spear. The engraving by Hans Sebald Beham, *Pacientia* (1540), in which she cuddles a lamb, is a later contemporary example of the frequent combination of this animal and the personified virtue. As our frontispiece reproduction shows, Patience is winged (as in Dürer's *Melencolia I*), sits on a column, and is oblivious to the monster baring his fangs at her. A set of eight virtues by Virgil Solis (Bartsch, IX:268, par. 197) includes *Paciencia*, who is represented with a lamb (Tate, pp. 35–36).

60. The anvil—prominent in numerous emblems concerned with endurance—is noted by Tuve (*Allegorical Imagery*, p. 166) as part of "the new iconography of the virtues" of the mid-fifteenth century. Chew cites the anvil as emblematic of Patience (p. 119 ff.) and Fortitude (p. 140) in *Pilgrimage of Life*. Tate notes that the anvil, traditionally the attribute of Fortitude, and the hammer, when combined in sixteenth-century engravings and emblems, conventionally suggest endurance or steadfastness.

61. Similarly, an anvil and hammers atop a large stone represent Constancy in La Perriére (*Le Théâtre des Bons Engins* [1539], no. 67, p. 144). The forge and fire are emblematic of Patience in Corrozet's *Hécatomographie* (1540), p 22: "Le tribulation vient prosperité." See also "plus il est dur, et plus il est ardent" in Le Moyne, *Devises héroiques et morales* (Paris, 1649), p. 103. Cf. also Junius (*Emblemata* . . . [Antwerp, 1565], no. LI), Ferro (*Teatro d'Imprese* [1695], II, no. 413), and Ruscelli (p. 129). See Hanna, note 37, in this volume.

62. *Constantia* is often related to Ceres and may wear a wreath of corn ears; see van Veen, *Spes optima nutrix* (no. 204), where wheat is combined with the anchor of Hope. Two of Wither's emblems relate harvests to hope in the midst of trials: I, no. 44—"if in honest Hopes, thou persevere / A joyfull Harvest will at last appeare." And in III, no. 10, a ploughing scene, we read that adversity's storms will not drown the seeds of hope when they are planted in affliction's ploughs and harrows.

63. The press as an iconographic motif of *Patientia-Fortitudo* is noted by Tuve, *Allegorical Imagery*, p. 60.

64. Camillo Camilli's collection of devices for royalty (II, no. 87) includes an impresa (*Pressa Tollitur Humo*) for Lucio Scarano depicting the same basket and acanthus plant. The same emblem is reproduced, e.g., in Ferro (II, no. 15). Chew's discussion of the camomile (*Pilgrimage of Life*, p. 118) is analogous: the more the herb is "trodden and pressed down, the more it spreadeth," Lyly says in *Euphues, the Anatomy of Wit*, in *Works of John Lyly*, ed. Bond (I:191); and note Falstaff's parody: "for Though the Camomile, the more it is trodden on, the Faster it grows, so youth, the more it is wasted the sooner it wears," *I Henry IV*, II.iv. 404–7. See Hanna (note 29) in this volume, for the medieval source of this image.

65. Heckscher, "Sturm und Drang." One survey of Spenser's emblematic sea images is provided by Kathleen Williams, "Spenser: Some Uses of the Sea and the Storm-tossed Ship," *Research Opportunities in Renaissance Drama* XIII–XIV (1970–71):135–42.

66. Quoted in F. E. Hulme, *The History, Principles and Practice of Symbolism in Christian Art*, 5th ed. (London, 1909), p. 211.

67. For this reference to the *Adagia*, I am indebted to Priscilla Tate, who also notes the connection between the ox and the story of Joseph (Gen. 41 and Deut. 33:17) and that, according to Irenaeus, the ox is specifically the figure of Christ as priest and sacrifice (*Against Heresies*, III:11, par. 8). See Hanna (note 14) in this volume, for a discussion of the ass.

68. Simeoni, *Le sententiose imprese* . . . (Lyons, 1560), no. 13; Pietrasanta, *De symbolis heroicis* . . . (Antwerp, 1634), no. 29; Typotius, I, no. 117.

69. As in Simeoni, nos. 13 and 29.

70. Horace is quoted as saying that patience can sustain what cannot be remedied (lib. i, ode 24).

71. Emblematic of patience as well as fidelity, friendship, vigilance, and melancholy (Tervarent, I:96).

72. Silence is the first means of curing impatience in others, according to J. Downame, *Consolations*, chap. 10. See also Martin le Roy Gomberville (*The Doctrine of Morality* [London, 1721], I, no. 28) and John Norden's description of the mouth of Patience sealed with the "honor of silence" (*A pathway to patience* [London, 1626], p. 10). The iconography of silence is treated by Karla Langedijk, "Silentium," *Netherlands Yearbook for the History of Art* CV (1964):3–18. See Capaccio's Patience with a bandage across her mouth, an emblem of silent endurance suggestive of the *Twelfth Night* image cited above (*Delle Imprese* [Naples, 1592], III, fol. 45r). See also Cousteau, *Le Pegme* . . . (Lyons, 1560), p. 144.

73. *Parthenia Sacra* (1633), ed. Iaian Fletcher (Aldington, 1950), IV, nos. 38–47; Freeman, *English Emblem Books*, pp. 192–93.

74. *Heliotropium seu Conformatio humanae voluntatis cum divina* . . . (Cologne, 1630). See also Freeman, *English Emblem Books*, pp. 25–29 and passim.

75. *Pilgrimage of Life*, p. 117. See my note 7.

Appendix

THE SCHOOL OF PATIENCE

A topical outline translation of *Gymnasium Patientiae*, by Jeremias Drexel, S. J., volume 2, pages 1–66, of *Opera Omnia* (Bruges, c. 1643).*

Part I (pp. 1–24)

Chap. 1. Which kinds of punishments, on which crosses, must be endured in the School of Patience
2. Why the students in this School have to endure so harshly and bitterly
3. Why some of the students are more tormented in this School than others
4. Five categories of punishments and afflictions are explained. . . .
5. Five more categories of types of punishment are also explained. . . .
6. Which guilty acts must be avoided in the School of Patience above all:
   —to be unaware of what has been taught
   —to chatter and tell tall tales
   —to be negligent about Scripture's daily assignment
   —to fail to attend without an excuse and to shun school
   —to quarrel violently or hit other students
   —to doodle, sleep, engage in trifling and to look out of the window
   —to feign illness
   —to lie or murmur against correction

Part II (pp. 24–44)

Chap. 1. Affliction teaches man fortitude and faith
   —The sweet waters of rivers and fountains have no effect on the saltiness of the sea; thus adversities will not affect the strong man's mind

*I am grateful to William S. Heckscher for his assistance with this translation.

—Calamity, and why it is a cause of virtue
—Why the School of Patience not only teaches fortitude but also faith
—We must be faithful and worthy of God

Chap. 2. Affliction teaches commiseration and abstinence
—For those in misery to have comrades in punishment is a solace
—He who has never been exposed to sad affairs is for that very reason inhuman to those in misery and why the Prince of the Apostles, Peter, was allowed to fall so heavily
—Temperance is taught in the School of Patience
—God at times will deprive us of our most treasured belongings so that we pay more attention to our own [spiritual] affairs
—There was no obstacle for him who seized Christ

Chap. 3. Affliction teaches us prayer and mortification
—Admonitions to prayer (David cited)
—a. Shouting to God in tribulation
—b. He who denies the existence of God is harsher than the Pharoah and more harmful than the devil
—The man who does not engage in work turns beastly and lecherous: for this reason God sends calamities in order to discipline us
—[Here Drexel quotes St. John Chrysostom in preferring silence, meditation, and true wisdom rather than feasts and rowdiness]
—[Quotes Constantine legend—prayer prevails—and quotes Psalm 49:15: "Invoke me in the day of tribulation and I will praise you and you will glorify me."]

Chap. 4. Affliction teaches prudence and modesty
—Punishment teaches prudence
—The bitterness of calamity is by far the best drug to heal us, not the voluptuousness of the world
—Why God handed the Law of Moses amid thunder and lightning
—Why God proscribed to Moses that he should put his hand in his bosom and when he withdrew it, it was leprous (in which manner, the School of Patience teaches wisdom and all humility)
—It is in keeping with modesty to recognize that in adversity we may be punished unfairly (whatever therefore has to be endured we must submit ourselves in all things to the divine scourge)

Chap. 5. Affliction is most useful in a variety of ways, and the majority of things which inflict damage teach us
—Water, in the pages of the divine Scriptures, acts as a symbol of affliction
—Why God in the Old Testament desired ashes to stand in such high honor
—Paradise was planted by God so that those created after His image, once they were expelled from it, would feel their tortures even more strongly; affliction is the remedy for evil
—Let not man hate the hand applying any of the scourges of God; under the impact of scourges let not our morale sink, for the scourge is a medicament for sin

Chap. 6. All afflictions and crosses, by whomsoever they be imposed, come from God
—Faith is needed in the School of Patience
—The people whom God loves most dearly are led to the Cross
—Prepare yourself not for ease and pleasure but for conflict and temptation
—If God is the origin of evil and of punishment, is he thus also the originator of sin?

—Good and evil, life and death, poverty and wealth are from God (Eccles. 2:14)

—In the School of Patience Christ . . . decrees that one be subjected to the other, and indeed that one be chastised by another [for his sins], yet only when he gives his assent thereunto

—But why, you will ask, does God make use of evil deeds. . . . Why do you inquire thus, curious man? God will give us no account concerning his reasons

—Yearly does the Church commemorate the Passion of Christ

—Even the most depraved people deserve all kinds of humane consideration

Part III (pp. 44–66)

Chap. 1. We must endure our afflictions patiently

—Definition of patience: the voluntary endurance which accepts without complaint what things soever happen or befall a man-other than he expected; a good man never cares what, but how well, he suffers

—Whence impatience comes: It is not evil to suffer bad things; not to know how to endure evil, *that* is bad

—Some documentation concerning patience:

Patience is enduring injuries

Patience is vindicated through self-restraint

Patience is used to restrain scourges

Patience is when goods are lost

Patience is to be preferred also in enduring others' afflictions

The dress and costume of Patience

The Praises [or attributes] of Patience

—We see from James the Anchorite that Patience is a remedy for all griefs; what saint was ever crowned without Patience?

—We are agitated by trifles and base things

—Often we forget that we are in banishment where all miseries should be borne with Patience

Chap. 2. We must meet our afflictions in a happy frame of mind

—"Do not yield to evils but go boldly against them" [Virgil, but no source cited]

—Endure humiliations for the name of Jesus

—Let us cheerfully run to the jail of suffering patiently

—Sadness [*Tristitia*] must be cast off

—The true and solid joy of a Christian is to be able to possess all joy (Example: King Wenceslas who was never as happy as when he was in prison)

Chap. 3. Affliction must be endured to the end in Constancy

—Many things that have started off well come to a miserable end in the School of Patience

—God loves Constancy in every decent human being

—Why do we not endure within the School of Patience?

—Considerations of Divine Will and Providence

—Spain has wines which are of a kind that, when drunk in their fatherland, taste horrible; yet, when exported over the seas, they will acquire a taste and a bouquet that is most attractive

Chap. 4. We must endure affliction in gratitude

—If anything hurt you or vex you, say thanks to God

—Tobias was not wroth at the Lord

—Under the Persian rulers, a man innocently flogged would offer thanks

—Thanks must be offered for everything

Chap. 5 We must encounter afflictions with premeditation
      —"Prepare thy mind for temptations" (Eccles. 2:1)
      —Nothing must be left to chance
      —You silence a wolf if you see him before he sees you
      —Premeditation acts therefore in adversity like a shield of steel
      —The source of pain and sadness in evil circumstances

Chap. 6. All afflictions must be seen through to the end by making the human will agree with that of the divine
      —There is no good volition that is not in complete agreement with divine volition
      —Patience makes us invincible
      —All students of Patience differ from each other
      —To array one's human will in conformity with the divine [will] should not appear hard to achieve for anyone
      —Evils confound many; why? That "why" must be banished from the School of Patience; as Augustine says, whatever happens in this world contrary to our will happens according to God's will
      —Resign and accommodate your will to God's goodness, patience, and Providence
      —Through adversity many thousands are brought to success [in life]; through prosperity, hardly anyone
      —A true student of patience brings the mind to condemn all afflictions and miseries
      —Epilogue or Recapitulation: Heaven is bought with labor and pains; life is a battle in which there is no rest nor ease. It is no sin to suffer but to do evil. . . . No one is ever to be accounted faithful who is not marked with this brand of Patience and Affliction

Patience Inventory

A. PRIMARY SOURCES

Adams, Thomas
  The happiness of the church. London, 1619.
  The three divine sisters, faith, hope and charity. Edited by W. H. Stowell. London, 1847.
Alanus ab Insulis (Alain de Lille)
  Liber in distinctionibus dictionum theologicalium. In *Patrologia Latina* (CCX:685–1012), edited by J. P. Migne. 221 vols. Paris, 1844–90.
Alciati, Andrea
  Andrea Alciati Emblematum flumen abundans, or Alciat's Emblems in their full stream. . . . Edited by Henry Green. Manchester, 1871.
  Diverse imprese accomodate a diverse moralita. . . . Lyons, 1551. Ed. prin., 1531.
  > Fortitude (no. 36), Hope (nos. 50–54). See also no. 28: *Obdurandum adversus urgentia* (palm tree blown in wind).
  Emblematum Libellus cum Commentariis. Padua, 1621.
Allestree, Richard [supposed author]
  The art of patience and the balm of Gilead under all afflictions. An appendix to the art of contentment. . . . London, 1694.
  > Frontispiece depicts undraped Patience seated on a cliff, holding a crown of thorns in one hand and a palm branch in the other, while angels hold a saintly crown above her head. The sections are entitled: "Of the connexion between Humility, Meekness and Patience"; "In time of Sickness"; "Afflictions of Conscience"; "Remedies against Temptations"; "Imbecility of Grace"; "Loss of Reputation"; "Of Publick Calamities"; "Loss of Friends"; "Of Poverty"; "Of Confinement"; "In Exile"; "Of Blindness and Deafness"; "Of Sterility"; "Want of Repose"; "Of Gray Hairs"; "Of Mortality"; "Of Judgment"; "Spiritual Conflicts"; "Character of Patience."
Ames, William
  The Marrow of Sacred Divinity. Translated as *The Marrow of Theology* from the 3d Latin ed. (1629), edited by John D. Eusden. London, 1643. Reprint. Boston, 1968.

This influential Puritan theologian defines patience as the virtue which moderates anger stirred up by grievous wrong (p. 315). See book II, chap. 2, no. 30: the third general expression of virtue is fortitude, which contains confidence, perseverance and constancy, and endurance and patience; no. 33: add "to continence patience (with which you may outlast any hardships for righteousness' sake)"; chap. 6 (Hope), no. 17: "the fruit and companion of hope is patience toward God whereby we constantly cling to him, seeking and expecting blessedness"; no. 18: "One fruit of this patience is the silence in which we rest on the will of God . . ." (pp. 229–30, 247–48).

Amman, Jost

293 Renaissance Woodcuts for Artists and Illustrators. Edited by Alfred Werner. New York, 1968. Ed. prin., 1599.

No. 68: *Allegory of Strength* (armed female with column seated on pedestal); no. 79 may be Patience (kneeling female looks heavenward amid rock and column).

Aneau, Barthélemy

Picta Poesis. London, 1552.

Anselm, Saint

Manuale Catholicorum. A Manuall for True Catholickes. Translated by William Carshaw. London, 1611.

Aquinas, Saint Thomas

Summa Theologica. 3 vols. Ottawa, 1941.

II-II, Q. 128: Fortitude. Cicero's four component parts—confidence, magnificence, patience, perseverance—are divided into two categories: aggressive (the first two) and enduring (the last two).

Arias, Francis

A Treatise of Patience. Translated 1630. English Recusant Literature, vol. XXI. Menston, 1970.

The Assaute and Conquest of heaven. Translated by Thomas Paynell. London, 1529.

Atkins, John

The Christians race. London, 1624.

Sermon asserts that patience is essential for every Christian's spiritual armor.

Attersoll, William

Three Treatises: Conversion of Ninevah; God's Trumpet; Physicke Against Famine. London, 1632.

Note especially "God's Trumpet," pp. 78–92: The end of God's patience ought to be our patience; patience abused breeds wrath; patience neglected breeds destruction.

Augustine, Saint

The De Bono Perseverantiae of St. Augustine. Edited and translated by Sister M. Alphonsine Lesonsky. Washington, D.C., 1956.

Saint Augustine on Christian Doctrine. Translated by D. W. Robertson, Jr. New York, 1958.

Austin, William

Devotionis Augustinianae Flamma, or Certayne Devout, Godly, and Learned Meditations. London, 1635.

Title piece features Patience with heart, yoke, anvil, and hammer in engraving by George Glover.

Baldacchini, Filippo

Dyalogo de Patientia. N.p., 1525.

Baptista Mantuanus

De patientia. Basel, 1499.

Among the many topics treated: patience defined (lib. I, cap. 31); how patience is the way to holiness and heaven, what virtues patience induces in men and what adversities it prevents (lib. II); the nature of faith, hope, charity, and long-suffering (lib. III).

Bargagli, Scipione
Dell'Imprese. . . . Venice, 1594.
Asprezza Cresce (no. 75—rock of constancy); *Giore spera* (no. 127); *Qui miglior Frutti Spero* (no. 190); *In Quascunque Formas* (no. 213—hammers, anvil); *Ut Feritur Ferit* (no. 274); *Alterius Sic Altera* (no. 335); *Iactata Magis* (no. 412); *Sine injuria* (no. 422); *Omnia mea mecum* (no. 461).

Barrow, Isaac
Of Contentment, Patience and Resignation to the Will of God. Several Sermons. London, 1685.
"Of Patience" (pp. 195–238).

Bartholome, Batman Uppon
His Booke De Proprietatibus Rerum. London, 1582.

Bateman, Stephen
A christall glasse of Christian Reformation. London, 1569.
Annotated woodcuts of virtues and vices in what is sometimes seen as the earliest emblem book in English. See Wrath (fol. ciiv): "A wrathful person provoketh contention: but he that is patient appeaseth debate."

Baudoin, Jean
Recueil d'emblèmes divers. 2 vols. Paris, 1638–39.

Bayly, Lewis
The Practice of Pietie Directing a Christian how to walke that he may please God. London, 1619.

Baynes, Paul
Briefe Directions unto a Godly Life. London, 1618.

Becon, Thomas
Prayers and other pieces of Thomas Becon. Edited by John Ayre. Cambridge, 1844.
"The Sick Man's Salve" (1561), pp. 87–191. See also "The Demands of Holy Scripture" (p. 621), and "The Pomander of Prayer" (pp. 81–82).

Beham, Hans Sebald
Pacientia (1540), engraving. In *Le peintre graveur* (no. 138), edited by Adam von Bartsch. 21 vols. Vienna, 1803–1921.
Discussed in Heckscher, "Shakespeare."

Berchorius, Petrus (Pierre Bersuire)
Dictionarium seu Reportorium Morale. 2 vols. Venice, 1583.

Bernard of Clairvaux, Saint
A Hive of Sacred Honie-Combes Containing most Sweet Heavenly Counsel: Taken out of the Workes of . . . S. Bernard. Translated by Antonie Batt. Doway, 1631.
Joy in Tribulation. London, 1631.

Beza, Théodore (de Bèze)
Christian meditations upon eight Psalmes of the Prophet David. Translated by "I. S." London, 1582.
Icones, id est Verae Imagines . . . . Geneva, 1580.

Bible
Biblia Sacra Vulgatae. Paris, 1922.
The Holy Bible (Authorized Version). London, 1611.

Boccaccio, Giovanni
Génealogie. Paris, 1531.
Historia de vera Patientia, quam ab Johanne Boccato vernacula Thuscorum lingua conscriptam latinitatae donavit Francis Petrarcha, ut iam lege cum voluptate et fructu ab omnibus posse. Paris, n.d.

Bocchi, Achille

Symbolicarum Quaestionum libri quinque. . . . Bologna, 1574.

Lib. II, symb. XLIX, p. C: *Disce pati quisquis vincere semper aves* ("Let him whose highest wish is to vanquish always learn to suffer"). A female figure, her head bowed, holds a staff topped by bucranium, helmet, and "winged hair"; she is stooped under a yoke, stands close to a barren tree, and is governed by the golden chain of being which appears from a cloud.

Boethius

The Consolation of Philosophy. Translated by "I. T." (1609). Rev. ed., Loeb Classical Library. Edited by H. F. Stewart. Cambridge, Mass., 1918.

Five Books of Philosophical Comfort, full of Christian consolation, written a 1000. yeeres since. London, 1609.

Boissard, Jean Jacques

Emblematum liber . . . . Frankfurt, 1593.

No. XXX: *Laesa Patientia Fit Furor* (frequent emblem of patience provoked).

Theatrum Vitae Humanae. Metz, 1596.

The Boke of Common Praier. 30th ed. London, 1594.

Bolton, Robert

Some Generall Directions for a Comfortable Walking with God. London, 1625.

Bonaventure, Saint

Opera omnia . . . . Edited by A. C. Peltier. Paris, 1867.

Borja, Juan de

Emblemata Moralia . . . . Berlin, 1697. Ed. prin., *Empresas Morales* (Prague, 1581).

Nitor in adversum (no. 10); *Ferendo Vinciam* (no. 17—rock of constancy amid rough seas); *Tranquilitatis Foecunda* (no. 18); *Ut Melius Tendere Possim* (no. 59—yoke); *Ne Te Quaesiveris Extra* (no. 60); *Irae Malum* (no. 66); *Tribulatio Optima* (no. 68); *Sapientia Animas* (no. 75—stone cube); *Incursionibus Solidatur* (no. 92—winds blow sturdy tree).

Bornitius, Jacobus

Emblemata Ethico Politica. Mainz, 1669.

I, no. 3: *Fata Viam Invenient*; II, no. 31: *Talis Fortuna.*

Boschius, Jacobus

Symbolographia. N.p., 1701.

See Class. III (*Symbola Ethica . . .*), Table XLIII: *Pater Fam. Patientiae* (no. 837—anvil, hammers); *In adversis exultat* (no. 838—dolphin); *Cedendo Restitit* (no. 844—trees blown by wind). Table XVIII: *Constantia* (no. 313—stone cube); no. 314 (anvil, hammers); no. 335 (laurel supported in wind storm).

Bourne, Immanuel

The True Way of a Christian, to the New Ierusalem. London, 1622.

Breton, Nicholas

I pray you be not angry. London, 1605.

The Pilgrimage to Paradise. London, 1592.

"The Praise of Patience" (1605). In *The Works in verse and prose of Nicholas Breton . . . .* Edited by A. B. Grosart. Edinburgh, 1879.

The Soules immortall crowne divided into seaven dayes works. London, 1605.

Bruck, Jacobus à

Emblemata moralia et bellica (1615). In Gabriel Rollenhagen, *Nucleus emblematum selectissimorum.* Magdeburg, 1611.

Emblemata politica. Cambridge, 1604.

Brune, Johan de

Emblemata of Zinne-werck. Amsterdam, 1624.

Bryskett, Lodowick

A Discourse of Civill Life. London, 1606.

"There is a kind of fortitude that hath no need of any ... anger .... And this is that blessed virtue which never suffers a man to fall from the height of his minde, being called by some men patience. . ." (p. 88); though not separate from the cardinal virtue of fortitude, patience means that he "who so beareth stoutly adversities deserveth greater commendation and praise than they which overcome their enemies, or by force win cities or countries, or otherwise defend their owne" (p. 89).

Bullinger, Heinrich
The tragedies of tyrants exercised upon the church. Translated from Latin by Thomas Twine. London, 1575.

Bunny, Edmund
A Booke of Christian Exercise, appertaining to Resolution .... London, 1584.
The coronation of David .... London, 1588.

Burges, Cornelius
A Chaine of Graces: Drawne out at length for reformation of Manners .... London, 1622. Chap. 6, "Of Patience" (pp. 113-57): its definition includes forbearance, taking injury without revenge, "a contented brooking of delayes"; sensible yet quiet bearing of all crosses and afflictions. Patience is a Grace of the Spirit. "It is the dutie of all Christians to get, and abound in supernatural patience, which may enable them to undergoe all labours, delayes and crosses. . .freely, cheerfully, and thankfully for God's honour, the benefit of the Church or Common-wealth, the preservation of their own faith and good conscience to the end" (p. 119). A patient man is like a bird in a cage, put there to be tamed; an impatient man is like a wild bull in a net (p. 134).

Calvin, John
Sermons of Master John Calvin, upon the booke of Job. Translated from the French by Arthur Golding. London, 1574.

Camerarius, Joachim
Symbolorum et emblematum ex re Herberia Desumtorum. .... Nuremberg, 1590.
Ardua virtutem (no. 5); *Gaudet Patientia Duris* (no. 58—acanthus plant); *Spes altera vitae* (no. 100).

Camilli, Camillo
Imprese Illustri di diversi, coi discorsi. .... Venice, 1586.
I: no. 10 (cypress); no. 31 (dead tree, green top); no. 52 (*Ardua virtutem*); no. 70 (column); no. 156 (rock, thorns); no. 180 (*Sperare nefas*). II: no. 27 (column); no. 87 (*Pressa Tollitur Humo*—acanthus).

Camus, John Pierre
A Spirituall Combat: A Triall in Temptation. Translated by "M. C. P." of the English College at Doway. Doway, 1632.
See Part I, chap. 19: "Patience accompaignied with courage, finds all things supportable . . ." (p. 103).

Capaccio, Giulio Cesare
Delle Imprese. Naples, 1592.
III, fol. 45r.: Patience with bandage (silent endurance) stands on square cube. For ox, see II, fols. 34-39.

Capel, Richard
Tentations: their nature, danger, cure. 2d. ed. London, 1635.
Not of major importance, but see p. 92: "We must bear temptation with a kind of impatient patience." Resistance to temptation comes through patience (pp. 126-29).

Case, John
Speculum moralium quaestionum in universam ethicam Aristotelis. N.p., 1585.

Cassian, John
Opera. Edited by Michael Petschenig. Vienna, 1886-88.

According to this influential fifth-century source, patience is the medicine which can cure all sins; he who is patient cannot be perturbed by anger, consumed by sloth, sadness, or pride (*Collatio*, XII.6).

The Castle of Perseverance (c. 1405). Edited by F. J. Furnivall and A. W. Pollard. London, 1904.

Cats, Jacob
Spiegel van den Ouden ende Nieuwen Tÿdt. Dordrecht, 1635.
Caussinus, P. Nicolao (Nicholas Caussin)
The Christian Diurnal. Translated by T. H. Paris, 1623.
    Part II ("The Practice of Virtues"), sec. iv: "Of Fortitude" (p. 221); "Of Patience" (pp. 222–23).
De Symbolica Aegyptiorum Sapientia. Cologne, 1633.
    Patientia: I, no. 62; VII, no. 102; X, no. 51 (palm=endurance); XI, no. 51 (patience alleviates evil). *Fortitudo*: VII, no. 53. *Perseverantia*: VII, no. 9. *Constantia*: VI, no. 63; IX, no. 60; XI, no. 1. *Pudicitia*: VII, nos. 29, 44. *Spes*: XII, no. 40.

Certain Sermons or Homilies Appointed to be Read in the Time of Queen Elizabeth. Dublin, 1767. Ed. prin., 1547.
    On the distinction between Stoic and Christian patience: "Histories be full of Heathen Men that took very meekly both opprobrious and reproachful words and injurious and wrongful deeds. And shall those heathen excel in patience us that possess Christ, the teacher and example of all patience . . . . Is it not a shame for us that possess Christ, to be worse than a heathen people, in a thing chiefly pertaining to Christ's religion? Shall philosophy persuade them more than Religion shall with us?" ("Of Contention," p. 113).

Chapelin, George, trans.
Christian Praiers, and consolations gathered out of sundrie places of the holie Scripture and learned writings of the ancient Fathers. London, 1601.
Chappuys, Gabriel
Figures de la Bible. Lyons, 1582.
Chartier, Alain
Delectable demaundes, and Pleasant Questions . . . . London, 1596.
    Weighted palm tree=constancy, no. 227.
Chytraeus, David
A soveraigne salve for a sicke soule. Translated by "W. F." London, 1590.
    A brief but valuable discussion of patience, defined as "a vertue that reverently submitteth itselfe to the will of God in bearing mildly and gently all griefs and miseries. . ." (fol. Aiiiir). In the eighteen chapters on the virtue, its parts, form, description, and necessity are delineated in conventional terms. Patience is called a singular gift of the Holy Ghost, and afflictions are seen as a school of wisdom.
Cicero
De Finibus Bonorum et Malorum. Translated by H. Rocham. New York, 1931.
De officiis. Translated by Walter Miller. New York, 1913.
Clerck, Nicolaes de
Const-Toonneel, Inhoudende de beschrijvinghe ende XL. Heerlijke Afbeeldindinghen. . . . Delft, 1609.
    No. 5 (*Fortitudo*—with column); no. 7 (*Spes*).
Coelho, Jorge
De Patientia Christiana. N.p., 1540.
Cogler, Johann
Similitudines Accommodate ad necessarias et praecipuas partes doctrinae coelistis. Wittenberg, 1561.

Patience rests her elbow on column (fol. 24r).

Colonna, Francesco

Hypnerotomachia, The Strife of Love in a Dream. London, 1592. Facsimile, edited by J. W. Appel, entitled *The Dream of Poliphilus, facsimiles of 168 woodcuts in the Hypnerotomachia Poliphili, 1499.* London, 1889.

> Note bucranium in nos. 18, 104; yoke in no. 107. N.B. the triumphal cars and ornamental altars in this influential art-romance, especially the *Triumph of Europa* (nos. 47–48), *Triumph of Cupid* (nos. 143–44). Also relevant to works such as the *Patientiae Triumphus* is the elephant (no. 12) with the inscription *Labor and Industry.* See also the translation by Robert Dallington (London, 1973).

Combe, Thomas

The Theatre of Fine Devices. Translated by Thomas Combe (from La Perrière, q.v.). London, 1614.

> No. 97: man treading crops ("The more saffron is trodden, the more it flourishes"). See Chew, *Pilgrimage of Life,* p. 118, and Freeman, *English Emblem Books,* pp. 63–64.

Comes (Conti), Natale

Mythologiae sive explicationes fabularum libri decem. . . . Venice, 1567.

Coornhert, Dirck Volckertszoon

Recht Ghebruyck ende misbruyck van Tÿdelÿck have. Leyden, 1585.

Corrie, G. E., ed.

Certain Sermons appointed by the Queen's Majesty 1574. Cambridge, 1850.

Corrozet, Giles

Hécatomographie de Gilles Corrozet (1540). . . . Facsimile, edited by C. Oulmont. Macon, 1905.

> *De tribulation vient prosperité* (p. 22); *Esperance en adversité* (p. 82); *Esperance conforte l'homme* (p. 98); *L'inconstant perit* (p. 122).

Cousteau, Pierre

Le Pegme de Pierre Cousteau, avec les Narrations Philosophiques. Lyons, 1560.

> Silence stands on altar with her hand over her mouth (no. 144); see also *Vertu surmonte tout* (no. 121).

Coverdale, Miles

Writings and Translations of Myles Coverdale . . . . Edited by George Pearson. Cambridge, 1844.

> "A Spiritual and Most Precious Pearl" (1550), pp. 84–194.

Cowper, William [Bishop of Galloway]

A Conduit of Comfort . . . . London, 1606.

A Defiance to Death . . . . London, 1610.

Good News from Canaan. Full of heavenly comfort and consolation . . . . London, 1613.

The Praise of Patience. London, 1616.

The Triumph of a Christian . . . . London, 1636.

Two Fruitful and Godly Treatises to Comfort the Afflicted. London, 1616.

> "The Praise of Patience" (chap. 2, p. 223 ff.): patience is the armor by which we may best defend the soul; patience is like the laurel tree which cannot be thunderstruck: so too persecution overcomes all except the patient (p. 270).

The Works, now newly collected into one volume . . . . London, 1626.

Cramer, Daniel

Emblemata Moralia Nova . . . . Frankfurt, 1630.

> *Spes et patientia* (p. 109): man's feet locked in *pedica*; anchor of hope.

Crowley, Robert

The Way to Wealth. London, 1550.

> A representative homiletic exhortation on patience: "Be sure, therefore, that if thou kepe thy selfe in obedience and suffer al this oppression patiently, not geving credite unto false prophecies that tel the of victorie but to the worde of God that telleth the thy

dutie: thou shalt at the time, and after the maner that God hath alredie pointed, be delivered" (sig. A7).

Cutreman, Philippe de
The true christian catholique. London, 1622.

Cyprian, Saint
De Bono Patientiae. Translated by A. J. Stephano. London, 1633.
See also Migne, *Patrologia Latina*, IV:623.
De Bono Patientiae. Edited and translated by Sister M. George Conway. Washington, D.C., 1957.

Day, John
Peregrinatio Scholastica. In *Works of John Day*, edited by A. H. Bullen. London, 1881.

Day, Richard
A Book of Christian Prayers. London, 1579.
Note *Patience over Wrath* woodcut (fol. 63v).

The declaracyon and power of the chrysten fayth. London, c. 1530.

Dekker, Thomas
The pleasant comedie of Patient Grissill. London, 1603.

De la Primaudaye, Peter
The French Academy. London, 1618.

Dent, Arthur
The Plaine Man's Path-way to Heaven. London, 1601.

Dod, John, and Robert Cleaver
Seven Godlie and Fruitful Sermons. Whereunto is Annexed, a Briefe Discourse, touching, 1. Extinguishing of the Spirit, 2. Murmuring in affliction. London, 1614.

Donne, John
Devotions upon Emergent Occasions. Edited by John Sparrow. Cambridge, 1923.

Downame, George
The christian arte of thriving. London, 1620.

Downame, John
Consolations for the Afflicted. London, 1622.
Summary of selected major points: Book I—Of afflictions; we must put on spiritual armor against our conflict with afflictions. Book II—Of patience in afflictions; there can be no true patience where there is no grief; patience must be joined with constancy, with cheerfulness in bearing crosses, and with joy; no one can attain perfection in patience but must labor after it; we have no true patience by nature but must seek it of God by prayer; there is no true patience among the heathens; we can have no patience unless we are sure that afflictions spring from God's love and are not punishments but fatherly chastisements; our afflictions advance the good of our neighbors; God by afflictions increases in us all those virtues which concern our neighbors and ourselves; some means whereby we may strengthen faith, hope, and patience are delineated.
A Treatise of Anger . . . . London, 1609.
The second means to subdue anger is "to labour for patience" (chap. 7, p. 65).

Drexel, Jeremias
Gymnasium Patientiae. In *Opera Omnia* (II:1–66). Bruges, c. 1643.
Translated by "D. L." (London, 1640) and by "R. S." (London, 1640) as *The School of Patience*; see my appendix.
*Heliotropium seu Conformatio humanae voluntatis cum divina. . . .*Cologne, 1630.
Chew (*Pilgrimage of Life*, pp. 179-80) notes that the final (fifth) plate includes Moses, a type of patience, leaning upon the rock of constancy.

Du Bartas, Guillaume de Salluste

The Divine Works and Weekes of Du Bartas (1614). Translated by Josuah Sylvester and edited by A. B. Grosart. 2 vols. Edinburgh, 1880.

Dürer, Albrecht

Melencolia I (1514), engraving. Reproduced in *The Complete Engravings, Etchings and Drypoints of Albrecht Dürer* (Fig. 79), edited by W. L. Strauss. New York, 1973.
> The winged central figure is in a conventional pose of patience (Heckscher, "Shakespeare," pp. 42–47).

Du Vair, Guillaume

De la constance et consolation des calamites publiques. Rouen, 1604.

The Moral Philosophy of the Stoicks, Englisshed by Thomas James (1598). Edited by Rudolf Kirk. New Brunswick, N.J., 1952.
> "We can do no more but to undertake a matter with wisdom, pursue it with hope, and be ready to suffer whatever may happen with patience" (p. 127). See also p. 111: Christian patience includes humility and faith, in contrast to Stoic patience.

Erasmus, Desiderius

Adagiorum Erasmi Epitome. Amsterdam, 1650.

Estella, Diego de

The contempte of the world, and the vanitie thereof.... Translated by "G. C." Doway?, 1589.
> Part I, cap. 31: "Of the profit of tribulations"; II, cap. 23: "Of patience in adversitie"; III, cap. 20: "Of silence."

Estienne, Henri

The Art of Making Devises. Translated by Thomas Blount. London, 1646.
> A translation of *L'art de faire les Devises* (Paris, 1645). Blount drew upon *The Faerie Queene* for inspiration; see Freeman, *English Emblem Books*, p. 81.

Farinator [Pistorious], Matthias

Lumen animae. Augsburg, 1477.

Featley, Daniel

Ancilla Pietatis; or the hand-maid to private devotion. London, 1626.

Ferro, Giovanni

Teatro d'Imprese.... Venice, 1623.
> Useful for its reliance on other emblematists. For emblems involving anvil, column, oxen, acanthus, etc., see II, nos. 15, 43, 52, 143, 213, 236, 413.

Feuille, Daniel de la

Devises et Emblems anciennes et modernes. Amsterdam, 1693.

Flamen, Albert

Devises et emblesmes d'Amour, moralisez .... Paris, 1653.
> *Spes Inde Serens* (no. 14); *Per Vincula Cresco* (no. 58); *Furor est Patientia Laesa* (no. 96).

Fleming, Abraham

The Diamond of Devotion. London, 1602.
> Only chap. 6 is of interest: "What we ought to do when God punisheth us with adversitie" and "Affliction in body and conscience, with an exhortation to patience" (Part I, pp. 24–25).

A Monomachia of Motives in the Mind of Man .... London, 1582.

Fletcher, Joseph

The History of the Perfect-Cursed-Blessed Man: Setting Forth Man's Excellency, Misery, Felicity by his Generation, Degeneration, Regeneration (1628). In *Poems* (pp. 23–119), edited by A. B. Grosart. London, 1869.

Fletcher, Phineas
  Joy in Tribulation, or Consolations for Afflicted Spirits. London, 1632.
    Not of major interest, but see chap. 5: "What comforts a Christian soule may gather from affliction itself."

The Florentine Fior di Virtu of 1491. Translated by Nicholas Fersin. Washington, D.C., 1953.
    Cicero is quoted (p. 75): "Man must be brave in battle and patient in adversity." Socrates, Homer, Solomon, and others are quoted on patience as perfect fortitude. See chap. 27, "Fortitude," and chap. 31, "Constancy."

Florio, John
  A Worlde of Wordes, or Most Copious, and exact Dictionarie in Italian and English .... London, 1598.
    See *Patiente* and *Patienza* (p. 262); *Perseverenza* (p. 270).

Francis de Sales, Saint
  An introduction to a devoute life. Translated by J. Yakesley. Rouen, 1614.
    Part II, chap. 3, "Of Patience" (pp. 217-26).

Freitag, Arnold
  Mythologia Ethica. Antwerp, 1579.

Friederich, Andreas, and Jacques de Zettre
  Emblemes Nouveaux .... Frankfurt, 1617.

Fulke, W.
  A Godly Learned Sermon Preached 26th Feb. 1580. London, 1580.

Gesner, Conrad
  Lexicon graeco-latinum. Basel, 1545.
    Holbein's title-border, featuring *Tristitia, Fortitudo,* and *Spes,* is reproduced in Doebler, *Shakespeare's Speaking Pictures* (plate 23).

Giovio, Paolo
  The Worthy Tract of Paulus Iovius. . . . Translated by Samuel Daniel. London, 1585.

Goltzius, Hendrik
  Patientia and Fortitudo, engraving. In *Le peintre-graveur* (III:37, 114-17), edited by Adam von Bartsch. 21 vols. Vienna, 1803-1921.

Gomberville, Martin le Roy [Le Roy, Marin, Sieur de Gomberville]
  The Doctrine of Morality; or a View of Human Life, according to the Stoick Philosophy. . . . Translated by T. M. Gibbs. London, 1721.
    A translation of *La Doctrine des Moeurs* (Paris, 1646) with 103 copperplate engravings; based on Otto van Veen. See I, no. 28: *Silence is the life of friendship;* no. 31: *Temperance is the sovereign good;* II, no. 2: *The fool always complains of his condition.*

Goodyere, Henry
  A mirrour of maiestie: or the badges of honour conceitedly emblazoned . . . (1618). Edited by Henry Green and James Croston. Manchester, 1870.

Gregory the Great, Saint
  Moralia in Job. In *Patrologia Latina* (LXXV, cols. 509-1162; LXXVI, cols. 9-782), edited by J. P. Migne. 221 vols. Paris, 1844-90.

Hall, John
  Emblems with Elegant Figures, 1658. Edited by John Horden. English Emblem Books, no. 17. Menston, 1970.
    II, no. 3 (hope); no. 6 (man, seated on rock, opens his heart and alludes to Augustine:

"For I carried my soul as it were torn in sunder, and gored with blood, and impatient even to be carried by me").

Halling, Arthur
The Cruell Shrew: or the patient man's woe. London, 1610.
Hawes, Stephen
The Example of Vertu. London, 1530.
   A poetic disputation between the Ladies Hardiness, Sapience, Fortitude, and Nature.
Hawkins, Henry [attrib.]
Parthenia Sacra. Or the mysterious and delicious Garden of the Sacred Parthenes. . . .
Rouen, 1633. Edited by Iaian Fletcher. Aldington, 1950.
   Violet (pp. 38–47); palm (pp. 153–64) as emblematic of bearing injuries and oppressions without shrinking. On the inseparability of patience and fortitude, see p. 155.
Heemskerck, Maarten van
Patientiae Triumphus, eight engravings by Dirck Coornhert. Antwerp, c. 1555.
Triumphus Cupidinis et Pudicitiae, six engravings after Petrarch by P. Galle. Antwerp, 1600.
Heyns, Zacharias
Emblemata, Emblemes Chrestiennes, et Morales. Rotterdam, 1625.
   I, fol. 2Gr (*Perfer et obdura*—diamond, anvil); fol. D2r (sunflower). II, fols. 43r and 47r (palm, thorns).
Hilton, Walter
Qui Habitat. In *Minor Works,* edited by Dorothy Jones. London, 1929.
The Scale of Perfection. Edited by Evelyn Underhill. London, 1923.
Hoefnaghel, Joris
Patientia. 24 politieke emblemata door Joris Hoefnaghel 1569. Facsimile of Rouen MS. Edited by R. van Roosbroeck. Antwerp, 1935.
   Of the twenty-four moral emblems by this Flemish miniaturist (done in London), nineteen of the verses are in Dutch, three in Spanish, two in French; the initial emblem is discussed and reproduced in Heckscher, "Shakespeare," pp. 49–50, Fig. 21.
Holland, Henry
Herologia Anglia . . . . Utrecht, 1620.
   Title plate (*Fortitude and Patience with Prudence and Religion Personified*) is reproduced in Heckscher, "Shakespeare," Fig. 15.
Hooker, Richard
A remedie against sorrow and feare. London, 1612.
Horapollo
Ori Apollinis Niliaci. . . . Paris, 1551.
   See *Labor* (bucranium), p. 221; *Ira,* p. 135.
The Hieroglyphics of Horapollo. Translated by George Boas. New York, 1950.
   I, no. 46; II, nos. 38, 72, 77.
Horozco y Corarrubias, Juan de
Emblemas Morales. Segovia, 1589.
   Note no. VII (altar and column).
Hugh of St. Victor
Tratto della patientia . . . Venice, 1541.
Hugo, Hermann
Pia Desideria Emblematis . . . . illustrata (1624). London, 1686.
   I, no. 11 (Psalm 68), no. 12 (Job 14); II, no. 13 (Psalm 72).
Hull, John
Saint Peter's prophesie of these last daies. London, 1610.
Hutchinson, Roger
The Works of Roger Hutchinson. Edited by John Bruce. Cambridge, 1842.
   See "Two Sermons on Oppression, Affliction and Patience," pp. 289–340.

Isidore of Seville
Etymologiarum sive originum, Libri XX. Edited by W. M. Lindsay. 2 vols. Oxford, 1911.
X, no. 201: *Patiens dictus a pavendo*; II, nos. 6 (*Fortitudo*), 24; VIII, nos. 2, 5 (*Spes*);
X, no. 40 (*Constans*).

Janua linguarum . . . cum translatione anglicana, by W. Welde. London, 1615.
1,200 sententiae in Latin and English. See no. 402 ("patience rejoiceth in adversitie"; no.
415 ("the palme tree groweth strong with weight").
Jeffray, William
The picture of patience, or a direction to perfection. London, 1629.
Jemin, Michael
A Commentary upon Ecclesiastes. London, 1639.
Jenner, Thomas
The Soules Solace; or Thirtie and one Spiritual emblems. London, 1626.
Note no. 3 (a remedy against despair).
John Chrysostom, Saint
A godly exhortation made unto the people of Antioch, touching Patience. London, 1591.
Junius, Hadrianus (Adriaan de Jonge)
Emblemata . . . . Antwerp, 1565.
Note nos. XXIII, XXXVII, LI.

Kis, Stephanus
Tabulae analyticae, de fide, caritate et patientia. N.p., 1593.
Knell, Thomas
An ABC to the christen congregacion. London, 1550?
Brief devotional poem includes this admonition: suffer Christ's cross when it is laid on
your back.
Knight, R. G.
"Characterisme of the Foure Cardinall Vertues." In *Panacea: or Select Aphorisms Divine
and Morall.* London, 1630.

La Faye, Antoine de
Emblemata et Epigrammata Miscellanea selecta ex Stromatis Peripateticus . . . . Geneva,
1610.
Fortiter adversa patiens, amara in dulcia convertit (no. 202).
La Perrière, Guillaume de
Le Théâtre des Bons Engins, auquel sont contenuz cent emblèmes moraulx (1539).
Facsimile, edited by Greta Dexter. Gainesville, Fla., 1964.
Nos. 19, 43, 65, 67 (Constancy with anvil, hammers, rock), 69, 70.
Latimer, Hugh
The Sermons and Life . . . of Hugh Latimer. Edited by John Watkins. 2 vols. London, 1858.
Legh, Gerard
The Accedens of Armory. London, 1568.
Fortitude (fol.A6v).
Leigh, Valentine
The Pleasaunt, Playne and Pythye Pathewaye leadynge to a vertues and honest lyfe.
London, 1550.
Leigh, William
*The christians watch: Or, An Heavenly Instruction to all Christians, to expect with pa-
tience the happy day of their change by death or doome.* London, 1605.

Le Moyne, Pierre
  Devises héroiques et morales. Paris, 1649.
    Pp. 43 (rose blown by wind: grace brings solace to afflicted ones), 71, 87 (dead tree
    with ivy), 101, 103 ("Plus il est dur, et plus il est ardent").
Ley, John
  A pattern of pietie; or the life and death of Mrs. J. Ratcliffe. London, 1640.
Licetus, F.
  Hieroglyphica, sive antiqua schemata anularium. . . . Padua, 1653.
Linche, Richard
  The Fountaine of Ancient Fiction. London, 1599.
Lipsius, L. Justus
  Iusti Lipsi De Constantia libri duo. . . . Antwerp, 1615.
  Monita et exempla politica. Antwerp, 1625.
    Note discussion of great people possessed of patience (pp. 202–8).
  *Two Bookes of Constancie, written in Latine by Iustus Lipsius; Englished by Sir John
  Stradling* (1594). Edited by Rudolf Kirk. New Brunswick, N.J., 1939.
    "Patience is a voluntarie sufferance without grudging of all things whatsoever can hap-
    pen to, or in a man." The true mother of constancy is patience and lowliness of mind,
    and the true nature of constancy is the steadfastness of a mind grounded in reason
    (book I, chap. 4, p. 79).
Loarte, Gaspare
  *The Exercise of a Christian life . . . with certaine verie devout Exercises and Praiers
  added thereunto.* Translated by James Sancer. Paris, 1579.
Lomazzo, G. P.
  Tracte Containing the Artes of Curious Paintinge, Carvinge & Buildinge. . . . Trans-
  lated by "R. H." [Richard Haydocke]. Oxford, 1598.
Longland, John
  A Sermon Spoken before the Kynge at Grenwich uppon good Fryday. London, 1536.
Lorens d'Orleans
  The Book of Virtues and Vices. Edited by W. Nelson Francis. London, 1942.
    A fourteenth-century English translation of the *Somme le Roi* of Lorens d'Orleans.
    Prowess, which displaces Sloth, has seven degrees: Magnanimity, Affiance (or Good
    Hope), Security, Patience or Sufferance (Tribulation forges and shapes sufferance . . .
    "without suffrance may no man ne womman come to parfitnesse," p. 167), Constancy
    (or Continuance), Magnificence (called Perseverance by Christ), Hunger and Thirst
    after Righteousness (pp. 164–70). See also Love (pp. 145–48), of which sufferance and
    forbearance are branches, and Meekness (pp. 130–32).

Maccio, Paolo
  P. M. Emblemata. Bologna, 1628.
    See especially nos. 38, 48, 78.
Maier, Michael
  Atalanta Fugiens. Oppenheim, 1617.
Masen, Jakob
  Speculum Imaginum Veritatis Occultae. Cologne, 1681.
    The third edition of this naked emblem book. See *Index Moralis: Patientia*, chaps. 77,
    78; *Patiens*, chap. 79; *Perseverantia*, chap. 83; *Fortitudo*, chaps. 11, 14, 31, 32;
    Constantia, chaps. 42, 77, 79; *Spes*, chaps. 12, 24, 77.
Maurer, Christoph
  XL Emblemata miscella nova. Zurich, 1622.
Maurus, Hrabanus
  "De Fortitudine patientiae." In *Patrologia Latina* (CXII:1632), edited by J. P. Migne. 221
  vols. Paris, 1844–90.

Metsijs, Cornelis
  Patientia, engraving. In *Le peintre graveur* (IV:111, 42), edited by Adam von Bartsch. 21
  vols. Vienna, 1803–1921.
    Reproduced in Heckscher, "Shakespeare," Fig. 16.
Migne, J. P., ed.
  Patrologia Latina. 221 vols. Paris, 1844–90.
Milton, John
  The Works of John Milton. Edited by F. A. Patterson. 18 vols. Columbia ed. New York,
  1931–38.
    Patience is that "whereby we acquiesce in the promises of God through a confident reli-
    ance on his divine providence, power and goodness, and bear inevitable evils with
    equanimity as the dispensation of the supreme Father, and sent for our good. Opposed
    to this is impatience under the divine decrees; a temptation to which the saints them-
    selves are at times liable" (vol. XVII, book II, chap. 3, p. 69).
Montenay, Georgette de
  Monumenta Emblematum Christianorum Centuria. . . . Zurich, 1584. Ed. prin.,
  Emblemes, ou devises chrestiennes (Lyons, 1571).
    Note especially nos. 31, 59, 60, 100; this last (*Patientia vincit omnia*) is reproduced in
    Henkel and Schöne, no. 353.
More, Saint Thomas
  Dialogue of Comfort against Tribulation. Edited by Miles Leland. Bloomington, Ind.,
  1966.
Mornay, Phillip of
  The Shielde and Rewarde of the Faithfull. London, 1620.
Moulin, Pierre de
  *A Preparation to Suffer for the Gospell of Jesus Christ, or a Most Christian Exercise full
  of Comfort and Consolation for these present times*. London, 1623.
    Patience is one of the most necessary virtues for a Christian, for it helps to preserve all
    others. . . . It is patience which bridles our affections, appeases our passions, moder-
    ates our violences, sways over our temptations, reduces errant reason into the right
    way, establishes the soul in her proper seat and residence. . . . There is no greater
    misery than to lack patience in a time of misery. . . . (pp. 43–44).
Mostaert, Gilles
  Patientia, drawing (1585).
    Reproduced in the Smithsonian Institution's *Antwerp Drawings and Prints, 16th–17th
    Centuries* (Washington, D.C., 1976), Fig. 24.
Musculus, Wolfgang
  Commonplaces of Christian religion. Translated by John Man. London, 1563.
    This learned treatise discusses patience extensively (fol. 521v): what patience is, its
    parts, types of patience, patience in Scripture, examples of the virtue, etc. It is defined
    in terms of expectation, abiding, and suffering. Note also "Impatience" (fol. 528v) and
    "Afflictions" (fol. 509r).
Myddleton, Richard
  Goodness; the blessed mans Badge; or, God's Character stampt on mans Conscience.
  London,1619.
    Sermon I: Love makes all difficult things easy (p. 113); Sermon II: the assurances of
    goodness are a lively faith, sound knowledge of God through Jesus Christ, temperance,
    "patience to bear sweetly whatsoever God shall please to lay upon him," obeying the
    Ten Commandments, brotherly kindness, love of God and man (p. 149).

Nani Mirabellio, Domenico
  Polyanthea novissimarum novissima. . . . Venice, 1630. Ed. prin. (less valuable), 1509.

Patientia (pp. 992–96); *Fortitudo* (pp. 484–93); *Spes* (pp. 1292–97); *Constantia* (p. 270).

Nixon, A.

The Dignitie of Man. Oxford, 1616.

For a catechism-like treatment of patience, see pp. 91–92; patience as part of fortitude, p. 87; tribulation, pp. 67–72.

Norden, John

A pathway to patience in all Manner of Crosses, Tryals, Troubles and Afflictions. . . . London, 1626.

Affliction is a school in which man learns patience; patience bears all things, brooks not a repining heart, is never idle, is a mark of God's choice; afflictions do not make a man miserable but honorable; ignorant men think patience is cowardice; we ought to embrace whatever God sends us; afflictions are medicines for our sins and the crown of the godly (pp. 2–20, closely paraphrased).

A poore mans rest. London, 1631.

Among the prayers (against temptations, despair, etc.) is the "Prayer for Patience in Affliction" (pp. 135–39), preceded by a definition: patience means bearing injuries with a willing mind without grudging.

Nowell, Alexander

A Catechism, or First Instruction of Christian religion (1571). Edited by G. E. Corrie. Cambridge, 1853.

Oraeus, Henricus

Viridarium hieroglyphico-morale. . . . Frankfurt, 1619.

Spes non confundit (no. X—ship, anchor, cross); *Patientia vincit omnia* (no. XXXII).

Paradin, Claude

Devises héroiques. Lyons, 1551. Translated by "P. S.," London, 1591.

No. 87: *Ardua deturbans, vis animosa quatit.*

Parsons, Robert

A Christian Directorie guiding men to their salvation. N.p., 1585.

1607 edition is reproduced in English Recusant Literature, vol. XLI, ed. D. M. Rogers (Menston, 1970).

The Seconde parte of the Booke of Christian exercise, appertayning to Resolution. London, 1590.

Partridge, John.

The worthie historie of the valiant knight Placidus. London, 1566.

Pavonius, Franciscus

Summa ethicae. N.p., 1633.

Peacham, Henry

The Garden of Eloquence. London, 1577.

Minerva Britanna, 1612. Edited by John Horden. English Emblem Books, vol. V. Menston, 1969.

See nos. 65, 71, 158 (rough seas=manly constancy); 163, 167 (cypress with green top= the greater the oppression, the greater the growth). As Chew observes (*Pilgrimage of Life*, p. 3), Peacham's melancholic man has his mouth bound and one foot fixed on the cube of constancy. Peacham, who drew upon Ripa, Whitney, and *The Faerie Queene*, is interesting for his references to color (e.g.,Constancy is dressed in blue with silver, the color of steadfastness).

Pearl Poet

The Complete Works of the Pearl Poet. Edited by Margaret Williams, R.S.C.J. New York, 1970.

Patience. Edited by Hartley Bateson. 2d ed. Manchester, 1918.

Peraldus, William [Guilelmus de Peraldus]

Summae virtutum ac vitiorum. Cologne, 1614. Ed. prin., Venice, 1497.

Book I (*Patientia*): *Christo assimilat; Jocunditatem expectat; Sustinendo coronat; Iram temperat,* etc. (pp. xviii-xix). *De Fortitudine* (Part III, chap. iv, pp. 208-44) includes description of patience (par. 6). See also Index (pp. 215-20; 237-38).

Perkins, William

A Golden Chaine. London, 1597.

Representative popular religious handbook.

Physicke for the soul in the agony of death. Translated by Henry Thorne. London, 1568.

Picinelli, Filippo

Mundus Symbolicus. Translated by Augustinus Erath. Cologne, 1694. Ed. prin., 1669.

Pietrasanta, Silvestro

De symbolis heroicis. . . . Antwerp, 1634.

Inclinata Resurgo (p. 39—weighted palm); *Pas à Pas* (p. 29); *Ardua virtutem* (p. 219); *Labore et Constantia* (p. 382—compass); *Et Peregrinum Alo* (p. 371); *Durate* (p. 341—storm-tossed ship).

Pliny

Naturalis historia. Venice, 1469.

The diamond's name means "indomitable" and it cannot be broken by anvil or hammer (book XXXVIII).

Polanus, Amandus

The substance of Christian religion. Translated by Thomas Wilcocks. London, 1600.

Chap. 16: of God's permission or sufferance; chap. 20: of affliction and the cross.

Pordrage, Samuel

Mundorum Explicatio or The Explanation of a Hieroglyphical Figure. . . . London, 1661.

Powell, Robert

The resolved christians. London, 1602.

Poyntz, Adrian

The treasure of the soule, newly translated from Spanish. . . . London, 1596.

Price, Lawrence

Bee patient in trouble. London, 1636.

Devotional ballad: "in affliction, give God thanks for all" (refrain).

The Primer Set Furth by the Kinges Maiestie, 1546. London, 1546.

Prudentius, Aurelius Clemens

Psychomachia. In *Prudentius,* translated by H. J. Thomson. Vol. I. Cambridge, Mass., 1949.

Pp. 274-343: *Patientia,* lines 109-77.

Quarles, Francis

Emblemes. London, 1635.

See Freeman, *English Emblem Books,* pp. 114-32 and passim.

Reusner, Nicolas

Emblemata . . . partim ethica, et physica: partim vero Historica et Hieroglyphica. Frankfurt, 1581.

Ripa, Cesare

Iconologia. Rome, 1603.

Patienza (p. 381—seated on rock, hands folded); *Speranza* (p. 469).

Nova Iconologia. Padua, 1618.
Rollenhagen, Gabriel
   Nucleus Emblematum Selectissimorum. Utrecht, 1613. Ed. prin., 1611.
      I: *Victrix Patientia Duri* (no. 28—tree green only on top); *In Silentio et Spe* (no. 61);
      Constante Fiducia (no. 69); *Spes Alit Agricolas* (no. 94—lady with anchor and oxen).
      II: *Facet Spera* (no. 7—female Hope with shovel, eyes downcast); *Labore et Constantia*
      (no. 9); *In Spe et Labore Transigo Vitam* (no. 16—Hope, with shovel and anchor,
      looks heavenward); *Virtus Inexpugnabilis* (no. 37—diamond, anvil); *Pas à Pas* (no.
      39); *Gaudet et Patientia Duris* (no. 74—man walking in thistles); *Furor fit Laesa
      Saepius Patientia* (no. 94); *Perseveranti Dabitur* (no. 100). See Wither, *A Collection of
      Emblemes*.
Ruscelli, Girolamo
   Le Imprese illustri. . . . Venice, 1584.
      Impresa for Ercole d'Este II, Fourth Duke of Ferrara, depicts Patience with arms
      crossed, eyes down, standing near rock with banner (p. 156); *Inclinata Resurgo*
      (p. 209—weighted palm); *Semper adamas* (p. 129—diamond, fire, hammers). *Sine
      Fine* (engraving) depicts Faith, Charity, Patience, and Fortitude (pp. 108-9). See also
      pp. 182, 287.

Sambucus, Joannes
   Emblemata, et aliquot, nummis antiqui operis. Quarta ed. Antwerp, 1584.
      Tolerantia (no. 136); *In Spe fortitudo* (no. 141); *Patientia laesa fit furor* (no. 271).
Sandys, Edwin
   The Sermons of Edwin Sandys, D.D. Edited by John Ayre. 2 vols. Cambridge, 1841-42.
Schoonhovius, Florentius
   Emblemata Florentii Schoonhovii I. C. Goudani. . . . Gouda, 1618.
      Patienter ferendum, quod necesse est (no. 184—farm scene with oxen features trapped
      starling which, though broken and provoked, remains constant); *Ardua quae pulchra*
      (no. 219—man climbs palm tree).
Schudder, Henry
   The christians daily walke in holy securitee and peace. London, 1628.
Seres, William
   A Tablet for Gentlewomen. London, 1594.
      Advocates silence for women.
Shakespeare, William
   The Complete Signet Classic Shakespeare. Edited by Sylvan Barnet. New York, 1972.
   Pericles. Edited by F. D. Hoeniger. London, 1963.

A short and pretie Treatise touching the perpetuall Reioyce of the godly, euen in this lyfe.
London, 1568.
      Printed with Edward Hake's translation of *The Imitation of Christ*.

Sicciolante, Giralamo
   Pazienza. Florence (Pitti Palace), 16th century.
      Reproduced in Heckscher, "Shakespeare," Fig. 22.
Simeoni, Gabriele
   Le sententiose imprese, et dialogo. . . . Lyons, 1560.
      For oxen, palm, column, stormy sea, etc., see nos. 13, 29, 37, 76, 78, 79, 118.
Southwell, Robert
   An Epistle of Comfort. Edited by Margaret Waugh. Chicago, 1966.
   Triumphs over Death (1591). Edited by J. W. Trotman. London, 1914.
Sparke, Michael
   The Crums of Comfort to Groans of the Spirit, The Second Part . . . *Whereunto is
   Added A Handkerchief for Wet-Eyes*. London, 1652.

Spenser, Edmund
  The Poetical Works of Edmund Spenser. Edited by J. C. Smith and E. de Selincourt.
  London, 1912.
Stephanus, Charles [Charles Estienne]
  Dictionarium Historicum, Geographicum, Poeticum. Paris, 1596.

Tasso, Torquato
  Jesusalem Delivered, an Heroic Poem. Translated by John Hoole. London, n.d.
Taurellus, Nicolaus
  Emblemata Physico-Ethica. Nuremberg, 1595.
    Chew (*Pilgrimage of Life*, p. 349, no. 19) cites sig. D6r: man hanging from palm tree
    teaches resistance to adverse fortune and victory to be gained by effort.
Taylor, Jeremy
  A Course of Sermons for all the days of the year. In *The Whole Works of Rt. Rev.*
  Jeremy Taylor, edited by Reginald Herber. Rev. ed. edited by Charles P. Eden. Vol. IV.
  London, 1848.
    See especially sermons 9–13 (1651 et seq.): "We have reason not only to be patient but
    rejoice when we are persecuted in a righteous cause: for love is the soul of Christianity,
    and suffering is the soul of love" (p. 449, "The Faith and Patience of the Saints"). See
    also "forbearance" (p. 478) and "long suffering" (p. 483).
Tertullian
  "Patience." In *Disciplinary, Moral and Ascetical Works.* Translated by R. Arbesmann et al.
  New York, 1959.
    See Migne, *Patrologia Latina,* I:1249–52.
Thomas à Kempis
  Of the Imitation of Christ. Translated by Thomas Rogers. London, 1580.
Thynne, Francis
  Emblemes and Epigrames (1600). Edited by F. J. Furnivall. London, 1876.
    Patience: no. 12, pp. 13–14, one of Thynne's naked emblems based on imaginary pic-
    tures. See Freeman, *English Emblem Books,* p. 67.
The Treasure of the Soule . . . newly translated into English by A. P. London, 1596.
    A moral allegory featuring Lady Humility, one of whose daughters is Poverty (Part I,
    chap. 20); Patience (Part II, chap. 1, pp. 173–82) includes the proverb, "There is no
    gaine without paine, no joy without annoy."
Turnbull, Richard
  An Exposition of the Canonical Epistle of Saint James. London, 1591.
Tyndale, William
  Doctrinal Treatises. Edited by H. Walter. Cambridge, 1848.
  The obedience of a christian man. London, 1528.
Typotius, Jacobus
  Symbola Divina et Humana Pontificum Imperatorum Regum (1601). Frankfurt, 1652.
    Book I: no. 20 (anchor, column); no. 124 (lady at sea with anchor); no. 117 (ox); no.
    114 (rock which saw cannot penetrate). II: no. 70 (anvil); no. 159 (shipwreck). III: no.
    1 (stone cube); nos. 5, 25, 34, 44, 47 (Patience, with arms folded across naked breasts, is
    chained to rock); no. 75 (weighted palm); no. 94 (diamond); *Fide et Patientia* (no.
    146—dog tied to tree).

Udny, Alexander
  The Voice of the Cryer. Containing 1. A Denunciation of God's Judgments. 2. An Invita-
  tion to Repentance to prevent the same. London, 1628.
    Be patient in waiting for God's mercy; he does not respect our crosses and calamities
    unless we join them with true repentance (p. 61).

Valeriano [Bolzani], G. Pierio [Joannes Pierius Valerianus]
   Hieroglyphica, sive de sacris Aegyptiorum. Basel, 1575.
      Lib. XLVIII, fol. 359b: *Patientia*; lib. XLI, fol. 306d: *Fortitudo* (diamond on rock). See
      also indexes: *Ira, Spes, Silentium, Constantia.*
Valerius, Cornelius
   *The casket of jewels: a playne description of morall philosophie. Out of Latin by J.
   Charlton.* London, 1571.
      This list of virtues and vices includes Fortitude (chap. xxix), Patience and Perseverance
      (chap. xxi: "the charge of patience is double: one in abiding injuries received, the other
      in suffering all calamities of fortune with an upright mind"), and Temperance (chap.
      xxxiii).
Veen, Jan van der
   Zinne-Beelden, oft Adams Appel. Amsterdam, 1642.
      No. II: Hope sits on rock with her hand on her head.
Veen, Otto van [Otho Vaenius]
   Emblemata sive Symbola. Brussels, 1624.
      No. 146 (stone cube=quiet); no. 204 (anchor with wheat).
Veghelman, S. (trans.)
   The Foundation of Christian Religion. . . . London, 1612.
      "A Treatise of Hope" (pp. 281–97).
Vennard, Richard
   The Right Way to Heaven. London, 1601.
      Chap. x: "An Exhortation to continue patient in Adversitie: the true Christian should
      be strongly armed with patience."
Verryke, E.
   Zederyke Zinnebeelden. Amsterdam, 1713.
      Nos. 5, 19, 22.
Vincent of Beauvais
   Speculum doctrinale. Venice, 1494.
   Speculum morale. Strasburg, 1476.
Voragine, Jacobus de
   The Golden Legend or Lives of the Saints. Translated by William Caxton, edited by F. S.
   Ellis. 7 vols. London, 1931.
      Stephen, the first Christian martyr and saint, was crowned for his patience (II:152).

Wakeman, Robert
   Jonah's Sermon and Ninivehs repentance. London, 1606.
      The homilist emphasizes the long-suffering of the Lord.
Warren, Arthur
   The poore man's passions and poverties patience. London, 1605.
      Two poems combining Christian allegory and classical allusions. "Poverties Patience,"
      containing 140 six-line stanzas, is worth noting for its association of poverty with
      patience.
Wastel, Simon
   A True Christians Daily Delight. London, 1623.
Webbe, George.
   A Posie of Spirituall Flowers, Taken out of the Garden of the holy Scriptures. London,
   1610.
   The Practice of Quietness: directing a Christian to live quietly in this troublesome world.
   London, 1618.
Webster, William

The plaine mans pilgrimage, or journey towards heaven. London, 1613.
> Not of major importance, but see chap. 4: "Christians ought to be thankful even in persecution, in thraldom, in adversity, in shame, in misery, and in death itselfe" (p. 138).

Whitforde, Richard
Here Foloweth dyvers holy instrucyons. London, 1541.

Whitney, Geffrey
A Choice of Emblemes (1586). Edited by Henry Green. Rev. ed., with introduction by Frank Fieler. New York, 1967.
> *Virescit vulnere virtus* (no. 98); *Constanter* (no. 129); *Constantia comes victoria* (no. 137); *Vincit qui patitur* (no. 220: with patience "wee must the combat wage").

Willet, Andrew
Sacrorum emblematum centuria una. Cambridge, c. 1591–92.

Wilson, Thomas (c. 1525–81)
The Arte of Rhetorique. Edited by G. H. Mair. Oxford, 1919.
> "Sufferance," "Continuance" defined (pp. 34–35).

Wilson, Thomas (1563–1622)
A Christian Dictionary. London, 1612.
> *Patience* (pp. 352–53): "1.) a suffering and bearing long with such as do provoke us, waiting till they amend . . . 'Have patience with me and I will pay thee all,' Matt. 18:29. 2.) the slowness of God to anger . . . sparing sinners that they may have space of repentance. 3.) quiet and constant suffering of afflictions for godliness. 4.) Hope, expectation or waiting. 5.) Perseverance in weldoing unto the ende." See also *Perseverance* (p. 358).

Wither, George
A Collection of Emblemes, Ancient and Moderne. . . . London, 1635.
> The same 200 emblems as in Rollenhagen, q.v., but treated differently. Book I: no. 23 ("Suff'rance" produces contentment); no. 26 (endure with patience); no. 28 (no grief can overcome a patient heart); no. 39 (Hope repels grief); no. 44 (persevere in hope for joyful harvest). Book II: no. 7 (Ixion, the impatient man, bound on a wheel resembling Lear's "wheel of fire"); no. 10 (dolphin-anchor, *festina lente*); no. 11 (Silence and Hope); no. 19 (Constancy on square cube, crowned like a saint); no. 44 (Hope-harvest-oxen); no. 46 (affliction as flail); no. 47 (value of affliction). Book III: no. 7 (Hope with shovel); no. 16 (Hope with shovel and anchor); no. 37 (diamond-anvil: true virtue will abide suffering); no. 38 (weighted palm tree); no. 39 (ox, *pas à pas*). Book IV: no. 1 (marigold); no. 9 (Hope's withered branch); no. 20 (stone cube); no. 24 (*Gaudet Patientia Duris*—man amid thistles); no. 44 (*Furor Fit Laesa Saepius Patientia*—boy attacked by lamb: "Who, Patience tempts, beyond her strength/Will make it Fury, at the length"). See also the facsimile edition edited by Rosemary Freeman and C. S. Hensley (Columbia, S.C., 1975).

Wollebius, John
The Abridgement of Christian Divinity. London, 1650.

Woolton, John
The Christian Manual. London, 1576.

Wright, Leonard
The Pilgrimage to Paradise. London, 1591.
> See especially chap. 5 (the passage to heaven compared to warfare) and chap. 6 (the arms and weapons of a Christian soldier); we should be "well and strongly armed, with the breastplate of equitie: the shield of undoubted faith in Christ: the helmet of assured hope . . . the girdle of truth, well buckled with patience, and constancie . . ." (p. 18). "He that in Paradise will come to joy with Christ must travell with patience under the crosse of Christ" (p. 20).

Zarate, Hernando de
    Discursos de la patienca Christiana. Alcala, 1592.
Zarlino, Gioseffo
    Utilissimo trattato della patientia, a tutti quelli chi desiderano vivere christiane-mente. . . . Venice, 1583.
        See female figure holding branch (laurel?) in title piece woodcut; also Flagellation woodcut (fol. 35r).
Zincgreff, Julius Wilhelm
    Emblematum Ethico-Politicorum Centuria. Heidelberg, 1616.

B. SECONDARY SOURCES

Alain-Peyrefitte, R. and M.
    Le Mythe de Pénélope. Paris, 1949.
Appleton, Leroy H., and Stephen Bridges
    Symbolism in Liturgical Art. New York, 1959.
Apteker, Jane
    Icons of Justice: Iconography and Thematic Imagery in Book V of the Faerie Queene. New York, 1969.
Auber, Marcel
    Histoire et Théories du symbolisme religieux. Paris, 1884.
Audsley, W. J., and G. A. Audsley
    Handbook of Christian Symbolism. London, 1865.

Bächtold-Stäubli, Hans
    Handwörterbuch des deutschen Aberglaubens. Berlin & Leipzig, 1921–42.
Bartsch, Adam von
    Le peintre graveur. 21 vols. Vienna, 1803–1921.
Baumgartner, Paul R.
    "Milton and Patience." *Studies in Philology* LX (1963): 203–13.
Berliner, Rudolf
    "Arma Christi." In *Münchner Jahrbuch der bildenden Kunst.* Munich, 1955.
        As the tools by which one overcomes sin, the *Arma Christi* can symbolize the two-fold essence of Patience: that he obediently endures and, through his suffering, ultimately triumphs. See "The Triumph of Patience," p. 130; Kirschbaum, *Lexicon*, III:185.
Bethune-Baker, J. F.
    An Introduction to the Early History of Christian Doctrine. . . . 5th ed. London, 1933.
Bloomfield, Morton W.
    The Seven Deadly Sins. East Lansing, Mich., 1952.
Bode, H. G., ed.
    Scriptores rerum mythicarum. Zelle, 1834.
Boyce, Benjamin
    "Stoic *Consolatio* and Shakespeare." *PMLA* LXIV (1949):771–80.
Bradbrook, M. C.
    "Virtue is the True Nobility." *Review of English Studies* I (1947):289–301.
Bréhier, Louis
    L'Art Chrétien, son développement iconographique des origines à nos jours. 2d ed. Paris, 1929.
Breidenbach, Herbert
    "Der Emblematiker Jeremias Drexel, S.J. (1581–1638), mit einer Einführung in die

Jesuitenemblematik und einer Bibliographie der Jesuitenemblembucher." Ph.D. dissertation, University of Illinois, 1971.

Bridoux, André
Le Stoicisme et son Influence. Paris, 1966.

Burger, C. P.
"Het hieroglyphen schrift van de renaissance." *Het Boek* XIII (1924):273-300.

Bush, Douglas
The Renaissance and English Humanism. Toronto, 1939.

Campbell, Lily B.
Shakespeare's Tragic Heroes, Slaves of Passion. Cambridge, 1930.

Chew, Samuel C.
"The Iconography of *A Book of Christian Prayers* (1578)." *The Huntington Library Quarterly* VIII (1945):293-305.
The Pilgrimage of Life. New Haven, 1962.
    Patience (pp. 116-22 and passim); Patience and grief (pp. 120-21); Constancy (pp. 66-67 ff.); Fortitude (pp. 133-34 and passim); Hope (pp. 111-13 and passim).
The Virtues Reconciled: An Iconographic Study. Toronto, 1947.

Clements, Robert J.
"Ars Emblematica." *Romantisches Jahrbuch* VIII (1957):95-109.
Picta Poesis: Literary and Humanistic Theory in Renaissance Emblem Books. Rome, 1960.

Collins Baker, C.H., and W. G. Constable
English Painting of the Sixteenth and Seventeenth Centuries. London, 1930.

Colvin, Sidney
Early Engraving and Engravers in England. London, 1905.

Crampton, Georgia Ronan
The Condition of Creatures: Suffering and Action in Chaucer and Spenser. New Haven and London, 1974.

Cross, Frank L., ed.
The Oxford Dictionary of the Christian Church. London, 1957.

Cuffe, Edwin D., S.J.
"An Interpretation of *Patience, Cleanness,* and *The Pearl* from the Viewpoint of Imagery." Ph.D. dissertation, University of North Carolina, 1951.

Curtius, Ernst R.
European Literature in the Latin Middle Ages. Translated by Willard R. Trask. New York, 1953.

Danby, John F.
Poets on Fortune's Hill. London, 1952.
    See especially pp. 47-70, 83, 110.

Davies, Horton
Worship and Theology in England from Cranmer to Hooker. Princeton, 1970.

Didron, Adolfe
Christian Iconography; or, the History of Christian Art in the Middle Ages. Translated by E. J. Millington. 2 vols. London, 1851.

Dieckmann, Liselotte
"Renaissance Hieroglyphics." *Comparative Literature* IX (1957):308-21.

Ditchfield, P. H.
Symbolism of the Saints. London, 1910.

Doebler, John

Shakespeare's Speaking Pictures: Studies in Iconic Imagery. Albuquerque, 1974.
    See especially pp. 122, 149 (fortitude), and the valuable bibliography.
Doering, Oskar
Christliche Symbole. Freiburg, 1940.
Drake, Maurice
Saints and their emblems. London, 1916.

Evans, Daniel
The Prayer Book: Its History, Language, and Contents. London, c. 1900.
Ewbank, Inga-Stina
"'More Pregnantly than Words': Some Uses and Limitations of Visual Symbols."
Shakespeare Survey XXIV (1971):13–18.

Fairchild, Arthur H. R.
Shakespeare and the Arts of Design. University of Missouri Studies, XII:1. Columbia,
    1937.
Ferguson, George
Signs and Symbols in Christian Art. New York, 1959.
Fletcher, Angus
Allegory, the Theory of a Symbolic Mode. Ithaca, N.Y., 1964.
Forstner, Dorothea
Die Welt der Symbole. 2d ed. Innsbruck, 1967.
    Cites Ignatius of Antioch: "Let baptism be your shield, Faith your helmet, Love your
    lance, and Patience your armor" (p. 480); also cites (p. 147) the diamond as symbolic of
    Christ (*Physiologus*, fourth century).
Freeman, Rosemary
English Emblem Books. London, 1948.
    Index of Emblems: Constancy (pp. 74, 145–47); Hope (p. 81); Sunflower (p. 23 ff.);
    Violet (p. 179 ff). General Index: Combe, Goodyere, Hall, Hawkins, Peacham, Quarles,
    Thynne, Whitney, Wither.
Frye, Roland M.
Shakespeare and Christian Doctrine. Princeton, 1963.

Garff, Jan, ed.
Tegninger af Maerten van Heemskerck. Copenhagen, 1971.
Gellert, Bridget
"The Iconography of Melancholy in the Graveyard Scene of *Hamlet.*" *Studies in Philology*
    LXVII (1970):57–66.
Giovannini, Giovanni
"Method in the Study of Literature and Its Relation to the Other Arts." *Journal of Aes-
    thetics and Art Criticism* VIII (1950):185–95.
Golden, Martha H. F.
"The Iconography of the English History Play." Ph.D. dissertation, Columbia Univer-
    sity, 1964.
Goldsworthy, W. L.
Shakespeare's Heraldic Emblems: Their Origin and Meaning. London, 1928.
Goodspeed, Edgar J.
A History of Early Christian Literature. Chicago, 1942.
Gottfried, Rudolf
"The Pictorial Element in Spenser's Poetry." *ELH* XIX (1952):203–13.
Green, Henry
Shakespeare and the Emblem Writers. London, 1870.

Hagstrum, Jean H.
  The Sister Arts: The Tradition of Literary Pictorialism from Dryden to Gray. Chicago, 1958.
Harris, William O.
  "Despair and 'Patience as the Truest Fortitude' in *Samson Agonistes.*" In *Critical Essays on Milton from ELH* (pp. 277–90). Baltimore, 1969.
  Skelton's Magnyfycence and the Cardinal Virtue Tradition. Chapel Hill, N.C., 1965.
Hart, A. Tindal
  The Man in the Pew, 1558–1660. London, 1966.
Hart, Alfred
  Shakespeare and the Homilies. Melbourne, 1934.
Hautecoeur, Louis
  Littérature et peinture en France du XVII au XX siècle. Paris, 1942.
Heckscher, William S.
  "Aphrodite as a Nun." *Phoenix* VII (1953):105–17.
  "The Genesis of Iconology." *Stil und Ueberlieferung in der Kunst des Abenlandes* III (1967):239–62.
  "Shakespeare in his Relationship to the Visual Arts: A Study in Paradox." *Research Opportunities in Renaissance Drama* XIII–XIV (1970–71):5–71.
  "Sturm und Drang: Conjectures on the Origin of a Phrase." *Simiolus* I (1966–67):94–105.
Henkel, Arthur, and Albrecht Schöne
  Emblemata. Handbuch zur Sinnbildkunst. . . . Stuttgart, 1967.
    See *Geduld* (pp. 122, 193, 297, 352, 360, 509, 536, 881, 1446). See also review by W. S. Heckscher, *Renaissance Quarterly* XXIII (1970):59–80.
Hind, Arthur M.
  Engraving in England: The Reign of James I. Cambridge, 1955.
Hollstein, F. W. H.
  Dutch and English Etchings, Engravings and Woodcuts, ca. 1450–1700. Amsterdam, n.d.
Hulme, F. Edward
  The History, Principles and Practice of Symbolism in Christian Art. 5th ed. London, 1909.

Jameson, Anna B.
  Sacred and Legendary Art. 2 vols. Boston, 1885.
Jong, H. M. E. de
  "Michael Maier's *Atalanta Fugiens:* bronnen van een alchemistisch emblemenboek." Ph.D. dissertation, Utrecht, 1965.

Katzenellenbogen, Adolf
  Allegories of the Virtues and Vices in Medieval Art. . . . London, 1939. Reprint. New York, 1964.
Kelly, Faye L.
  Prayer in Sixteenth Century England. Gainesville, Fla., 1966.
Kerrich, Thomas
  A Catalogue of the Prints . . . after Martin Heemskerck. Cambridge, 1829.
Kirchner, Gottfried
  Fortuna in Dichtung und Emblematik des Barok. Tradition und Bedeutungswandel eines Motifs. Stuttgart, 1970.
Kirschbaum, Englebert, ed.
  Lexicon der Christlichen Ikonographie. 6 vols. Rome, 1968.
Klein, H. Arthur

Graphic Worlds of Peter Brueghel the Elder. New York, 1963.
Knipping, J. B.
De Iconografie van de Contra-Reformatie in de Nederlanden. Hilversum, 1939.

Langedijk, Karla
"Silentium." *Netherlands Yearbook for the History of Art* CV (1964):3–18.
Lanoe-Villene, Georges
Le livre des Symboles. Paris, 1926–29.
Leclercq, Jean
Etudes sur le vocabulaire monastique du Moyen-Age. Rome, 1961.
Lee, Rensselaer W.
Ut Pictura Poesis: The Humanistic Theory of Painting. New York, 1967.
Lessing, Theodor
Symbolik der menschlichen Gestalt. Celle, 1925.
Levitsky, Ruth M.
"Shakespeare's Treatment of the Virtue of Patience." Ph.D. dissertation, University of Missouri, 1959.
Lightfoot, J. B.
St. Paul and Seneca. Cambridge, 1869.

Machie, G. M.
A Dictionary of Christ and the Gospels. New York, 1909.
Mack, Maynard
King Lear in Our Time. Berkeley, 1965.
    See pp. 111–12: the tragic fate of man in the play is best defined in terms of patience.
Mâle, Emile
L'Art Religieux après le Concile de Trente. Paris, 1951.
Religious Art from the twelfth to the eighteenth century. New York, 1958.
Marle, Raimond van
Iconographie de l'art Profane au Moyen-Age et à la Renaissance. . . . The Hague, 1931.
    Vol. II, chap. i, Figs. 2–11 (Psychomachia, Strasbourg, etc.); Figs. 19, 39, 53, 68, 69 (Hope); Figs. 23, 26, 58 (Courage); Fig. 66 (Patience—bronze medallion depicts her seated with lamb, her hands extended prayerfully).
McKeon, Richard, ed. and trans.
Selections from Medieval Philosophers. 2 vols. New York, 1929–30.
Mehl, Dieter
"Emblems in English Renaissance Drama." *Renaissance Drama,* n.s. II (1969):39–57.
Meikle, W.
"The Vocabulary of 'Patience' in the Old Testament" and "The Vocabulary of 'Patience' in the New Testament." *Expositor* XIX (1920):219–25, 304–13.
Meiss, Millard
De Artibus Opuscula XL: Essays in Honor of Erwin Panofsky. 2 vols. New York, 1961.
Molsdorf, Wilhelm
Christliche Symbolik der mittelalterlichen Kunst. Liepzig, 1926.
Monroy, Ernst Friedrich von
Embleme und Emblembücher in den Niederlanden (1560–1630). Utrecht, 1964.
Morse, H. K.
Elizabethan Pageantry. London and New York, 1934.
Muller-Hofstede, J.
"Zum Werke des Otto van Veen, 1590–1600." *Bulletin des Musées Royaux des Beaux-Arts* (Bruxelles) VI (1957):158–60.

Noble, Richmond
    Shakespeare's Biblical Knowledge and Use of the Book of Common Prayer. London, 1935.

Oetinger, F. C.
    Biblisches und emblematisches Wörterbuch. Stuttgart, 1776.

Panofsky, Erwin
    Meaning in the Visual Arts. Garden City, N.Y., 1955.
    Studies in Iconology: Humanistic Themes in the Art of the Renaissance. New York, 1939.

Parker, M. D. H.
    The Slave of Life. London, 1935.

Passavant, J. D.
    Le peintre-graveur. 6 vols. Leipzig, 1860.

Patch, Howard R.
    The Goddess Fortuna in Medieval Literature. Cambridge, Mass., 1927.

Pauli, Gustav
    Hans Sebald Beham. Strasbourg, 1901.

Pellegrini, Guiliano
    "Symbols and Significances." *Shakespeare Survey* XVII (1964):180-87.

Poot, Hubert Korneliszoon
    Het groot Natur, en Zedekundigh Werelttoneel of Woordenboek. 3 vols. Delft, 1743-50.

Praz, Mario
    "The English Emblem Literature." *English Studies* XVI (1954):129-40.
    Studies in Seventeenth Century Imagery. 2d ed. Rome, 1964.

Preibisz, Leon
    Maerten van Heemskerck. Leipzig, 1911.

Prosser, Eleanor
    Hamlet and Revenge. Stanford, 1967.

Réau, Louis
    Iconographie de l'art Chrétien. 3 vols. Paris, 1955.
        Fortitude: I, no. 189.

Reznicek, E. K. J.
    Die Zeichnungen von Hendrik Goltzius. Utrecht, n.d.
        Fig. 85: *Patientia?* (c. 1595); Fig. 220: *Fortitudo* (1592); Fig. 78: *Sieben Tugenden* (1588).

Richardson, Alan, ed.
    A Theological Word Book of the Bible. New York, 1951.
        Patience (pp. 164-65).

Richardson, George
    Iconology. London, 1779.

Roberts, Alexander, and James Donaldson, eds.
    The Ante-Nicene Christian Library. Edinburgh, 1867-72.

Roder, Helen
    Saints and Their Attributes. . . . London, 1955.

Ronchetti, G.
    Dizionario illustrato dei simboli. Rome, 1922.

Ross, Lawrence J.
    "Art and the Study of Early English Drama." *Renaissance Drama* VI (1963):35-46.

Salis, Arnold Von
   Antike und Renaissance. Erlenbach-Zurich, 1947.
Saunders, Jason L.
   Justus Lipsius: The Philosophy of the Renaissance Stoicism. New York, 1955.
Saxl, Fritz
   "A Spiritual Encyclopedia of the Later Middle Ages." *Journal of the Warburg and Courtauld Institutes* V (1942): 82–142.
Schaff, Philip, ed.
   A Select Library of the Nicene and Post-Nicene Fathers of the Christian Church. New York, 1888.
Schazmann, Paul E.
   Siegende Geduld; Versuch der Beschichte einer Idee. Bern, 1963.
Schiffhorst, Gerald J.
   "Art and Design in *Pericles*: A Study in Shakespearean Experimentation." Ph.D. dissertation, Washington University, 1973.
Schmidt, Alexander
   Shakespeare-Lexicon. 2 vols. London, 1874.
      Patience defined as calm temper in grief and suffering; quiet perseverance in waiting for something; calmness or composure; and indulgence or forbearance.
Seltman, Charles
   Women in Antiquity. London, 1956.
Seznec, J.
   The Survival of the Pagan Gods. Translated by B. F. Sessions. Bollingen Series, no. 38. New York, 1953.
Siefken, Ortgies
   Das geduldige Weib in der english cen Literatur bis auf Shakspere. Rathenow, 1902.
Skibbe, Martin
   Die ethische Forderung der Patientia in der patristichen Literatur von Tertullian bis Pelagius. Munster, 1964.
Smith, Charles G.
   Shakespeare's Proverb Lore. Cambridge, Mass., 1963.
Snyder, Susan
   "The Left Hand of God: Despair in Medieval and Renaissance Tradition." *Studies in the Renaissance* XII (1965):18–59.
Sonn, Carl R.
   "Spenser's Imagery." *ELH* XXVI (1959):156–70.
Spevack, Marvin
   A Complete and Systematic Concordance to the Works of Shakespeare. Hildesheim, 1970.
Spicq, C.
   "Hypomena, Patientia." *Revue des sciences philosophiques et théologiques* (Paris, 1930): 95–106.
Steadman, John M.
   Milton and The Renaissance Hero. Oxford, 1967.
Stechow, Wolfgang
   Northern Renaissance Art, 1400-1600: Sources and Documents. Englewood Cliffs, N.J., 1966.
Stridbeck, Carl Gustav
   Brueghelstudien. . . . Stockholm, 1956.
Sypher, Wylie
   Four Stages of Renaissance Style. New York, 1955.

Tabor, Margaret E.
   The Saints in Art. . . . London, 1908.

Tate, Priscilla
"The Triumph of Patience; a set of eight original engravings in the Duke Art Museum by Maarten van Heemskerck and Dirck Volckertszoon Coornhert: an Art-Historical Study in Iconography and Typology." Master's thesis, Duke University, 1974.
Tervarent, Guy de
Attributs et symboles dans l'art profane 1450-1600. 2 vols. Geneva, 1958-59.
I: p. 2 (lamb as first attribute of Patience); p. 96 (dog can symbolize patience, vigilance, as well as fidelity, friendship, and melancholy); p. 173 (lady chained=patient endurance).
Thorpe, L.
"Montaigne and the Emblems of Jacob Cats." *Modern Language Quarterly* X (1949): 419-28.
Tilley, Morris P.
A Dictionary of the Proverbs in England in the Sixteenth and Seventeenth Centuries. Ann Arbor, 1950.
Timmers, J. J. M.
Symboliek en Iconographie der Christelijke Kunst. Roermond-Maaseik, 1947.
See register, s.v. *Geduld* (pp. 595, 1163, 1165, 1214, 1215, 1259, 1261, 1764, 1780). See also plate 92 (Hope seated on Cube), fifteenth-century engraving.
Trench, R. C.
Synonyms of the New Testament. Cambridge, 1880.
Tuve, Rosemond
Allegorical Imagery: Some Medieval Books and Their Posterity. Princeton, 1966.
Index: Patience (pp. 59, 60, 74, 96, 166, 184), Fig. 15 (p. 74), and appendix (p. 443); Fortitude (pp. 59, 63, 66, passim); see also Wrath, Constancy.
"Spenser and Some Pictorial Conventions. . . ." In *Essays by Rosemond Tuve* (pp. 112-38), edited by T. P. Roche, Jr. Princeton, 1970.
Twining, Louisa
Symbols and Emblems of Early and Medieval Christian Art. London, 1885.

Vignau-Schuurman, Theodora
Die emblematischen Elemente im Werke Joris Hoefnagels. 2 vols. Leiden, 1969.
Vochon, Marius
La femme dans l'art. Paris, 1892.
Volkmann, Ludwig
Bilderschriften der Renaissance. Hieroglyphik and Emblematik in ihren Beziehungen und Fortwirkungen. Leipzig, 1962.
The Roman origin of the bucranium as symbolic of patience (p. 17).
Vries, Anne Gerard Christiaan de
De Nederlandsche Emblemata. . . . Amsterdam, 1899.
"The most detailed bibliography of emblem books ever made" (Praz, "English Emblem Literature," p. 237); but see Henkel and Schöne.

Warren, Austin
"Baroque Art and The Emblem." In *Richard Crashaw. A Study in Baroque Sensibility* (pp. 63-76). Baton Rouge, 1939.
Wellek, René
"The Parallelism between Literature and The Arts." *English Institute Annual 1941* (1942):29-63.
Welzig, W.

"Constantia und barocke Beständigkeit." *Deutsche Vierteljahrsschrift* **XXXV** (1961): 416–32.
Wenzel, Siegfried
  The Sin of Sloth: Acedia in Medieval Thought and Literature. Chapel Hill, 1967.
Wheasley, H. B., ed.
  The History of Patient Grissel. London, 1855.
White, Helen C.
  English Devotional Literature. Madison, 1931.
  Social Criticism in the Popular Religious Literature of the Sixteenth Century. Madison, 1943.
  The Tudor Books of Private Devotion. Madison, 1951.
Whittick, Arn
  Symbols, Signs and Their Meaning. London, 1960.
Williams, Kathleen
  "Spenser: Some Uses of the Sea and the Storm-tossed Ship." *Research Opportunities in Renaissance Drama* XIII–XIV (1970–71):135–42.
  Spenser's World of Glass: A Reading of the Faerie Queene. Berkeley, 1966.
Wind, Edgar
  Pagan Mysteries in the Renaissance. Rev. ed. New York, 1968.
Wittkower, Rudolf
  "Patience and Chance: The Story of a Political Emblem." *Journal of the Warburg Institute* I (1937–38):171–77.
Wölfflin, Heinrich
  Principles of Art History. Translated by M. D. Hottinger. London, 1932.
Wood, D. T. B.
  "Tapestries of the Seven Deadly Sins." *The Burlington Magazine* **XX** (1912):210–22, 277–89.

Zanta, Leontine
  La Renaissance du stoicisme au XVIe siècle. Paris, 1914.
Zavadil, Joseph B.
  "A Study of Meaning in *Patience* and *Cleanness.*" Ph.D. dissertation, Stanford University, 1961.
Zockler, Otto
  Handbuch der theologischen Wissenschaften. . . . 4 vols. Nördlingen, 1885–86.
  Die Tugendlehre des Christentums, geschichtlich dargestellt in der Entwicklung ihrer Lehrformen. . . . Gütersloh, 1904.

Some Commonplaces of
Late Medieval Patience Discussions:
An Introduction

RALPH HANNA III

ften in the later Middle Ages, knowledge of fundamental Christian truths, including information about the virtues, was communicated to the laity through Sunday sermons. The priests who delivered these sermons acquired their knowledge through compendia of various types—confessional manuals and handbooks, *exemplum* collections, handbooks on vices and virtues, commonplace collections, encyclopedias—compilations written specifically for this purpose and use.[1] In spite of the scant remains (and skimpier published versions) of what was a flourishing oral literature, the outlines of "later medieval common knowledge" about the vices and virtues, as well as moral theology generally, may readily be ascertained by scrutinizing the materials to which priests seeking information for lay instruction had habitual recourse.

To discover what constitutes "common knowledge" about patience or any other virtue, two types of materials are especially useful, since they are ubiquitous in provenance and frequently similar in format: the handbooks on vices and virtues and the *exemplum* books. Typically, both types are carefully arranged by topic and present for the priest's use an awesome variety of commonplace materials, much of it inherited from the Fathers. But although the external organization of the works is often meticulous, within individual articles or entries they frequently achieve a fine—and I think deliberately provocative—disorder, which allows ample room for the initiative and imagination of the individual cleric. In such materials one finds discussions of the various virtues copiously yet irrationally divided into topics: these divisions, through their rubrics, or marginal notations, form the finding marks for the individual priest, who is usually searching for explanatory filler for a virtue-oriented division of a *sermo modernus*. Within each topic are heaped together a variety of materials, some perhaps repeated elsewhere several times in the discussion. No distinction among sources or degrees of authority will be found in the presentation: God's word in the form of biblical citations, snippets of patristic teaching, *exempla*, moralized natural history, and figural readings of Scripture will nestle cheek by jowl, as a not untypical praise of patience from William Peraldus' influential *Summa de virtutibus* will attest:

> Octavo quod [patientia] mira facit. Gregorius: "Ego virtutem patientiae signis et miraculis majorem puto. Si patientiam habens aliquid mortiferum biberit, non ei nocebit. Sermo venenatus quem audit convertitur ei in medicina patienti. Nox adversitatis ut dies illuminabitur: ita enim clare videt in nocte adversitatis sicut in die prosperitatis, vel etiam clarius ei implet dominus illam promissionem." *Isaiae* 43:2, "Cum pertransieris per aquas, tecum ero, et flumina non operient [t]e; cum ambulaveris in ignem, non combureris." Homo patie[n]s est ut rubus ardens absque lesione, *Exodi* 3:2. Homo patiens est ut pueri quos deus in igne babilonicae fornacis illesos servavit, *Danielis* 3:49–50. Accidit homini patienti sicut accidit Beato Tiburtio qui, cum nudis plantis incederet super carbones ardentes, videbatur ei quod super flores roseos incederet. *Proverbiorum* 6:27–8, "Nunquid potest homo ambulare super prunas et non comburentur plante eius:" homo patiens potest.

> Eighth because patience performs wonders. Gregory: "I consider the virtue of patience greater because of the signs and miracles associated with it. If a patient person drinks anything deadly, it will not hurt him. A poisoned word which he hears will be converted into medicine for the patient man. The night of adversity will be as bright as day for him: he will see just as clearly in the night of adversity as in the day of prosperity, or indeed the Lord will fulfill that promise for him more clearly than for others." Isa. 43:2,

"When you journey across the waters, I will be with you, and the rivers will not overwhelm you; when you walk in the fire, you will not be burned." A patient man is as the bush burning without injury, Exod. 3:2. A patient man is as the children whom God saved uninjured in the fire of the Babylonian furnace, Dan. 3:49-50. A patient man has experiences just like Blessed Tiburtius, to whom, when he walked barefoot over burning coals, it seemed as if he walked upon rosy flowers. Prov. 6:27-28, "A man may never walk over coals without burning the soles of his feet"; but a patient man can.

This brief passage, one of sixteen rather disconnected commendations of patience,[2] typifies the form of handbook discussions of the virtues. A variety of texts from quite diverse sources are linked together; and, as the discussion proceeds, the reader may with some justice wonder how the materials adduced refer to the announced topic. The discussion begins to clog under the weight of its own imagery, an imagery suggestive of topics Peraldus will discuss elsewhere (tribulation as the proverbial "through fire and flood," for example).[3] But the very lack of focus within the presentation, its tendency to fall into separable items, insures its usefulness: in the dissipation of announced context, the individual priest is left free to construct his sermon, to provide connections which would yoke any single piece of virtue lore to the announced sermon division, to insert additional *figurae* or *exempla* which the allusiveness of the cited materials calls to mind.[4]

But within this evocative diffuseness, the plethora of individual scriptual passages and idiosyncratic *figurae*, constants occur in the manuals' presentations of the virtues. Some topics prove conventional, even if the exact parameters of the discussion remain highly individualistic. For the most part, these conventional topics are provided by the legacy of patristic thought. And in their turn, the Fathers depended upon a consensus of views in order to define the objects of their interest. Standard definitions of vices and virtues exist, and the emphases inherent in these definitions frequently provided conventional topics which gave some formal imperatives to the later medieval authors of handbooks. In this paper I will discuss the three most commonly cited definitions of the virtue patience, the assumptions about the virtue which these have in common, and the way these assumptions are reflected in the form and content of the handbooks.

All three definitions immediately recommend themselves by their brevity. Cicero's—the first, most venerable, and most honored—is by far the longest: "Patientia est honestatis aut utilitatis causa rerum arduarum ac difficilium voluntaria ac diuturna perpessio" ("Patience is the willed and continuous endurance of laborious and difficult things for the sake of virtue or benefit"). The two Christian examples are shorter still. Augustine says that patience is "aequo animo mala tolerare" ("to endure evils with an even mind"). And Gregory the Great defines the virtue as "aliena mala aequanimiter perpeti" ("to endure external evils with equanimity").[5] These three statements are universally known: nearly every patience discussion I have seen utilizes one of them; a majority include at least two of the three. Their ubiquity as platitudes can be gauged by the widespread use of the nearly identical Gregorian and Augustinian versions in ordinary Sunday sermons.

The regular citation of these differing definitions reflects the agreement among handbook writers about major issues involved in the practice of patience. Thus, by examining these inherent issues, one can determine the topics important to all the authors. Four topics seem central to all definitions: first, the nature of those acts which typify the patient or impatient man; second, the definition of the cause which should produce a display of patience; third, those external situations in which the virtue proves useful; and fourth, the mental qualities associated with the *habitus* of patience.

On the first of these topics, the acts of the patient man, there is nearly universal agreement. In the definitions these acts are indicated through the use of related verbs—*perpeti* and *tolerare* ("to endure"); equally sanctioned are such obvious synonyms as *sustinere* ("to bear up"), *suffere*, and the simplex *pati* ("to suffer"). The external visible act most strikingly associated with patience is simply unswerving and silent endurance, passive bearing-up under all hardship, even to the point of death.

In their general insistence upon the endurance of suffering, the verbs imply a particular context for patient action: adversity. But the association of patience with this state is not absolute in medieval discussions, although several traditions combine to make it usual. From classical times patience (and fortitude, of which it is a "part")[6] is defined as a virtue actuated only in the face of *difficilia* or *mala*, one only perfected in adverse conditions. (For writers through the fourteenth century this tradition remains vital through the widespread distribution of Senecan proverbial commonplaces, e.g., "Virtus in infirmitate perficitur" ["Virtue is made perfect by hardship"].)[7] Further, in continuing this classical topos, early discussions of the cardinal virtues use spatial metaphors to describe the virtuous man as protected from incursions on all sides. In these metaphors authors link fortitude (and its associated virtues) with the *sinistrum latus* of *adversitas* or *tribulatio* and thus oppose it to the *dextrum latus* of *prosperitas* where protection comes from temperance, which moderates concupiscent desires. In this schema, patience, as part of fortitude, deals with bearing incommodities. These quasi-pictorial metaphors recur in important twelfth-century discussions which preserve these views for the later Middle Ages.[8]

However, there coexists with this usual association of patience and the endurance of adversity a second, more complicated definition.[9] As the author of the *Fasciculus morum* expresses this related topic, "Patientia est quae in prosperis non elevatur, nec in adversis frangitur" ("Patience is that virtue which is neither elated in prosperity nor broken in adversity"). Patience here becomes a virtue for all occasions, an expansiveness associated in the history of the virtue with fifth- through seventh-century efforts to generalize its use and remove it from primary reference only to blood martyrdom. This transformation is effected by intensifying the strong connections of patience and humility (or spiritual poverty) and by arguing for the patient man's strength as proof against prosperity's temptations of pride and cupidity. The equanimity always associated with patience (the fourth topic I will discuss below) insures a moderated response to all external events: it includes not simply the ungrudging endurance of difficulty that this virtue shares with *fortitudo in adversis*, but also the ideal of indifference to wealth and high estate which medieval Christianity inherited from late classical ethical systems, as well as gospel injunction. The patient man remains unmoved by temptations just as by persecutions, and this stability is another form of his passion.

As the *Fasciculus morum* citation above suggests, the verbs conventionally associated with this passion and with virtuous responses to it— *pati, tolerare, sustinere*—have traditional antonyms. Of such oppositions, the most commonplace juxtaposes *pati* and *frangere* ("to break") although such ready substitutes as *flectere* ("to bend"), *curvare* ("to bow"), *mollire* ("to become soft") and *tumere* ("to swell with passion") occur.[10] The impatient man cannot face situations which demand heroic passivity: in such contexts he will lose his self-possession and forfeit his equanimity. This inner decomposition of a unific and controlled personality is the situation patristic writers identify as that of the "broken man." Typically, such a fracture is associated with lapses into two of the Seven Deadly Sins—either *acedia* (implicit in the widespread use of *dolor* or *tristitia* ["sorrow"] as alternatives to patience), or, almost universally, *ira* (commonplace anger-words include *contumelia* ["scornful words"], *ultio* ["revenge"], and *vindicta* ["vengeance"]). Oppressive fear of pain, the emotional certainty that one cannot succeed at a certain task, a small faith that forgets that God tempts no man above his strength, or the melancholy that may result from such anxieties will lead the impatient man to doubt his own strength or the value of his own efforts. Eventually he may despair of any possible virtuous success. At the other extreme, he may resent his persecutor, be provoked into an angry verbal response, or, worse, long to subject his tormentors to the same pain he feels.[11]

The second topic inherent in these definitions concerns the cause for which the patient man suffers. For Cicero, this topic is broached tautologically within the definition—either *honestas* (the very nature of virtue) or utility to the state (only a different definition of virtue) determines the moral value of the patient man's actions. But for Christian authors, somewhat more expansive discussions are necessary, and these eventually become commonplaces of later patience tracts.[12]

Augustine makes the central contribution to this discussion, for he sees clearly that triumphant endurance of pain is a great virtue but that some triumphs are not worth suffering for. The later medieval citation-version of Augustine puts the matter most succinctly: "Non facit martyrem poena, sed causa" ("Not suffering, but a good cause, makes a martyr"). In addition, Augustine introduces the usual theological standard for measuring the value of a cause, the eighth Beatitude: "Beati qui persecutionem patiuntur propter justitiam, quoniam ipsorum est regnum caelorum" ("Blessed are they who suffer persecution for righteousness' sake, for theirs is the kingdom of Heaven"). By investing the *justitia* of the Beatitude with the full weight of connotation he normally associates with the word *caritas*, Augustine redefines the nature of the virtuous cause—it becomes the cause of God alone.[13]

Consequently, suffering for a cause which is not God's is viewed throughout the Middle Ages as less than meritorious, as indeed sinful. The term usually attached to this fictive patience, the patience of a *martyr Sathanis*, is *duritia*, although *negligentia* occurs sporadically. Most normally *duritia* is defined as a hardness that amounts to perverse insensitivity to pain: it is the zeal of the worldling which enables him to pursue a base goal, e.g., riches, without reckoning carefully the costs involved in his effort. As some later writers would have it, this patience is purely *asinaria* or *mercenaria*.[14] *Negligentia* can function as a synonym because of its frequent sense of "heedlessness, recklessness"; but more frequently, negligence is opposed to *duritia* as that excess softness which inclines one not to suffer. It is typically the sin of those bishops or superiors who do not recognize the goodness of the cause they should pursue and who thus neglect their duties through a fear of the difficulties involved in prosecuting some worthwhile action.[15]

In the later Middle Ages, the concept of the "good cause" becomes entwined with discussions of the "degrees" of patience, those levels of performance which separate the merely "good" from the perfect. In this context, classical materials are regularly introduced to give a fuller paradigm. In thirteenth-century scholastic discussions of the *habitus* proper to fortitude, it is usual to attempt some distinction between acts which appear courageous and those which are in fact so. In this discussion, the schoolmen draw their examples of perverse fortitude from a lengthy discussion in the *Nichomachaean Ethics*. There Aristotle defines five types of boldness which fall short of true virtue, the consuetudinal indifference to hardship of the professional soldier, for example. This passage, reduced to its bare bones and its examples, becomes attached to a good many later patience discussions; in this context it functions to define the lower degrees of patience, to provide examples of the pursuit of a bad cause.[16]

Inherent in Cicero's, Augustine's, and Gregory's definitions is a third topic: the specification of the *difficilia* or *mala* which the patient man faces with indifference. Here conventional patience discussions prove truly expansive in their descriptiveness because medieval writers find insuperable difficulties in discussing the patient man's activities as the reflection of a mental *habitus*. Particularly, given the conspicuous overlapping of Christian virtues, they only with difficulty can separate psychic states specifically *patiens* from those specifically *humilis, mitis, mansuetus, benignus, obediens* ("humble, meek, mild, loving, obedient").[17] As a result, authors tend to define, not a *habitus*, but situations in which patience may be exercised and the external forms of the patient man's behavior. This form of definition, in which discussion is amplified through a series of illustrative anecdotes or static icons, accounts in part for the expansive and rather disorganized form of most patience discussions.

But in spite of this expansive attention to the *mala* which the patient man faces, these discussions often have a relatively careful, implicit organization inherited from a single patristic locus. This contribution reflects Gregory the Great's persistent effort to make the virtue central to the daily Christian life. As he says in his thirty-fifth homily on the Gospels, the most quoted single discussion of the entire Middle Ages: "Sine ferro vel flammis esse possumus martyres, si patientiam veraciter in animo custodimus" ("Without iron or flames we may be martyrs, so long as we keep patience truly in our minds"). Later in the same homily, Gregory, in an attempt to solidify this connection of patience with daily life, provides a *distinctio* frequently used to shape late medieval patience discussions:

> Tribus modis virtus patientiae exerceri solet. Alia namque sunt quae a Deo, alia quae ab antiquo adversario, alia quae a proximo sustinemus. A proximo namque persecutiones, damna, et contumelias, ab antiquo vero adversario tentamenta; a Deo autem flagella tolleramus.[18]

> The virtue of patience usually is expressed in three types of action. For we must bear some things which are from God, some from our ancient adversary the devil, and some from our neighbor. We endure persecution, loss of possessions, and scornful words from our neighbor; from the devil, temptations; from God, scourgings.

This passage goes on to outline the virtuous responses which each situation should evoke—as usual, through negation, indicating the acts the patient man will not perform.

From this Georgian locus is derived the overwhelming tendency in later medieval discussions to treat patience in conjunction with two other themes—tribulation and temptation.[19] The first of these includes both "God's scourgings"—corrective tribulation which emerges from divine good will—and the ill-intentioned persecutions of one's neighbor, persecutions which through sufferance may become meritorious and pleasant to God and the patient man. Demonic incursions, especially sinful suggestions which may assail the patient man in situations of apparent nonadversity, form the second theme. Late medieval treatises follow Peraldus by interrupting the direct praise of patience with the commendation of tribulation; many, but far from all, include also a discussion of temptation and of the passive warfare against the devil's blandishments.

The first of these themes, the *flagellum divinum*, includes a variety of "natural" calamities which can befall the Christian in this world. The conventional lists of these tribulations include those painful occasions mentioned by Paul in two famous catalogues, most normally the *vigilia, fames, sitis, jejunia, frigor*, and *nuditas* ("wakes, hunger, thirst, fastings, cold, nakedness") of II Cor. 11:27.[20] To these, authors quite frequently add *infirmitas* ("sickness") or *afflictio* ("hardship"), the loss of loved ones, and poverty. The very naturalness of these states, their position as expected incommodities of human experience, demonstrates that they form part of man's merited punishment, one result of his fall into sin. And that this punishment is deserved is demonstrated by the obdurate human propensity to see oneself as victimized by traumatic experiences, rather than to endure them with patience.

For the scourgings of God are designed to recall the Christian to himself and thus to the divine:

> Tribulatio hominem incitat ut dominum requirat. . . . *Hebraeos* 4:11, "Festinemus ingredi in illam requiem." Saltem deberet qui a deo flagellatur intelligere quod jumentum percussum videtur agnoscere, quod sive percutiatur quod errat extra viam unde reddit ad viam, vel quia nimis lente incedebat unde gressum accelerat. Sic qui flagellatur a deo, si extra viam erat per mortale peccatum, debet redire ad viam, peccatum deserendo. Si in via erat sed lente incedebat pauca bona agendo, accelerare debet gressum plura bona agendo.[21]

> Tribulation spurs man as God may require. . . . Heb. 4:11, "Let us hasten to enter that repose." The man who is scourged by God should at least understand what a beaten ox appears to recognize— that he is struck either because he wanders out of the way [and beaten until he returns to it] or because he was going too slowly [and beaten until he speeds up]. Similarly the man struck by God, if he left the way through mortal sin, should return and desert his sin. If he followed the way but moved slowly, performing few good deeds, he should speed his pace, doing more.

On the basis of Heb. 12:5–11 and Apocalypse 3:19, medieval commentators regularly link the impetus to return to the *via recta* with God's position as a loving father who corrects an errant child. The patient man should recognize such unpleasant events, not as random ill fortune, but as a controlled Providential act with the goal of bringing sinners to penance and purgation. "Kicking against the pricks" merely reduplicates Adam's primal sin—substitutes man's judgment for God's, attacks Providence itself.[22]

The theodicy inherent in this discussion forms for the later Middle Ages a conspicuous literary topic—one where patience discussions, the tradition of spiritual consolation, and amatory topics merge. Gregory, immediately after the passage quoted above, identifies *murmuratio* (in Middle English *grucchinge* or *plainte*) as the expected impatient response to God's flagellation. In the presentation of such late medieval antiheroes as the dreamer of *Pearl* or Chaucer's Dorigen, characterization proceeds largely by playing out the implications of *grucchinge*, the effort to limit God's plan to man's least enlightened desires. Quite similar are several centuries' worth of disgruntled lovers,[23] all of whom, deprived of their amatory objects, question the governance of the universe at large. And at a more exalted level, all these literary discussions receive a philosophic framework from the popularization of Boethian consolatory topics during the period.[24]

Although Gregory's division of the forms which persecution by one's neighbor may take remains a standard theme, it frequently alternates with a different *distinctio*, one which mediates between it and the *flagellum* materials we have just scanned. In this five-part discussion, tribulations are distinguished, not in terms of the specific act which persecutes, as in Gregory's division, but through the ultimate purpose the tribulation serves in the providential scheme. This topic emerges in Bede's analysis of Matt. 9:5 but achieves nearly universal currency in the form given by Peter Lombard in his *Sentences*.[25] As with several other distinctions, it succeeds as a topic because it comes with exemplary material built in: widespread distribution for odd pieces of patristic information frequently seems assured when these include data to be adduced at a variety of points in a discussion. Bede's topic has this flexibility; for example, it gives strong impetus to the widespread use of Miriam's leprosy (Num. 12:10) as an emblem of tribulation sent to coerce a sinner to penance. It is also responsible for the development of an irregular list of biblical figures— Herod Agrippa (Acts 12:23), Antiochus (II Macc. 9:5 ff.), Pharoah (cf. Exod. 12:28–30), Herod of Ascalon (cf. Matt. 2:19?), and the persecutors of Dan. 3:22—for whom tribulation repays irrevocable obduracy and begins the sufferings of Hell in this world.[26]

When not deprived of its high place by Bede's distinction, the Gregorian division of tribulation from one's neighbor usually appears intact in its tripartite form—*contumelia verborum, damna rerum, cruciatus corporis* ("scornful words, loss of possessions, physical torture") are the most frequent late-medieval tags. Two other topics are occasionally attached to this time-honored triad: invariably they occur as fourth members and never, so far as I know, coexist. The first, *angaria operum* ("enforced works"), emerges in standard readings of Matt. 5:41 as a companion to *cruciatus* and *damna*; through typical late-medieval efforts at concording all discussions, it thus becomes their companion in tribulation materials.[27] Most typically *angaria* is associated, as in Chaucer's *Parson's Tale*, with Christ's actions at the crucifixion. The second topic derives support from a variety of religious preoccupations: its original form, witnessed by John of Wales' *Breviloquium,* is "moderatio in correctionibus disciplinarum" ("moderation in correcting one's pupils"). But this statement appears to have been felt too limiting, and related topics which expand the field prove more commonplace—moderation in *correctio fraterna* ("brotherly correction") and enduring *correptio* ("chastisement") with patience, for example.[28] Both *angaria* and *correctio* remain interlopers, intruders into the Gregorian scheme, however; one may gain some sense of the tentativeness with which they are inserted by noting the proclivity of writers to invert both topics. Thus may each be introduced not simply to exemplify proper patience under duress from one's neighbor but also to discuss its antithesis, *negligentia.* Many Christians resemble Simon the Cyrene and must be coerced by *angaria* to take up their cross and follow Christ; many prelates and vicars find peaceful living more satisfying than daring to arouse their flocks by proper correction.

The Gregorian division of persecution by one's neighbor, however, much it may be fleshed out with other topics, is the vehicle for some of the richest and most conventional parts of later medieval patience discussions. Here the authors of vice and virtue books proceed by expansion and inclusiveness, large infusions of brief *exempla,* of *figurae* (moralized objects, frequently derived from the juncture of Scripture and natural history, the ancestors of Renaissance emblems),[29] and of moralized biblical and hagiographic narratives. The metaphoric richness and profusion of this material constantly brought priests back to such works as Peraldus' *Summa,* for in such writings they found compendia of late medieval symbolic thought in all its evocative power as well as its bewildering confusions and inconsistencies.[30] Typically in the description of the patient Christian put upon by his persecutors, argument takes the form of symbolic imagery.

Within this symbolic framework, argumentation tends to become standardized, even if specific topics in their breadth prove capable of dazzling individual adaptations, the wit of sermon delivery. For example, the persecutor who provides the Christian with the opportunity to exhibit his patience regularly is described as *dei virga,* "the scourge of God," the instrument of His correction. Viewed through one set of *figurae,* the persecutor is thus as evanescent as any other form of evil. As merely God's instrument, he is thoroughly expendable: just as a father or teacher may throw his rod in the fire after his chastising has affected his son or pupil, so the unrepentant persecutor may expect only Hell as his reward. Or, to shift figural perspectives, the patient man sustains his passion by viewing the domination of his attacker as apparent only; in fact, one's persecutor is one's servant, and (by the blows he rains upon one) he fashions, with no effort on the part of the sufferer, an eternal crown of glory. Or, from yet another perspective (in this case based on a figural reading of Esther 5:2), all Christians may choose to which rod they will bow—the golden rod of tribulation in this world with its promise of salvation, or the iron rod of eternal correction in Hell.[31]

Or the handbook writer may press the *virga* further, taking it into the area where it joins with originally independent *figurae*. Tribulation purifies, or as a "Gregorian" proverb has it: "Quod lima ferro et flagellum grano et fornax auro, hoc facit tribulatio viro justo" ("Tribulation affects the righteous man as the file does iron, the winnowing flail wheat, and the furnace gold").[32] To trace out the development of even a single member of this sentence would involve lengthy discussion: the gold image, with its overtones of smithy or foundry, proves particularly expansive. In these terms, the *virga* coexists with or is analagous to the *fornax*, in which the dross of sin is separated from the refined metal.[33] The image might be further extended; the gold could be the material of a crown of glory or of a precious vessel for God's house. That extension would produce further ramifications: allusions to the *vas fictilis* ("earthen vessel") or the *vas electionis* ("vessel of election"), allegorization of the process by which cups are molded from molten metal (*tribulatio solidat*—"tribulation makes firm"), discussion of the actual decoration of the golden object (probably by using a *malleus* ["hammer"] or *lima*, leading by a "*commodius vicus* of recirculation" back to the *virga* again). The imagery has the flexibility one associates with literary language at its best, a resonance and wit which provokes both thought and further innovation.[34]

Temptation, the last of the *mala illata* named by Gregory as occasions of patient action, falls somewhat outside the usual preoccupations of patience discussions. The reason for including some treatment of the topic is obvious: temptation is a tribulation daily encountered, a blandishment which the Christian must continually face. As a result, a number of traditional patience topics coalesce with temptation topics; for example, the general commendation of temptation relies on the same data which commend tribulation as a divinely sent testing of merit. But, on the whole, temptation was always a topic of more general relevance than discussions of patience, especially insofar as it was associated with arguments over the nature of sin. Thus, the subject developed patterns of emphasis removed from the normal center of patience discussions. Hence temptation tracts emphasize the dramatic encounter of sinner and temp-

tation, the external acts relevant to vanquishing man's three foes, and the
tools which may create the Christian's inner stability (especially *oratio*
["prayer"], on the basis of Matt. 26:41). Such discussions take the handbook writers far away from topics directly associated with patience.[35]

The fourth topic broached in the conventional definitions of patience is
implied by the Latin root *aequ-* ("even"): the central psychological act of
the patient man is a voluntary indifference to external pain and a resulting inner equipoise. Again the topic occurs in Gregory's homily, a
commentary on Luke 21:19: "In patientia vestra possidebitis animas
vestras" ("In your patience you will possess your souls"). This model of
self-government is universally praised in patience discussions.

Historically, this material probably owes more to classical antecedents
than any other single patience topic. *Aequanimitas* ("equanimity"),
tranquillitas animi ("untroubled mind"), or *pax animi* ("peace of mind")
represents the Christianization of the central Stoic virtue *apatheia*, the
indifference to externals and to one's own passions. But although
Christian writers readily use the classical images which describe the
passions as a storm, a *perturbatio*, the Christianizing of *apatheia* requires
one fundamental omission. For the Stoic sage, the passions, or *affectūs*,
must be fully extirpated; for the patient Christian such extirpation is
impossible, so long as he is a fallen man in this world. Christian patience
presupposes a continual inner effort to control aspects of post-Edenic
man which cannot be dismissed; patience is elevated to a fully heroic self-
control, the constant recreation of an ordered inner kingdom. And this
inner citadel may be created only through continuous adjustment of the
will to follow reason, unlike the instantaneous and mysterious Stoic
conversion experience.[36]

The acts of the patient man, especially when he is persecuted, reflect in
a slightly different way this effort to recognize and yet control the
emotions. Discussions of equanimity are always paradoxical, for the
patient man is viewed as if simultaneously hard and soft. From without
he appears to hold himself as a rock, infrangibly strong in his endurance
of all insult and pain. But the hardness is only apparent, like that of the
adamant which attracts the iron of martyrdom and cannot be injured by
it. The adamant can, after all, shatter under an effusion of *sanguis
hircinus* ("kid's blood"), the memory of Christ's love as expressed in the
crucifixion.[37] Although hard without, the Christian patient proves soft,
loving, sweet, and compassionate as a human being. His triumph, as
Langland's Patience knows, rests upon his love of those who persecute
him.[38]

This height of equanimity, as most medieval authors see it, is expressed in the active practice of charity, even in persecution. The patient man, through his equanimity, can follow the counsel of perfection, can love his enemies. In his suffering, his passion, he finds a compassion which extends to his tormentors. In his pain, he can bless them, for they speed his journey to eternal life. Further, he can pray for them, ask God to put an end to their fury and provide for their conversion. In his death as martyr, to take the most extreme case, the patient man provides a role model for his persecutor, illustrates (as countless *exempla* remind the medieval reader)[39] that true conquest, the conversion of souls through grace, comes without bold physical action, through the suffering passivity of love.

The materials which I have briefly reviewed are the commonplaces which give some structure to conventional medieval patience discussions. No writer, least of all the compiler of a handbook for parochial use, can ignore such important matters as the nature of patient action, the distinction of patience from mere endurance, the situations which demand patience, or the general *habitus* underlying the virtue. All of these materials, inherent in the standard definitions with which nearly all treatments begin, occupy writers (and the sermon orators who pillage their works) through the later Middle Ages. They provide the frame into which vast amounts of other, equally conventional material may be placed—the biblical citations, figures, and examples which contribute to the vitality and informativeness of patience discussions. This vitality was the center of religious instruction—palpable examples supporting abstract doctrine—and the form in which most late medieval Christians became aware of the imperative to virtuous endurance, the imitation of the suffering Christ.

NOTES

1. This paper expands a brief talk presented to MLA Seminar 282, San Francisco, December 28, 1975, a seminar ably chaired by Gerald Schiffhorst. It represents a tentative first contribution in a projected series of studies concerning the history of the virtue patience to the year 1430, the use of patience materials in fourteenth-century English literature, and the transmission of patristic information in England in the later Middle Ages. In preparing the paper I have incurred three particular indebtednesses: Siegfried Wenzel has been unstinting in helpful suggestions and generous in giving me access to his collection of unpublished materials, both microfilms and personal transcriptions; William O. Harris has made numerous suggestions about method and argumentation; and NEH and University of

California research grants have helped defray many of the costs associated with the research and its preparation for publication.

All my notes attempt to be evocative rather than exhaustive; here I cite a single outstanding example of each genre of compendium. For confessional manuals, S. Raymond de Penyaforte, *Summa de poenitentia et matrimonio* (Rome: Ioannes Tallini, 1603; reprint ed., Farnborough: Gregg, 1967); see also Amédée Teetaert, "La 'summa de poenitentia' de Saint Raymond de Penyaforte," *Ephemerides Theologiae Louvanienses* V (1928):49–72, and *Dictionnaire de théologie catholique* XIII, II:1806–23; and on the work's waning later reputation, Leonard Boyle, "The *Summa Confessorum* of John of Freiburg," in Armand A. Maurer et al., eds., *St. Thomas Aquinas 1274-1974: Commemorative Studies*, 2 vols. (Toronto: Pontifical Institute, 1974), II:245–68. For *exemplum* collections, John Bromyard, *Summa praedicantium*, 2° (Nürnberg: Anton Koberger, 1485), or Etienne de Bourbon, *Liber seu tractatus de donis*, partially ed. A. Lecoy de la Marche, *Anecdotes historiques, légendes, et apologues* (Paris: Renouard, 1877); I customarily cite Etienne's expansive patience discussion from the unique manuscript, Bibliothèque Nationale MS lat. 15970, ff. 659vb–686ra. For vice-virtue books, William Peraldus, *Summa aurea de virtutibus et vitiis*, 8° (Venice: Paganinus de Paganinis, 1497); see also A. Dondaine, "Guillaume Peyraut, vie et œuvres," *Archivum Fratrum Praedicatorum* XVIII (1948):162–236. For an interesting commonplace book of primarily patristic and canonistic selections, Johannes de Mirfield's *Florarium Bartholomaei* (I cite the imperfect version of Cambridge University Library Mm.ii.10); see also Sir Percival Horton-Smith Hartley and Harold Richard Aldridge, *Johannes de Mirfield of St. Bartholomew's, Smithfield: His Life and Works* (Cambridge: Cambridge University Press, 1936). For a widely used encyclopedia written specifically for sermon use, Bartholomaeus Anglicus, *De proprietatibus rerum*, available now in John Trevisa's Middle English translation, ed. M. C. Seymour et al., 2 vols. (Oxford: Clarendon, 1975); see also Gerald E. Se Boyar, "Bartholomaeus Anglicus and his Encyclopaedia," *Journal of English and Germanic Philology* XIX (1920):168–89. For sermons in general, materials of English provenance (almost all unpublished) are surveyed in G. R. Owst's two volumes, *Preaching in Medieval England: An Introduction to Sermon Manuscripts of the Period c. 1350-1450* (Cambridge: Cambridge University Press, 1926) and *Literature and Pulpit in Medieval England: A Neglected Chapter in the History of English Letters and of the English People*, 2d ed. (New York: Barnes and Noble, 1961). Standard on the rhetorical prescriptions peculiar to *sermones moderni* is Th.-M. Charland, *Artes praedicandi; Contribution à l'histoire de la rhétorique au moyen âge* (Paris: Vrin, and Ottawa: Institut d'Etudes Médiévales, 1936).

2. Peraldus, VIII.vii, ff. n 7rb–n 7va. As in all Latin citations not from standard modern editions, I have silently expanded abbreviations, normalized spellings to those of classical Latin, provided punctuation and capitalization, and regularized biblical citations (including silent correction of miscitations and addition of verse numbers). The Gregory citation is a pastiche from a variety of loci: the first sentence from *Dialogi* I.ii (*Patrologia Latina*, LXXVII:161—hereafter cited as *PL*), the second and part of the third from *Homeliae in Evangelia* II.xxix.4 (*PL*, LXXVI:1215, a reading of Mark 16:18). The fourth sentence I have not located, though it vaguely resembles a number of passages; cf. *Moralia* V.ii.2 (*PL*, LXXV:680). A good deal of work needs to be done on the vagaries of Gregorian references, a topic which will recur in these notes. For some useful data on the early stages of the tradition, see René Wasselynck, "Les 'Moralia in Job' dans les ouvrages de morale du haut moyen âge latin," *Recherches de Théologie Ancienne et Médiévale* XXXI (1964):5–31 (hereafter cited as *RTAM*); and "La presence des Moralia du S. Grégoire le Grand dans les ouvrages de moral du xiie siècle," *RTAM* XXXV (1968):197–240, and XXXVI (1969):31–45.

3. This topic, *tribulatio* as *ignis* and/or *aqua*, is a fixed piece of virtue discussions. The second topic, the storm of tribulation, has been discussed with reference to Shakespeare by W. S. Heckscher, "Shakespeare in His Relationship to the Visual Arts: A Study in Paradox," *Research Opportunities in Renaissance Drama* XIII–XIV (1970-71):5–71. Both are

based on patristic readings of isolated passages of Scripture; they first appear together fully formed either in William of Auvergne's *Summa de vitiis et virtutibus* or Peraldus' *Summa*. See William, "De Moribus" XI, in *Opera omnia*, 2 vols. (Orleans: F. Hotet, and Paris: Andraea Pralard, 1674; reprint ed., Frankfurt am Main: Minerva, 1963), II:249ᵇ–53ᵃ; Peraldus, VII.ix, ff. o 1ʳᵃ–o 2ʳᵃ, o 4ʳᵃ–o 4ʳᵇ.

4. For example, Gregory's initial allusion to Mark 16 might suggest the legend of Saint John, who survived a poisoned drink; cf. any *Legenda Aurea* derivative *sub* December 27, e.g., John Mirk, *Festial*, Early English Text Society (hereafter cited as EETS), es 96, p. 31.

5. For the texts, see respectively *De inventione* II.54.163, ed. E. Stroebel, *Scripta quae manserunt omnia, fasc. 2: Rhetorici libri duo qui vocantur de inventione* (Stuttgart: Teubner, 1965), p. 149; *De patientia* II.2 (*PL*, XL:611); *Homeliae in Evangelia* II.xxxv.4 (*PL*, LXXVI:1261–62). The Ciceronian definition is that used by Aquinas, *Summa theologica* IIªIIᵃᵉ, Q. 128, art. uniq.

6. The best treatment of the relationship understood in naming certain virtues *partes* of the cardinals is Rosamond Tuve's *Allegorical Imagery* (Princeton, N.J.: Princeton University Press, 1966), p. 70.

7. Cf. II Cor. 12:9. For other examples of the proverb, see *Florilegium morale oxoniense*, ed. Ph. Delhaye and C. H. Talbot, 2 vols. (Louvain: Nauwelaerts, and Lille: Giard, 1955–56), I:75 (inserted in a quotation of Apuleius, *De Platone* II.12); William of Pagula, *Oculus sacerdotis* II, "De tribulatione," British Museum MS Royal 8.C.ii, f. 111ᵛᵇ and "Postquam," Cambridge University Library MS Ff.i.17, f. 92ᵛᵃ (cf. also the Middle English translation included in *Memoriale credentium*, British Museum MS Harley 535. f. 86ʳ). On Pagula, see Leonard E. Boyle, "The *Oculus Sacerdotis* and Some Other Works of William of Pagula," *Transactions of the Royal Historical Society*, 5th ser. V (1955):81–110; on "Postquam," see Siegfried Wenzel, "The Source of the 'Remedia' of the *Parson's Tale*," *Traditio* XXVII (1971):433–53. Behind this proverb lies a tradition based on such statements as Seneca's "Calamitas virtutis occasio est" ("Disaster is the primary opportunity to display one's virtue"—*De providentia* 4.6); similar items are enshrined in such collections as Publilius Syrus' *Sententiae*, the pseudo-Senecan *De moribus*, and Walter Burley's *De vita et moribus philosophorum*. In Christian contexts, the parallel adages are Gregorian: "Fortitudo autem nonisi in adversitate ostenditur, unde et mox post fortitudinem patientia subrogatur" ("Fortitude is not shown except in adversity, and immediately thereafter patience takes the place of fortitude"—*Moralia* V.xvi.33, *PL*, LXXV:697) and "Nunquam est patientiae virtus in prosperis" ("The virtue of patience never exists in prosperity"—*Moralia* XI.xxxiv.47, *PL*, LXXV:975).

8. For examples of this topic, see Etienne de Bourbon, f. 653ʳᵇ; John Felton, *Sermones*, British Museum MS Harley 868, ff. 32ᵛ and 40ʳ (a collection of exemplary sermons made for those lacking access to handbooks, riddled with commonplaces); and Bromyard, P.1.iv.10 (lacks the full *temperantia* moralization). The same idea, without directional markings but with the two virtues as *alae* or *columnae*, occurs in a series of important pseudo-Abelardian texts—*Epitome theologiae christianae* xxxii (*PL*, CLXXVIII:1751), *Sententiae parisienses* III, *Ysagoge in theologiam* I (both ed. Arthur Landgraf, *Ecrits théologiques de l'école d'Abelard: Textes inédits* [Louvain: Spicilegium sacrum lovaniense, 1934], pp. 52–53, 75)— and in William of Conches' *Moralium dogma philosophorum*, ed. John Holmberg (Uppsala: Almqvist and Wiksells, 1929), p. 8. Cf. also, more distantly, Richard of St. Victor, *Benjamin Minor* 25 (*PL*, CXCVI:17). On the importance of these materials for later virtue lore, see Tuve, pp. 60–65; on the *Moralium*, see Ph. Delhaye, "Une adaptation du *De officiis* au xiiᵉ siècle: Le *Moralium dogma philosophorum*," *RTAM* XVI (1949):227–58, and XVII (1950): 5–28.

9. William O. Harris, *Skelton's "Magnyfycence" and the Cardinal Virtue Tradition* (Chapel Hill: University of North Carolina Press, 1965), ably argues for the persistence of this tradition. Harris traces the earliest form of this view to Julianus Pomerius' *De vita contemplativa* III.xx.2: "tunc est vera patientia, si fuerit justa: et in eis justa est patientia

quorum *nec doloribus, nec voluptatibus cedit mentis invicta constantia.* . . . . Fortitudo nostra est, quia ita nos contra omnia vitia invicta protectione corroborat, *ut animum nostrum nec blanda dissolvant, nec adversa dejiciant* ("Then true patience exists, when it is righteous, and they have such a patience whose minds are never swayed from unconquerable constancy either by sorrows or vain delights. . . . This is our fortitude, because it strengthens us with an unconquerable protection against every vice, so that neither blandishments dissolve nor harsh things cast down our spirit"), *PL,* LIX:504, italics added. I cite *Fasciculus morum* in the next sentence from Frances A. Foster's transcript of Bodleian Library MS Rawlinson C.670, f.27^v. The transcript, which is at the Beinecke Library, Yale, was kindly lent me by Siegfried Wenzel. For the standard study of *Fasciculus,* see A. G. Little, *Studies in English Franciscan History* (Manchester: Manchester University Press, 1917), pp. 139-57. For other examples of this view of patience, see *The Book of Vices and Virtues* (one of numerous Middle English translations of Frere Lorens' *Somme le roi*), EETS 217, pp. 123, 162; and *The Lay Folk's Catechism* (Archbishop Thoresby of York's translation of the Pecham constitutions on instruction of the laity), EETS 118, lines 430-39. See also the fine articles of F. N. M. Diekstra, "Jonah and *Patience*: The Psychology of a Prophet," *English Studies* LV (1974):205-17, and "*The Wanderer* 65b-72: The Passions of the Mind and the Cardinal Virtues," *Neophilologus* LV (1971):73-88.

10. Related images underscore further the implications of verbs like *frangere.* The mind of the patient man is described through such adjectives as *fixus, immobilis, stabilis, immutabilis, erectus, firmus, solidus,* or *cunctus.* Similarly, the patient is frequently enjoined to *refraenare* ("bridle") his emotional impulses, sometimes to bind them with a *vinculum* or *funiculus* ("bond" or "cord").

11. The opposition of *ira* and patience is commonplace from Stoic discussions of the first century; there, *tranquillitas mentis* regularly opposes the *furor* of wrath. Cf. Seneca, *De ira* II.xii.6: "Nos non advocabimus patientiam, quos tantum praemium expectat, felicis animi immota tranquillitas? Quantum est effugere maximum malum, iram, cum illa rabiem, saevitiam, crudelitatem, furorem, alios comites eius adfectus" ("Shall we not summon ourselves to patience when it promises so great a reward, the unmoved serenity of a happy mind? How great a happening it would be to avoid the worst evil, anger, and with it insanity, savagery, cruelty, fury, and its other henchmen, the passions"). This opposition occurs already in very early Christian writings (e.g., Cyprian, *De zelo et livore* 16 [*PL,* IV:649], and Prudentius, *Psychomachia,* lines 109-77), and by the later Middle Ages septenaries which arrange the Seven Deadly Sins against seven remedial virtues regularly juxtapose *ira* and *patientia.* See Tuve's lengthy treatment of the septenary, pp. 85-114; and Maurice Hussey, "The Petitions of the *Pater Noster* in Mediaeval English Literature," *Medium Aevum* XXVII (1958):8-16. The *acedia-patientia* discussions are nearly as widespread: in part, these opinions reflect the view that fortitude—spiritual strength—corrects the debilities of sloth. Thus patience, as a "part" of fortitude, may stand for the whole virtue. See Harris' discussion, *Skelton's "Magnyfycence"*; and his article, "Despair and 'Patience as the Truest Fortitude' in *Samson Agonistes,*" in *Critical Essays on Milton from ELH* (Baltimore: Johns Hopkins Press, 1969), pp. 277-90. For examples of this tendency, see "Postquam," f. 92vb; Gregory, *Cura pastoralis* III.9 (*PL,* LXXVII:61); and such proverbs as "Cuivis dolori remedium est patientia" ("Patience is a cure for any sorrow") and "Viriliter feras quod necesse est; dolor enim patientia vincitur" ("You should bear in a manly fashion whatever is necessary; sorrow is conquered by patience")—Publilius Syrus 96 and ps-Seneca, *De moribus* 6, respectively).

12. For example, the Augustinian source of the short definition of patience cited above reads in full: "Patientia hominis, *quae recta est atque laudabilis et vocabulo digna virtutis,* ea perhibetur qua aequo animo mala toleramus, ne animo iniquo bona deseramus, per quae ad meliora perveniamus" ("That patience which is proper, praiseworthy, and deserving the name 'virtue,' is produced by that quality by which we endure evils with an even mind; otherwise we should in an unjust spirit desert those good things through which we may pass

to better things")—*PL*, XL:611, italics added. Similarly, Peraldus (VII.vi, f. n 5vb) finds it necessary to gloss Cicero in order to put the language òf late classical ethics within a Christian context: "'Honestatis causa' est perpessio ut cum quis pro fide Christi potius eligit mori quam negando eam salvare vitam suam. 'Utilitatis vero causa' ut cum quis pro salute gregis mori eligit. 'Voluntaria' vero ideo dicitur, quia qui omnino invitus patitur non habet laudem vel meritum. . . . [cites I Pet. 4:15–16 as a proof-text] 'Diuturna dicutur, quia ad verum patientem pertinet ut patiendo perseveret." (*For the sake of virtue* means such indifference to pain as when someone chooses to die for the Christian faith rather than save his life by renouncing it. *For the sake of some benefit* is when someone chooses to die for the salvation of the flock. *Voluntary* is also included in the definition because one who suffers with extreme reluctance is neither praiseworthy nor meritorious. *Longlasting* is also included because a truly patient man should persevere in his suffering.) This gloss is also cited by Alexander Carpenter (Fabricarius), *Destructorium vitiorum*, 2° (Köln: Heinrich Quentell, 1480), VI, 76, f.R. 1vb. On Carpenter, see G. R. Owst, "The *Destructorium Vitiorum* of Alexander Carpenter" (London: S.P.C.K., 1952).

13. The Augustinian catch-phrase comes from *Epistle* 204.4 (*PL*, XXXIII:940) and in context refers to heretics who will suffer for their false beliefs: "monstravimus non eos posse habere martyrum mortem, quia Christianorum non habent vitam; cum martyrem non faciat poena, sed causa" ("We have shown these to be incapable of dying as martyrs because they did not have a Christian life; for not pain, but a good cause, makes a martyr"). The fullest discussion of the value of the eighth Beatitude as a touchstone occurs in *De patientia* III–X, especially X.8 (*PL*, XL:615); cf. also *Sermons* 274 (*PL*, XXXVIII:1253) and 293.V.4 (*PL*, XXXVIII:1287–88). The expansion of charity to form the *habitus* of all virtues typifies Augustinian discussions; cf. Gösta Hök, "Augustin und die antike Tugendlehre," *Kerygma und Dogma* VI (1960):104–30. This Augustinian discussion animates Aquinas, *Summa theologica* II^a.II^{ae}, Q. 136, art. 3 ("Utrum patientia possit haberi sine gratia"—"Whether one may possess patience without grace"); see Etienne Gilson, "La vertu de patience selon Saint Thomas et Saint Augustin," *Archives d'Histoire Doctrinale et Littéraire du Moyen Age* XV (1946):93–104.

14. The *martyr Sathanis* topic occurs regularly in sermons. For some other uses cf. Bruno of Asti, *Sententiae* II.8 (*PL*, CLXV:926); ps.-Vincent of Beauvais, *Bibliotheca mundi seu Speculi maioris*, vol. III, *Speculum morale* (Douai: Balthazar Belieri, 1624; reprint ed., Graz: Akademische Druck., 1964), col. 463; Saint Thomas More, *Dialogue of Comfort* I.10. The two deprecating terms for this patience are provided by the author of "Postquam," f. 93vb; he associates the ass with that patience which endures divinely sent affliction only when sent as a rebuke for past sin. Contrary to the emphases of later medieval symbolic traditions, the donkey nearly always functions in patience discussions as a figure *in malo*; cf. Peraldus, VII.xii, f. p. 1ra: "Asinus non discernit quid sibi imponatur, utrum aurum vel lutum" ("The donkey does not distinguish what load is placed on his back, whether gold or mud"), or William of Auvergne, II. 249^b: "Patientia asinaria . . . est sicut durities in lateribus equorum et in natibus asinorum ex assuetudine stimulationis" ("Donkey-like patience is as the hardness which develops in the sides of a horse or the buttocks of an ass from the regularity with which it is goaded").

15. *Negligentia* regularly appears in discussions of the prelate's duties, for, as William Alnwick, bishop of Lincoln (1437–49), put it: "Cure nobis [episcopis] est mores in populo et clero nobis subditis reformare, virtutes plantare, et vitia sarculo correctionis ordinarie evellere et extirpare" ("The charge given us bishops is to reform the habits of the laity and clerics in our care, to plant virtues, and to tear out and root up vices with the hoe of ordinary correction"); cited by A. Hamilton Thompson, *The English Clergy and their Organization in the Later Middle Ages* (Oxford: Clarendon, 1947), p. 41n. The duty of correction is an absolute imperative, enjoined by canon law; see Gratian's lengthy proof that correction is not sin, nor form of vengeance, nor violation of Christian patience, but in fact a duty of charity, *Decretum*, pars. 2^a, C. 23, Q.4 *in extenso*, and Q.5, cc. 1–7, in *Corpus Juris Canonici*,

ed. A. I. Richter (rev. Aemilius Friedberg), 2 vols. (Leipzig: Tauchnitz, 1879; reprint ed., Graz: Akademische Druck., 1955–59), I:899–931. For other discussions, see John Waldeby, *Sermones in diversis*, Gonville and Caius College, Cambridge, MS 334, f. 177[rb]; Robert Grosseteste, "Deus est," ed. Siegfried Wenzel, *Franciscan Studies* XXX (1970):264; and Thomas Brinton, *The Sermons*, ed. Mary Aquinas Devlin (Camden Society, 3d series, 85–86), pp. 68–71, 120–21, 480–81, et alibi.

16. The Aristotelian source is *Nichomachaean Ethics* III.viii.1116 a 16–1117 a 18. For discussion and analysis of Aristotle's examples and their importance, see Albertus Magnus, *De bono*, Tract. 2, Q. 1, art. 5; Aquinas, *Summa theologica* II[a] II[ae], Q. 123, art. 1, ad 2[m]; Giles of Rome, *De regimine principum* I.ii.14; Peraldus, VII.xii, ff. p 1[ra]–p 1[rb]; Etienne de Bourbon, ff. 660[vb]–661 .

17. Cf., as examples, the patience discussion in the Middle English *Consilia Isidori*, ed. C. Horstman, in *Yorkshire Writers*, 2 vols. (London: Swan Sonnenschein, and New York: Macmillan, 1895–96), II:369, and its Latin parallels, Anselm's *Exhortatio* (*PL*, CLVIII:681), and ps.-Bernard's *Liber de modo bene vivendi* XL, 101 (*PL*, CLXXXIV:1261): "Esto mansuetus, esto patiens, esto mitis, esto modestus. Serva patientiam, serva modestiam" ("Be mild, be patient, be meek, be modest. Serve patience, serve modesty"); or the *tabula* entry for patience from William of Pagula's *Speculum praelatorum*, Merton College, Oxford, MS 217; f. 446[va]: "Patientia, secunda parte, titulo lxxiiii....Adde benignitas, clementia, mansuetudo, obedi[enti]a, placere, placentia, convicium, consolatio, ira, tribulatio, sapientia, silentium" ("Patience, in the second part, title 74. . . . See also loving one's neighbor, tranquil compassion, mildness, obedience, to please, courtesy, abuse, consolation, anger, tribulation, wisdom, silence"). This manuscript, the unique and imperfect copy of the work, is unfoliated; I follow the best description, given by Leonard Boyle, *Monumenta Iuris Canonici, Series C: Subsidia* I (1965):454.

18. The first citation occurs at *Homeliae in Evangelia* II.xxxv.7 (*PL*, LXXVI:1263), where it concludes a moral reading of Matt. 20:22, the history of the two sons of Zebedee, James and John; the passage is cited *in extenso* by John of Mirfield, ff. 113[vb]–114 . In the Gregorian text, the phrase "vel flammis" does not occur, but it already formed part of the Gregorian quotation tradition by the time of Alcuin; cf. *De virtutibus et vitiis* IX (*PL*, CI:619). The lengthier quotation occurs in the same homily, par. 9 (*PL*, LXXVI:1264); for quotation of this passage or its use to divide a discussion, see Bromyard, P.1.ii.3; ps.-Vincent, col. 448; and "John of Hoveden," *Speculum laicorum*, ed. J. Th. Welter (Paris: Picard, 1914), p. 61. On Gregory's effort to "routinize" the use of the virtue patience, see Alfred C. Rush, "Spiritual Martyrdom in St. Gregory the Great," *Theological Studies* XXIII (1962):569–89.

19. Some idea of the emphasis given these two topics can be gained from viewing the proportions of Peraldus' patience tract. The whole discussion occupies forty-seven columns (ff. n 5[vb]–p 1[rb]); of these, thirty-one are given over to tribulation and temptation (tribulation, ff. n 8[vb]–o 4[va]; temptation, ff. o 4[vb]–o 8[va]). Even in tracts where topics are not so clearly separated out as in Peraldus', the proportions do not vary much, the majority of the discussion being given over to situations which should inspire patience, rather than to the virtue itself.

20. The other Pauline catalogue occurs at II Cor. 6:4–10. It appears quite infrequently in the Middle Ages as an exhaustive division of the occasions that call forth patience. For the only examples I have found, see Bruno the Carthusian, *Expositio in omnes epistolas Pauli* (*PL*, CLIII:245), and Robert Ripon (subprior of Durham, c. 1400), *Sermones*, British Museum MS Harley 4894, ff. 56[r]–56[v]. The Pauline use of *jejunium* may be responsible for some associations of patience with the proper endurance of the third stage of penance, *satisfactio*; cf. Raymond de Penyaforte, III.xxxiv.38, 49, pp. 470[b], 479[b]–80[b].

21. Peraldus, VII.ix, f. o 2rb.

22. For elaboration of such views, see (among others) Brinton, p. 454; Waldeby, f. 195va; and Robert Holcot's lengthy discussion of the Wisdom of Solomon 1:11, *Super Sapientiam Salomonis*, 4° (Köln: Conrad Winters, 1479), lectio 9, ff. B 7ra–B 9rb.

23. One thinks immediately of Chaucer's Palamon and Arcite, for whom failure in love is a sign that "the world is out of joint," or of the lovers of Lydgate's *Black Knight* and *Temple of Glass*, who find peace only when the complete (mythographic) fabric of the cosmos is explicated for them.

24. Specifically consolatory materials lie somewhat outside the scope of normal Christian discussions, in that Boethius and other writers in the genre presuppose that reason easily triumphs over pain, an attitude foreign to most religious discussions (see note 35). Indeed, the only commonplace patience figure specifically Boethian is the anecdote of *Consolatio* II, p. 7, with its punch line, "Philosophus fuisses, si tacuisses" ("You would have been a philosopher had you kept your mouth shut"). Cf. Langland, *Piers Plowman* B XI:*post* 416 (Kane-Donaldson numeration); Etienne de Bourbon, f. 680ra; ps.-Vincent, col. 470; Holcot, lectio 55, ff. M 4ra-M 4rb.

25. See Bede, *Matthaei Evangelii expositio* II.9 (*PL*, XCII:46); Peter Lombard, *Sententiae* IV, Dist. 15.1 (*PL*, CXCII:873): "Quinque enim modis flagella contingunt: vel ut justis per patientiam merita augeantur, ut Job; vel ad custodiam virtutum, ne superbia tentet, ut Paulo; vel ad corrigenda peccata, ut Mariae lepra; vel ad gloriam Dei, ut de caeco nato; vel ad judicium poenae, ut Herodi, quatenus hic videatur quid in inferno sequatur" ("Divine scourgings occur for five purposes: that the rewards of the just may be increased by patience, as with Job; or to preserve virtue, lest pride should tempt a man, as with Paul; or to correct sins, as with Miriam's leprosy; or for the glory of God, as with the man born blind; or as a judgment of deserved punishment, so that one may see in this world what will follow in hell, as with Herod"). Examples appear in *The Chastising of God's Children*, ed. Joyce Bazire and Eric Colledge (Oxford: Blackwell, 1957), pp. 149-50; William of Pagula, *Oculus*, ff. 110va, 110vb, 111rb; in truncated three-part form in Holcot, lectio 107, f. a 3va; and More, *Dialogue of Comfort* I.7-10.

26. For Miriam as an example of impatience needing correction and as an invitation to patience, see Felton, f. 88r; Penyaforte, III.xxxiv.41, pp. 473b-474a (as an argument for extreme penances); *Memoriale credentium*, f. 87r. For variously expansive lists of the negative examples, see Etienne de Bourbon, f. 668ra; Waldeby, f. 193ra; ps.-Vincent, cols. 464-65.

27. The *Glossa* in *Biblia cum glossis*, 2°, 4 vols. (Venice: Paganinus de Paganinis, 1495), f. 1027vb, reads: "Malum [with reference to "malo," Matt. 5:39] temporale dicit quid tribus modis sit: cruciatu corporum, de quo dicit 'Si quis te percusserit'; damno rerum, unde ait, 'Et ei, qui vult tecum &c'; angariis operum, unde ait, 'Et quicumque angariaverit te &c' " ("He speaks of the triple evil of this world: of bodily torture . . . of loss of possessions . . . of enforced work . . . , etc."). For discussions of *angaria*, see the *Parson's Tale* I, 666-69; its source, "Postquam," ff. 92ra-92rb; and the second Middle English translation of this material, *Memoriale credentium*, f. 36r. For Simon the Cyrene as a negative example, see Peter Cantor, *Verbum abbreviatum* CXIV (*PL*, CCV:302).

28. Discussions which utilize *correptio* as a topic rely on the following rather discrete traditions: (1) John of Salisbury, *Polycraticus* III, xiv (*PL*, CXCIX:506-12) discusses the patience of various classical figures as their ability to keep their tempers when corrected by detractors of inferior station. (The most famous of these anecdotes, that of Alexander and the pirate [col. 508], was known to Chaucer; see *Manciple's Tale* I, 223-34, with the narrator's customary inversion of morality.) Many of the same examples recur in *Breviloquium* IV, 8, where John of Wales adds *correptio* to the traditional three topics; for further dependent use, see Alexander Carpenter, f. R1vb. (2) The first of the so-called "spiritual works of mercy," the correction of the sinner, clearly is also relevant, especially as the fifth and sixth of these "works," bearing wrongs patiently and forgiving one's enemies, are standard patience topics. Only rarely do medieval authors refer directly to these "works" in organizing patience discussions; Carpenter, who shapes parts of his discussion around the spiritual works, is a conspicuous exception. (3) Already mentioned (note 15) is the universal insistence on the episcopal duty of correction. (4) In influential late-medieval eighteen-part divisions of *acedia*, the last six steps (the stage known as "worse ending") describe the sin-

ner's obdurate refusal to be corrected, his anger at his spiritual physician. Indeed, the fourteenth step is known as "impatience," a fact which solidifies connections between enduring corrective penance and following patience. For discussion, see Siegfried Wenzel, *The Sin of Sloth: "Acedia" in Medieval Thought and Literature* (Chapel Hill: University of North Carolina Press, 1967), pp. 76, 79–82.

29. For example, the camomile or the trodden plant which springs anew has as a medieval precursor the *granum sinapis* (ultimately based on the mustard grain of Matt. 13:31–32). See Nicholas of Lyra, "Prothemata in Job," in *Biblia*, f. 473ra; Etienne de Bourbon, f. 679va; Waldeby, f. 150va.

30. See the discussion of the ass in patience materials (note 14) or compare the strange use of *cetus* as a figure *in bono*, of interest perhaps to readers of the Middle English *Patience*, by William Auvergne, II:252^b; Peraldus, VII.ix, f. o4^{ra}; Carpenter, f. R3^{vb}; Etienne de Bourbon, f. 683rb.

31. I cite one example for each permutation: for the rod which is burnt, see Carpenter, f. i 6rb (based on the reference to Assur at Isa. 10:5 as *virga furoris*, the rod of anger); for the rod as an implement which works salvation, see *Ancrene Wisse*, EETS 249, f. 49^r / 8 ff.; for God's two rods, see Peraldus, VII.viii, f. n 8va.

32. The sentence is probably not Gregorian; cf. *Moralia* XVI.xxxii.39 (*PL*, LXXV:1141), a discussion of one of several biblical uses of this idea, Job 23:10: "Quasi aurum ergo quod per ignem transit probantur animae justorum" ("The souls of the righteous are tested just as gold which passes through the fire"). *Moralia* XX.xxxix.76 (*PL*, LXXVI:183–84) has similar material, together with references to *granum*, to *flores inter spinas*, to *rosa* as a camomile. For examples of this sentence and expansive discussions based on it, see Felton, ff. 7^v, 90^v; the Middle English *Twelve Profits of Tribulation*, version C, in Horstman, II: 48–51, and its source, Peter of Blois, *De Duodecim Utilitatibus Tribulationis* (*PL*, CCVII: 992–95). On *Twelve Profits* and related popular theological materials, see Albert Auer, *Leidenstheologie im Spätmittelalter* (St. Ottilien: EOS Verlag der Erzabtei, 1952), Kirchengeschichtliche Quellen und Studien 2.

33. This figure forms a traditional part of the discussion of *ignis* as a figure for tribulation: *ignis purgat* ("fire cleanses") and the *palea* ("dross") or *feces peccati* ("dregs of sin") are removed from the metal alloy. (See note 3.) A near variant of this figure, the golden coin which may or may not be counterfeit with baser metals, occurs widely; see Chaucer, *Clerk's Tale* E, 1166–69; Langland, *Piers Plowman* XV:349–55 (in a general discussion of sin and hypocrisy); and Felton's elaborate moralization, ff. 105^v–107^r.

34. Again I cite only single examples of each permutation: for the idea of the precious vessel, see *Ancrene Wisse*, EETS 249, f. 77^v / 19 ff.; for a connection with the *vas fictilis* (cf. II Cor. 4:7) which must be fired to subsist, see John of Mirfield, f. 7vb (citing Chrysostom), and cf. the near variant, the *tegula* ("tile") used by William of Pagula, *Oculus*, f. 115vb, and *Speculum religiosorum* 16, ibid., f. 31vb; for tribulation as the mold giving substantial form to the patient, see William of Auvergne, II:250^a; and for the *malleus* (and *tunsio* ["pounding"] as a metaphor for tribulation), see Peter of Blois (*PL*, CCVII:1001) or Peter Damian, *Opusculum* 40.1 (*PL*, CXLV:649). As an example of wit and expansiveness inherent in the image, cf. Deguilleville's use of the anvil as a figure for the patient man who will imitate Christ's actions at the buffeting, *The Pilgrimage of the Lyf of the Manhode*, ed. William Aldis Wright (London: J. B. Nichols and Sons, 1869), I:111–12, pp. 58–59. The figure occurs elsewhere, of course, and is, at least in part, inspired by Psalms 128:3, the anvil being the implement on which "Supra dorsum meum fabricaverunt peccatores" ("Sinners build upon my back"). Cf. also Bartholomaeus Anglicus' derivation of *tergum* ("back") from *terrendo* ("beating"), V.xxxii (in the Trevisan translation, p. 230/15–7).

35. The Peraldus discussion, VII.x–xi, ff. o4^{vb}–o8^{va}, and William of Pagula's discussion at the end of *Oculus* II, ff. 111va–15vb, provide good examples of these tendencies. Among other themes which recur both in temptation tracts and in more straightforward patience discussions, one may cite the insistence on humility and self-abnegation, especially fasting

and abstinence as *modi repugnandi diabolum* ("ways of repelling the devil in battle"; cf. the Penyaforte citation, note 20); insistence on temptation as a corrective to possible pride, with the standard example of Paul based on II Cor. 12:7 (cf. the materials grouped in note 25); frequent discussion of the legitimacy of *fuga* to avoid temptation (cf. note 38); and common use of *Vitae patrum* anecdotes which regularly appear in patience discussions (especially *exempla* associated with Saint Anthony; see note 39 for a rather typical apologue of this sort).

36. The conversion of the Stoic concept into Christian terms has been brilliantly treated by Erich Auerbach, "Excursus: *Gloria Passionis*," in *Literary Language and Its Public in Late Latin Antiquity and in the Middle Ages*, trans. Ralph Manheim (Princeton: Princeton University Press, 1965), pp. 67–81. Especially important for my argument in subsequent paragraphs, Auerbach underscores the influence of two widely quoted Bernardine loci, both of which insist upon the necessity of loving in one's suffering. Also useful on this topic, especially for its collection of patristic passages, is Johannes Stelzenberger, *Die Beziehungen der frühchristlichen Sittenlehre zur Ethik der Stoa* (München: Hueber, 1933), esp. pp. 247–77. Virtually a convention of early Christian patience tracts is an attack on the nondivinely inspired *patientia philosophorum*: Macrobius debunks the value of unaided human virtue, *Commentarii in Somnium Scipionis*, I.viii.9, esp.; other broadsides occur in Tertullian, *De patientia* 1–2 (*PL*, I:1249–52); Cyprian, *De bono patientiae* 2–3 (*PL*, IV:623); Lactantius, *Institutiones divinae* VI.17 (*PL*, VI:694–95); Augustine, *De civitate dei* XIX.iv.3–5 (*PL*, XLI:628–31). Cf. also notes 12–13. Obviously the need for such sharp definition of Christian patience as differing from Stoic *apatheia* declined in the course of the Middle Ages; this decline allowed the later pillaging of Stoic aphorisms and opinions as commendations of patience. But later medieval writers still show aversion to the complete extirpation of the passions: cf. Peter Damian, *Opusculum* 40:9 ("Naturam quippe possum ex ratione compescere, non omnino delere; possum linire, non prorsus exstinguere": "I can curb my nature rationally, but not completely obliterate it; I can cover it, not completely extinguish it"—*PL*, CXLV:659–60); Peraldus, VII.xi, f. o 7va ("non sumus eradicatores cogitationum sed luctatores contra eas": "we are not the eradicators of our evil thoughts but contenders against them"); or Thomas More, *Dialogue of Comfort* I.1.

37. I adopt to my own use one somewhat unusual patience figure; for examples, see Prudentius, *Psychomachia*, lines 125–30; "Postquam," f. 93ra; *Fasciculus morum*, f. 28^r; John of Wales, *Breviloquium* IV, 7, Libreria comunale di Cortona MS 58, f. 184^r; Bromyard, A.18.ii.8; Felton, f. 90^r. The *Fasciculus morum* version reads: "Bene comparatur [patiens] adamanti qui secundum Ysidorum, nulli cedit materiae ut ferro, nec igni [sic] frangitur nec umquam incalescit, unde *adamas* grece, *vis indomita* latine dicitur; sed dum sic invictus fuerit ferri ignisque contemptor, hircino tamen sanguine maceratur. Revera sic verus patiens nulla vi ferri aut ignis frangitur aut dissolvitur, et tamen amore sanguinis Christi Jesu statim ad compassionem emollitur" ("The patient man may well be compared to the adamant which, according to Isidore, yields to no material, even iron. Nor is it broken or heated at all by fire. Hence it is called *adamas* in Greek and *invincible strength* in Latin. But when it stands invincibly, despising both iron and fire, it may nevertheless be softened with a kid's blood. Thus the true patient is neither broken nor dissolved by any strength of iron or fire, and nevertheless is immediately softened to compassion by the love of Christ's blood").

38. One should note that canonistic discussions adopt a more realistic view, one which does not place value on unnecessary suffering. Legal writers strongly dissuade their audience from following the injunction of Matt. 5:39 in a literal manner and adduce more common sense considerations. See particularly Gratian, *Decretum*, pars. 2^a, C.23, Q.1, esp. *ante* c.1, c.2, and *post* c.2 ("Precepta patientiae non tam ostentatione corporis quam preparatione cordis sunt retinenda": "The commands to follow patience are to be held not so much by displaying one's body to injury as by preparing one's heart"); cf. Augustine's *Epistle* 138.12–14 (*PL*, XXXIII:530–31), in some sense the ultimate source of *Hamlet*'s "the readiness is all,"

and Q.3, I:889–92, 895–98. Also cf. the legal commonplace translated by Chaucer at *Reeve's Prologue* A 3912: "a jure concessum est ut vim vi repellamus" ("law grants us the right to repel force with force"), originally the wording of *Digest* IX.ii.45 (2), adopted in a canon of Alexander III, which is promulgated in Gregory IX's collection *Extra* 5.39.3, *Corpus Juris*, II:890.

39. One of the most widely diffused examples, cited by de Voragine, *Legende aurea, sub* April 28 (Saint Vitalis); "Postquam," f. 91vb; and, in the following form, by Peter Cantor, *Verbum abbreviatum* CXIV (*PL*, CCV: 300–301): "Haec virtus [patientia] prae caeteris arreptitium curavit, arreptitio triumphavit. Eremita cum venisset ad civitatem, ut venderet opuscula sua, praebente ei aliam maxillam percutiendam cum unam praebuisset, a quo daemon exiens, hujusmodi vocem emisit: 'In sola patientia victus sum, hac sola amisi vas, quod firmiter possedi,' et haec est examen virtutum, et boni viri, quod non alia virtus" ("This virtue before all others has cured and exultingly triumphed over demonic seizures. A certain hermit went to the city so that he might sell his handiwork. After he had offered a certain man one cheek to strike, upon offering him his other cheek, a demon left his persecutor and exclaimed: 'I am conquered by patience alone; by patience alone I have lost the container which I possessed completely.' And this is a true test of virtues and of a good man, and no other virtue is").

"Who Suffreth More Than God?" :
Narrative Redefinition of Patience in
Patience and *Piers Plowman*

Elizabeth D. Kirk

haucer's Franklin, placing patience among the conditions for love without *maistrye*, links two apparently contradictory elements in one typically pragmatic formulation:

> Pacience is an heigh vertu, certeyn,
> For it venquysseth, as thise clerkes seyn,
> Thynges that rigour sholde nevere
>   atteyne. . . .
> Lerneth to suffre, or elles, so mot I goon,
> Ye shul it lerne, wher so ye wol or noon. . . .[1]

This formulation embodies a paradox almost too unobtrusive to be noted as a contradiction. Patience is the attitude that can bring about what action and exigence are powerless to effect; patience is a matter of stomaching what will surely happen, whether we accept it or not. Patience is both active and passive, both creative and cynical. This paradox, implicit in medieval thought about patience, provides the informing structure for two major Middle English treatments of the subject, *Patience* and the B-text of *Piers Plowman*. Both were written early in the last quarter of the fourteenth century, and both treat patience in connection with the idea of patient poverty; most probably *Patience* influenced Langland.[2] More significantly, these two poems, so diverse in length and in genre, present actions in which an initial, simple, and essentially negative view of patience is cumulatively redefined until, as the poem's perspective widens, this conception is subsumed into a positive one grounded in a new sense of man's place in a theocentric universe.

Patience, much the shorter treatment and probably the earlier, is one of the four poems attributed to the poet of *Sir Gawain and the Green Knight* and *Pearl*, and has been so overshadowed by them that the sophistication of its intellectual and dramatic structure has been insufficiently appreciated.[3] The bulk of the poem's 531 lines consists of a retelling of the biblical Book of Jonah. This story, however, is framed by a first person narrator's account of his own need to acquire patience in the face of poverty.[4] Consequently, Jonah is presented primarily as an anti-type of patience, an inherently comic situation and one which appears at first sight to conflict with traditional interpretations of Jonah.[5] Jonah was commonly regarded, because of his three-day sojourn in the whale's belly, as a type of Christ's descent into Hell and resurrection, and is so presented in liturgy and biblical commentary, on the authority of several New Testament passages.[6] Most artistic treatments of Jonah have been pictorial rather than literary,[7] presumably because the contrast between the largely satiric view of Jonah implicit in the Old Testament narrative and the contrary aura that surrounds Jonah in his typological role can be dealt with in pictures of individual moments but cannot be evaded in a consecutive narrative. *Patience*, however, far from evading this problem, makes it central. One previous comic literary treatment of Jonah does exist which may shed light on the connection between the narrative frame and the story proper. This is a Goliard poem, "Fama tuba dante sonum," attributed to the Arch-poet of Cologne, a begging letter to a patron which makes Jonah a type not of Christ but of the impoverished poet.[8]

Patience begins with the narrator presenting an explicit definition of patience:

Pacience is a poynt, þaȝ hit displese ofte.
When heuy herttes ben hurt wyth heþyng oþer elles,
Suffraunce may aswagen hem and þe swelme leþe,
For ho quelles vche a qued and quenches malyce.
For quo-so suffer cowþe syt, sele wolde folȝe,
And quo for þro may noȝt þole, þe þikker he sufferes.

þen is better to abyde þe bur vmbe-stoundes,
þen ay þrow forth my þro, þaȝ me þynk ylle. (lines 1–8)

Patience is a point [target? feat? position reached?] though it is often
unpleasant. When heavy hearts are wounded by scorn or other
things, sufferance can assuage them and calm the flame, for she
subdues every evil and quenches malice. For anyone who knows
how to endure misfortune, happiness would follow, and whoever
can not endure because of his anger, the more he suffers. Then it is
better to endure the wind occasionally than always to give vent to
my anger, though it seems ill to me.[9]

The narrator places these reflections in the context of the Beatitudes,
which he translates. The first and last of them, with their praise of the
poor in spirit and the patient, he links together, and chooses Dame
Poverty and Dame Patience as the ladies he must embrace since he will
have to put up with their company in any case. This highly Stoic attitude,
which avoids cynicism only by its poignancy, is embodied in his translation of the eighth Beatitude. Where the Vulgate reads "Beati qui
persecutionem patiuntur propter iustitiam"[10] ("Blessed are they who suffer persecution for the sake of justice"), the poet translates "þay ar
happen also þat con her hert stere" (line 27): "Blessed are those also who
can steer [discipline, direct, govern] their hearts." Positive action for a
great cause is transformed into control of the feelings. Since there is no
evicting Dame Poverty once she has moved into one's house, one can
only accept her with her inevitable companion, Dame Patience:

Thus pouerte and pacyence are nedes play-feres;
Syþen I am sette with hem samen, suffer me by-houes;
þenne is me lyȝtloker hit lyke and her lotes prayse,
þenne wyþer wyth and be wroth and þe wers haue. (lines 45–48)

Thus poverty and patience are necessarily play-fellows; since I am
beset by them together, it behoves me to acquiesce; for it is easier to
like it and praise their manners than fight against it and be the worse
off.

Clearly, the poet is characterizing a complex state of mind. The narrator's ideas, in one sense, reflect the traditional view of patience as the
quality which makes possible the endurance of external evil; Saint
Thomas formulates it in terms that present patience as the antidote to
two destructive forms of passivity, depression, and sloth: "Unde necesse

est habere aliquam virtutem per quam bonus rationis conservetur contra tristitiam, ne scilicet ratio tristitiae succumbat. Hoc autem facit patientia"[11] ("It is necessary to have a virtue to safeguard the good of reason against sorrow, lest reason give way to sorrow. This patience achieves"). But this element has become intertwined with two others. One involves problems in the psychology of those attempting patience. Medieval awareness of this is clearest in discussion of the Book of Job, particularly in Saint Thomas' great commentary and in the *Glossa Ordinaria*'s presentation, especially Nicholas of Lyra's analysis and the additions of Paul of Burgos.[12] The *Glossa* cross-references its discussion with another key biblical treatment of patience, James 1:12–15. These commentaries recognize explicitly that, while suffering should ideally be penance or, better still, a smelting of the personality that refines it, in practice suffering is likely to produce depression, sloth, despair, and anger hardening into hatred.[13] Even when one successfully combats these tendencies, patience is too likely to remain merely negative, an avoidance of action, an attempt to keep oneself to oneself. One maintains a rigid mental control because one realizes that any other course would merely make things worse. The *Patience* narrator argues in this way (line 53): "What grayþed me þe grychchyng bot grame more seche?" ("What would complaining achieve but to seek more pain?") Such a state of mind cannot be equated with real patience, and while it does avoid hatred, it achieves only an armed truce with anger and depression.

But even the virtue itself has an inherently negative character. This led Saint Thomas to differentiate it from the positive virtue of fortitude and to deny it the role of greatest virtue:

> Directius autem ad bonum ordinant hominem virtutes quae sunt constitutivae boni, quam illae quae sunt impeditivae eorum quae abducunt a bono. Et sicut inter illas quae sunt constitutivae boni tanto aliqua potior est quanto in maiori bono statuit hominem, sicut fides, spes et caritas quam prudentia et iustitia; ita etiam inter illas quae sunt impeditivae retrahentium a bono, tanto aliqua est potior quanto id quod ab ea impeditur magis a bono retrahit. Plus autem a bono retrahunt pericula mortis, circa quae est fortitudo, vel delectationes tactus, quae est temperantia, quam quaevis adversa, circa quae est patientia. (II-II, 136, 2, r)

> Now those virtues which constitute good incline a man more directly to good than those which are a check on those things which lead man away from good; and just as among those that bring about good, the greater is that which establishes man in a greater good (so

that faith, hope, and charity are greater than prudence and justice),
so too among those that are a check on what draws man away from
good, the greater virtue is the one which is a check on the greater
obstacle to good. But dangers of death, with which fortitude is concerned, and pleasures of touch, with which temperance is concerned, withdraw a man from good much more than any sort of
hardship, with which patience is concerned.

The *Patience* narrator's attitude, however well-meaning, divorces
patience from positive development of the personality. He does his best
to rise to full acceptance of his situation, but can get no further than self-
control and endurance. To illustrate to himself the uselessness of fighting
one's fate, he turns to the story of Jonah.

One of the hardest literary effects to define is that of high comedy. Yet
such comedy is *Patience*'s greatest achievement. The poem is suffused
with a delicately ironic sense of Jonah's predicament. From Jonah's own
point of view his story is one of tyranny heroically defied and catastrophe
and danger stoically endured. From the reader's less limited perspective,
it is one of cowardice, self-pity, rationalization, and naiveté. In the larger
perspective of God's action, the dangers Jonah runs are revealed to be no
dangers at all, but part of God's unceasing care for him, the very security
he thought to achieve by escaping from God. It is undignified in the
extreme to posture heroically when you are in fact perfectly safe. The
cosmic point of view alone would render Jonah farcical and distasteful;
his own perspective alone would make him a Prometheus. By super-
imposing the larger perspective on a shrewdly convincing and not
unsympathetic portrayal of Jonah's thoughts, and by a subtle trans-shifting
between the human and the cosmic scale, a distinctive tone is achieved, a
sophisticated, comic tone which provides the resolution to the problem of
man's status in a world he did not make and cannot control.[14] Much of
this effect is achieved by delicate exaggerations of pace or of statement,
and by inherently deflating juxtapositions of scale or of two points of
view on the same thing. Particularly important for our purposes is the
way the poet suggests echoes of Jonah's typological role as Christ in the
midst of speeches in which Jonah displays his most un-Christlike aspects.
Jonah's thoughts when ordered to Nineveh show either rising hysteria or
realistic visualization of danger, depending on one's point of view:

If I bowe to his bode and bryng hem þis tale,
And I be nummen in Ninniue, my nyes begynes.

> He telles me þose traytoures arn typped schrewes;
> I com wyth þose tyþynges, þay ta me bylyue,
> Pyneȝ me in a prysoun, put me in stokkes,
> Wryþe me in a warlok, wrast out myn yȝen." (lines 75-80)

If I submit to his command and bring them this story, and I am captured in Nineveh, my troubles begin: He tells me those traitors are utter villains; I come with those tidings—they grab me at once—they torture me in prison—put me in the stocks—fetter me in a foot shackle—gouge out my eyes.

He sets off for Tarsa, naively reflecting that God won't notice and that, after all, a man must look out for himself:

> Oure syre syttes, he says, on sege so hyȝe,
> In his glowande glorye, and gloumbes ful lyttel
> þaȝ I be nummen in Ninniue and naked dispoyled,
> On rode rwly to-rent with rybaudes mony. (lines 93-96)

Our Sire sits, he says, on so high a seat, in his resplendent glory, that he would scarcely even frown if I were captured in Nineveh and dispoiled naked, miserably torn on a cross by many ruffians.

When Jonah thus visualizes himself crucified, the typological Jonah is momentarily superimposed on the comic one, and Jonah's picture of a thoughtless tyrant is juxtaposed with the biblical God who deals with evil by suffering its worst himself. This kind of treatment effects a major shift in the poem's structure, whereby patience ceases to mean human self-control and is redefined as the attitude of God toward His creation.

This transformation becomes explicit once the reluctant Jonah has delivered the message and every Ninevite, from the king (who dashes from his throne, tearing his robe, to repent naked on the nearest ash heap) to nursing babies and the very horses and oxen, has joined in national prayer and mourning. Jonah's objection to preaching the destruction of Nineveh is as nothing to his objection to having that destruction not take place; he even claims that it was a fear of looking silly in the latter eventuality that made him refuse the commission in the first place. God, on the other hand, defends his concern for his creatures apart from any wisdom or virtue they may possess. When Jonah loses the woodbine God grew for him, his usual recriminations are addressed to God in His capacity as creator:

A, þou maker of man, what maystery þe thynkeȝ
Þus þy freke to forfare forbi alle oþer?   (lines 482–83)

Ah, you maker of man, what do you think you are achieving, thus
to ruin your own man more than any other?

It is precisely as creator that God responds:

If I wolde help my honde-werk, haf þou no wonder.
Þou art waxen so wroth for þy wod-bynde,
And trauayled neuer to tent it þe tyme of an howre. . . .
Þenne wyte not me for þe werk, þat I it wolde help,
And rwe on þo redles þat remen for synne;
Fyrst I made hem myself of materes myn one,
And syþen I loked hem ful longe and hem on lode hade.
And if I my trauayl schulde tyne of termes so longe. . . .
Þe sor of such a swete place burde synk to my hert.   (lines 496–507)

Don't be surprised if I want to help my handiwork. You are so
angry for your woodbine, and yet you never worked to tend it so
much as an hour. Then do not accuse me about my work, that I want to
help it and pity those miserable people that cry out for their sin. First
I made them myself, out of elements that are mine alone, and after I
took care of them a long time and had them under my guidance, and
if I should lose my trouble over so long a time, sorrow for such a
sweet place ought to go to my heart.

(Note that the biblical God's argument was based simply on the relative
impermanence of woodbines, not on who created them.) The poet goes
on to link God's sufferance and creativity with Christ's suffering, a point
for which the groundwork was laid, as we noted, in ironical echoes of
Jonah's typological role as Christ. God continues his rebuke of Jonah:

Wer I as hastif as þou, heere, were harme lumpen;
Couþe I not þole but as þou, þer þryued ful fewe. (lines 520–21)

If I were as hasty as you, sir, disaster would befall; if I didn't know
any way to suffer except your way, few would thrive.

Patience is a distinctive way of suffering which God knows and Jonah
does not, a way by which God completes his act of creation *ex nihilo*.
Such a redefinition of patience as God's sufferance makes the narrator's
desperate efforts at self-control look almost as antithetical to it as Jonah's
overt rebelliousness. God needs to be as patient with him as with Jonah

or the Ninevites. God's final rebuke (line 524)—"Be nouȝt so gryndel, god-man, bot go forth þy wayes" ("Don't be so angry, man, but go on your way")—addresses the tenacious narrator as much as the mercurial Jonah.[15] God's speech brings the narrator back from his vicarious experience of a world of impatience to conclude the poem with a line that differs from the first line in only one word. But that word is an essential one which gives the line entirely new meaning: "pacience is a nobel poynt, þaȝ it displese ofte."

This positive definition of patience as *imitatio dei* or *imitatio christi* is based on seeing a continuity between God's creative and salvific roles. This would seem to contrast with Saint Thomas' narrower view. But Saint Thomas' discussion shows a similarly expanding movement. He grounds an initial, restricted view of patience, similar to that of the *Patience* narrator, in a larger view of God's action. In the article immediately following the one in which he compares patience unfavorably with fortitude and temperance, he raises the question of whether it is possible to have patience without grace. In replying that it is not—and that even famous pagans who exercised patience must have been sustained by God's grace—he places patience in a very different light from the stoical one:

> Quod autem aliquis praeferat bonum gratiae omnibus naturalibus bonis ex quorum amissione potest dolor causari, pertinet ad caritatem, quae diligit Deum super omnia. Unde manifestum est quod patientia, secundum quod est virtus, a caritate causatur: secundum illud I *ad Cor.* 13, 4: Caritas patiens est. (II-II, 136, 3)

> Now the fact that a man prefers the good of grace to all natural goods, the loss of which may cause sorrow, depends on charity, which loves God above all things. Hence it is evident that patience, as a virtue, is caused by charity, according to I Cor. 13, 4: Charity is patient.

Thomas concludes his discussion of fortitude, of which patience is a subdivision, by arguing that fortitude corresponds to the fourth Beatitude, "Blessed are they that hunger and thirst after justice," since patience and perseverance are the fruits of fortitude (II-II, 139, 2 ad 2). This completes a movement away from his initial terms. It also may suggest a reason for the *Patience* poet's associating his subject so centrally with the Beatitudes.[16]

Saint Thomas reveals a central element in the structure of patience in still another way. In *Patience*, all suffering, danger, and poverty are referred to the responsibility of God, whether or not they have human agents. Jonah actually attributes them to God's callousness or lack of interest.[17] There is an organic connection between this aspect of the poem and the fact that its resolution is based on a revelation of God as creator. Both elements suggest the Book of Job, medieval commentary on which is a revealing context for an understanding of patience. Unlike Jonah, whose defiant "I do well to be angry" (Jonah 4:10) is definitively rebutted, Job demands an accounting from God and is praised by God for refusing to accept his friends' rationalizations. On the other hand, he receives no accounting, but rather a revelation of the divine power couched entirely in terms of God's role as creator: "Where were you when I laid the foundations of the earth?" (Job 38:4). This had presented insuperable difficulties to biblical commentators before Saint Thomas. Previous exegetes had confined themselves to extracting moral and allegorical meanings and refused to deal with the literal meaning, arguing that the Book of Job must not have had a literal meaning, since the literal meaning it appeared to have was blasphemous and portrayed an ostensibly good man cursing the day he was born and accusing God of having become a tormentor: "pereat dies in qua natus sum" (3:1) and "mutatus es mihi in crudelem" (30:21).

It was only in the later Middle Ages that these issues were addressed. Saint Thomas was the first to attempt a complete commentary *ad literam*, which was considered then and is still considered one of his greatest contributions to biblical exegesis.[18] Saint Thomas was willing to take Job as a poem on a historical subject, and to accept that it had been written as a poem precisely to make the reader feel with maximum intensity what a man in Job's position would say in giving vent to his feelings,[19] feelings aroused not merely by his suffering but by an entirely justified conviction that this suffering is not deserved on any ethical grounds.[20] Saint Thomas could take this view because he was prepared to face the question of whether God is in fact cruel, and to regard it not as a blasphemous question but as one which is central to Christian theology if we are to understand how a good God can rule a world which so obviously appears filled with injustice. Patience and acceptance of the will of God must rest on a view of God's relationship to human suffering, which poses special problems for the Judaeo-Christian tradition. Manichean religions permit a "good" God of spirit to blame evil and suffering on a second "bad" God of matter. Religions which set nothingness as the goal of the enlightened can see suffering as a problem inherent in finite existence. But in trying to account for the presence of evil in a world made *ex nihilo* by one God, the

Judaeo-Christian tradition must ultimately lay the responsibility at God's door: "Can there be evil in the city and the Lord not have done it?" (Amos 3:6). Hence God's role as creator must be completed by his choice to save the world, and to do so not by legislation or conquest but by participation in the suffering, through the Incarnation and the Atonement. Therefore, for man as well, true sufferance of the workings of the finite universe must involve not mere self-control but participation in God's creative sufferance of evil.

When we turn to the portrayal of patience in the B-text of *Piers Plowman*, precisely the issues raised by the structure of *Patience* are again central.[21] Here, however, the matter is more complex. So much in *Piers Plowman* remains problematical, and, furthermore, patience is not the whole subject here but one of a series of interwoven factors. The two passūs in which the main treatment of this subject appears are transitional, linking the part of the B-text which incorporates the action of the A-text and presents a resolution of its problems, with the vast historical and apocalyptic vision of the later B-text. Patience appears at a crucial, transitional point in the poem's development, a point where the poem casts a retrospective eye over its own progress in order to reorient its action toward the sweeping portrayal of God's work in history which is to follow. The fact that Patience is here a character among other characters creates a quite different situation from *Patience*. He is important for what he says and does, and even more for the way he is associated with characters and themes crucial to the previous development of the poem. These characters are the Dreamer, Clergy, Scripture, Conscience, and a Friar. The Dreamer, for the last five passūs, has been searching for answers to the questions raised by the A-text, questions answered only when he has learned to view them with patience, not rebelliousness, a point to which we will return. Conscience was a central character in the early part of the poem, one of the key actors in the attempt to set up a just society, the opponent of Lady Meed and the ally of Reason. Clergy (or Learning) has been controversial throughout the poem; his ambivalent qualities have been highly repugnant to the Dreamer and were largely responsible for the rebellion which interrupted his search for the truth and provoked him to his first praise of patient poverty. Scripture, Clergy's wife, preached the sermon on predestination which was broken off by the Dreamer's abandonment of his search and presided over his reacceptance of membership in the body of Christ. The corrupt Friar sums up the abuses of the order and of learning which have been a major theme in the poem. But Patience is also associated with another character. He enters the poem at the point when we receive the first news of its vanished hero, Piers the Plowman. Piers had been the dominant figure of its earlier action until Truth sent him a pardon whose contents looked like a mere reiteration of the Law; this pardon he tore up, and quoting "Though I walk through the valley of the shadow of death, I shall fear no evil, for thou art with me," and "My tears shall be my bread day and night" (Psalms 22:4 and 41:4, Vulgate), he enigmatically vanished for the intervening five passūs in which the Dreamer has been the central character.[22]

The five characters meet at a banquet given by Clergy and Scripture, which is one of the finest scenes of the B-text, and one which, like *Patience*, is suffused with the spirit of high comedy. That both poems approach patience through such a tone may be the clearest indication that they both look to patience for the reestablishment of a "comic" vision of the human predicament. Patience is first presented as having the characteristics of the traditional conception. Unlike the Dame Patience of *Patience*, Langland's Patience is male, a pilgrim and a beggar, who is set to eat at the side table along with the equally disreputable Dreamer. The group at the high table are served appropriately: the Friar gorges himself on "Wombe-cloutes and wylde braune and egges yfryed with grece" ("Tripe and wild boar and eggs fried in fat" [B XIII, line 63]); and Scripture sets before Clergy and Conscience "sondry metes manye,/Of Austyn, of Ambrose • of alle the foure euangelistes" ("many various meats, of Augustine, of Ambrose, of all four gospels" [lines 38–39]). At the low table, Patience and the Dreamer are marked as penitents by being served sour loaves of *agite-penitenciam* washed down with *diu perseverens* ("do penance"—"long lasting") to which Patience adds from his own supplies such further delicacies as *Miserere-mei-deus* ("God have mercy on me"). Even so, Patience thoroughly enjoys himself—"he made hym mirthe with his mete" (line 60)—whereas the Dreamer remains morose; and when the Dreamer becomes so enraged at the Friar's behavior that he threatens to make a scene, he calms him down by giving a humorous prediction of what the Friar will do next and persuades him to wait until the Friar's behavior provides its own punishment, alimentarily if not otherwise.

So far Patience differs from the *Patience* narrator largely by his sense of humor and capacity for enjoyment, which contrasts with patience conceived as an uneasy mixture of submission, wrath, and depression. But when Patience begins to act, much more is added. The guests, like everyone else in the *Vita de Dowel*, offer definitions of that elusive personage.[23] But then Clergy tells us with obvious bafflement that a certain Piers the Plowman has given definitions of DoWell and DoBetter which

Clergy cannot fully understand but which pull the rug out from under the whole discussion since Piers bases them on rejection of intellectual learning:[24]

> [he has] sette alle sciences at a soppe saue loue one,
> And no tixte ne taketh to meyntene his cause
> But *dilige deum* and *domine quis habitabit*, &c. (lines 124-26)

> He values all kinds of knowledge at nearly nothing except love only, and does not base this argument on any text except "Thou shalt love the Lord thy God"—Matt. 22:37-38—and "Lord, who will dwell in thy temple"—Psalm 14:1.

Faced with this impasse, Conscience calls on the one person who can speak from experience since, as a pilgrim, he has been everywhere, and who, since *pacientes vincunt* ("the patient triumph"), is the only sure winner in this situation. Like Piers' *dilige deum*, Patience's definition focuses on love and he learned it from "A lemman [lover] that I loued • Loue was hir name" (line 139). He then expounds the "science" of love which culminates in loving one's enemies:

> Bothe with werkes and with wordes • fonde his loue to wynne;
> And lay on hym thus with loue • til he laughs on thee.
> (lines 145-46)

> With words and deeds strive to win his love; apply such a salve to him with love?—attack him with love?—until he smiles on you.

In fact, he tells them, he actually has DoWell with him, wrapped in his bundle, as a talisman against all suffering and enmity, since *caritas nihil timet* ("love fears nothing"—cf. I John 4:18) and *pacientes vincunt*. Instead of showing DoWell to them, however, he describes it in a riddle:

> I bere [there in a bouste] faste ybounde Dowel
> In a signe of the Saturday that sette firste the kalendare,
> And al the witte of the Wednesday of the nexte wyke after;
> The myddel of the mone is the miȝte of bothe. (lines 152-55)

> I carry DoWell tied up safe in a box, in a sign of the Saturday that first set the calendar and all the wisdom of the Wednesday of the week after; the middle of the moon is the power of both.

This riddle has been the despair of *Piers Plowman* scholars. But though solutions to it do not entirely agree, it is clear that DoWell's power, and Patience's general position, are based on central biblical accounts of charity, especially that of Saint Paul in I Cor. 13; and that the Sunday and the Wednesday refer to the creation and the crucifixion, the two modes of God's action in which, for the *Patience* poet, God's embodiment of a redefined patience inheres.[25] But we are not dependent for an understanding of this scene on an ability to solve the riddle. What has been overlooked is the fact that in the very next passus Patience opens his bundle and we see the contents:[26]

> But I listnede and lokede with liflode it was
> That Pacience so preisede and of his poke hente
> A pece of þe *paternoster* and profrede vs alle
> And banne was it *fiat voluntas tua* sholde fynde vs alle.
> (B XIV, lines 47–48)

> But I listened and looked to see what sustenance it was that Patience praised so highly and took out of his bundle: a piece of the Lord's Prayer, and [he] offered it to us all; and it was *thy will be done* that would supply everything.

"Thy will be done" is the phrase that links man's daily acceptance of God's will with Christ's acceptance of the Passion in the Garden of Gesthemane. Clearly, for Langland, as for the *Patience* poet, any positive definition of patience must see it as *imitatio christi*.

This perspective becomes even clearer in the rest of passus XIV. Conscience has abandoned Clergy and Scripture in order to accompany Patience and the Dreamer on their pilgrimage, and the three meet Hawkin the Active Man. Without entering into the larger questions about Hawkin and his role,[27] we can note that it is Conscience who questions Hawkin and brings out his confession of his sinful state, whereas it is Patience who offers to supply Hawkin with whatever he needs to do well, hence his opening his bundle. Having offered Hawkin the mysterious talisman, Patience explains the sovereign effects of poverty patiently accepted and links the whole subject with Charity:

> There parfit treuthe and pouere herte is and pacience of tonge,
> There is Charitee, the chief chaumbrere [chamberlain] for god
> hymselue. (B XIV, lines 99–100)

This development through the two passūs in which Patience appears is better appreciated if we remember that the scenes in which Patience appears *as a character* are only part of Langland's treatment of patience, which is a major theme in the passūs on either side. Patience has been a key issue in earlier portrayals of the Dreamer. His impatience broke off the search for DoWell, and his reacceptance of the very issues he could not understand or tolerate before, when Scripture's sermon is renewed, marks the crisis in his development. After this scene, he sees a vision of nature in which all creatures except man are governed by Reason. Instead of trying to learn from Reason, he criticizes him for not controlling man as well. Reason rebukes him sharply, making his own permissiveness part of the larger mystery of God's sufferance: "'Who suffreth more than god?' quod he, • 'No gome, as i leue!/He miȝte amende in a minute-while • al that mys standeth'" ("'Who puts up with more than God does?' he said, 'No man, I think. He could put right in a minute everything that has gone amiss'"). This sufferance Reason links not with the Passion but with the creation (line 388 ff.). In the next scene, Imagination repeats this lesson as a prelude to resolving the Dreamer's earlier intellectual difficulties, and it is immediately after meeting Imagination that the Dreamer goes to Clergy's banquet.

Similarly, in the passus after our last glimpse of Patience comforting the weeping Hawkin, we see the completion of the development implied in the character Patience. The Dreamer meets Anima, whose account of his nine names or functions places the soul's ostensibly active and ostensibly passive aspects on the same footing. The grounding of patience in Charity is worked out in detail in Anima's speech on Charity as a "fre, liberal wille" (B XV, lines 145–46) which lives on "loue in goddes passioun" (line 250). Here at last the connection between patience, charity, and the Passion is made as fully explicit as the earlier connection with the creation:

Amonges Cristene men • this myldnesse shulde laste;
In alle manere angres • haue this at herte—
That though thei suffred al this • god suffred for vs more,
In ensample we shulde do so • and take no veniaunce
Of owre foes that doth vs falsenesse • that is owre fadres wille.
For wel may euery man wite • if god hadde wolde hymselue,
Sholde neuere Iudas ne Iuwe • haue Iesu don on rode. . . .
                                                            (lines 253–59)

Among Christian men this mildness should last, in all kinds of anger they should have this in their hearts: that though they suffered all this,

God suffered more for us, as an example that we should do the same and take no vengeance on our enemies who do us wrong; that is our father's will. For every man can know that, if God had not willed it, neither Judas nor Jew would have put Jesus on the cross.

Finally, in one of the poem's most controversial passages, we see why Piers Plowman had to be included in the Banquet Scene. Charity itself is linked with the *imitatio christi*. When the Dreamer wants to know Charity, Anima tells him he cannot do so without the help of Piers Plowman because one cannot know charity by words or deeds but only through the will: "And that knoweth no clerke ne creature in erthe/But Piers the Plowman • *Petrus id est Cristus*" ("Peter, that is, Christ")— lines 205–6.[28]

Having seen the view of patience that emerges from these two probing Middle English treatments of the subject, we can turn to a terse and conventional formulation like that of Chaucer's Parson and see that, in a sense, it contains everything written large in *Patience* and *Piers Plowman*:

Patience, that is another remedie agayns Ire, is a vertu that suffreth swetely every mannes goodnesse, and is nat wroth for noon harm that is doon to hym. . . . This vertu maketh a man lyk to God, and maketh hym Goddes owene deere child, as seith Crist. This vertu disconfiteth thyn enemy. And therfore seith the wise man, If thow wolt venquysse thyn enemy, lerne to suffre. . . . And understond wel that obedience is parfit, whan that a man dooth gladly and hastily, with good herte entirely, al that he sholde do.

Parson's Tale, lines 658–61, 674

But to see this while reading the *Parson's Tale* would be another matter. The essential boldness and imaginativeness of the two poems lies in their having created dramatized contexts within which our capacity to understand and react to traditional meaning, which we are inoculated against by its familiarity and abstractness, is re-created. The different elements so tersely joined by the Parson are separated so that they can be encountered sequentially and their full problems and implications perceived, subsumed into a new kind of knowledge that is both intellectual and experiential.

NOTES

Much of the research for this essay was made possible by sabbatical leave from Brown University, a grant from the American Council of Learned Societies, and the hospitality of the Pontifical Institute of Mediaeval Studies, Toronto.

1. *The Canterbury Tales*, F, lines 773–78. All Chaucer quotations follow F. N. Robinson, ed., *The Works of Geoffrey Chaucer*, 2d ed. (Boston: Houghton Mifflin, 1957), and are identified by fragment and line number.

2. See the discussion of dating and influence in the editions of *Patience* by Hartley Bateson, 2d ed. (Manchester: Manchester University Press, 1918), pp. xxiv–xxviii, and J. J. Anderson (New York: Barnes and Noble, 1969), pp. 20–22; and E. Talbot Donaldson, *Piers Plowman: The C-Text and Its Poet* (New Haven: Yale University Press, 1949), p. 171. All quotations from *Patience* follow the Anderson edition.

3. The best discussion of *Patience* is A. C. Spearing, *The Gawain-Poet: A Critical Study* (Cambridge: Cambridge University Press, 1970), chap. 3, which disposes once and for all of the earlier view that Patience is merely a "quaint" biblical paraphrase, or naive.

4. See Charles Moorman, "The Role of the Narrator in *Patience*," *Modern Philology* 61 (1963):90–95.

5. See Anderson, pp. 16–19, and William Vantuono, "The Structure and Sources of *Patience*," *Mediaeval Studies* 34 (1972):401–21.

6. See Matt. 12:40 and Luke 11:30.

7. See Otto Mitius, *Jonas auf den Denkmälern des christlichen Altertums* (Freiberg, 1897).

8. Text and facing translation appear in George F. Whicher, *The Goliard Poets* (New York: New Directions, 1949), pp. 120–25.

9. The appended translations attempt only to provide a trot. Though those for *Patience* are heavily indebted to Anderson's notes and glossary, they are not necessarily in agreement with his interpretation.

10. Anderson prints the Vulgate passages relevant to *Patience*, pp. 70–72.

11. *Summa Theologiae*, de Rubeis, Billuart, P. Fancher, O.P. et aliorum, cum textu ex recensione Leonina (Rome: Maurietti, 1948), II-II, 136, 1. All quotations from the *Summa* follow this edition; appended translations generally follow the translation by the Fathers of the English Dominican Province (London: Burns, Oates & Washbourne, 1922), vol. 12.

12. *Bibliorum Sacrorum cum Glossa Ordinaria . . . et Postilla Nicolai Lyrani, Additionibus Pauli Burgensis, ac Matthias Tmoryngi Replicis* (Paris, 1590). Nicholas of Lyra's commentary (1322–30) could influence *Pacience* and *Piers Plowman* where Paul of Burgos' additions (c. 1435) could not, but as the latter defend Saint Thomas against Nicholas they shed much light on fourteenth-century ideas. See Fr. C. Spicq, *Esquisse d'une histoire de l'exégèse Latine au moyen âge* (Paris, 1944), pp. 335, 339.

13. *Glossa*, vol. 3, p. 406; vol. 6, p. 1268; vol. 3, p. 84. That suffering produces *tristitia, ira*, and *odium* is discussed particularly in vol. 6, p. 1266.

14. Spearing, pp. 28–32, has an excellent discussion of the *Gawain*-poet's comic vision, which is applied to *Patience*, pp. 78–90.

15. It is not clear exactly where the break between the story and the frame should be deemed to come. See Anderson's note on line 524.

16. Elizabeth B. Keiser points out illuminating parallels between Saint Thomas' treatment of magnanimity and magnificence (which are parts of fortitude) and of temperance, and *Cleanness*, the *Patience*-poet's other biblical paraphrase, in "Perfection and Experience: The Celebration of Divine Order and Human Sensibility in *Cleanness* and *Patience*" (Ph.D. diss., Yale, 1972).

17. Though the poem's opening lines refer to "heþyng oþer elles" and to poverty as inde-

pendent evils, it is soon clear that the narrator sees them in terms of the necessity and
inevitability of obeying one's "lege lorde," God.

18. See the introductory material, especially pp. *17-*27, *Sancti Thomae de Aquino
Opera Omnia iussu Leonis XIII P. M. edita*, tomus XXVI, *Expositio Super Iob ad Litteram*
(Rome, 1965). Roland of Cremona's commentary a generation earlier had incorporated
some comments on the literal sense. Albertus Magnus' commentary on Job, which takes it
as a scholastic disputation, is probably later than Thomas'.

19. See *Expositio*, p. 21, lines 135-42, and p. 212, lines 370-79.

20. *Expositio*, pp. 21, 41, 213, and the introductory discussion, p. *26.

21. All B-text quotations follow W. W. Skeat, ed., *The Vision of William Concerning
Piers the Plowman in Three Parallel Texts*, 2 vols. (London: Oxford University Press, 1866),
because its accessibility and the pertinence of the parallel passages are useful for such a
study. Readings in square brackets, however, have been introduced from the new edition of
the B-text by George Kane and E. Talbot Donaldson (London: Athlone Press, 1975) where
differences are significant. This essay focuses on the B-text, even though concern with
patient poverty and with the Dreamer's impatience begins at the end of the A-text, and
these subjects are important in the C-text, both revisions and additions (see Donaldson,
especially pp. 169-80). Patience, rather than Patient Poverty, will be the focus, and the
influence of *Patience* on Langland will not be an explicit concern, though major parallels in
the structures of the poems would appear to confirm earlier belief on this point (see note 2).

22. For the role of these characters, and the function of patience in the poem, some of the
many analyses of the B-text are especially useful: John Lawlor, *Piers Plowman: An Essay in
Criticism* (New York: Barnes and Noble, 1962); P. M. Kean, "Love, Law and *Lewte* in *Piers
Plowman*" (1964), reprinted in Robert J. Blanch, *Style and Symbolism in Piers Plowman*
(Knoxville: University of Tennessee Press, 1969), pp. 132-55; John Burrow, "The Action of
Langland's Second Vision" (1965), reprinted in Blanch, pp. 209-27. My own views are
presented in *The Dream Thought of Piers Plowman* (New Haven: Yale University Press,
1972), of which pp. 40-43, 80-100, 114-26, and 129-46 are especially concerned with the
context for the passūs in which Patience appears, which cannot be presented here. Note
that, in the C-text, Piers actually arrives at the Banquet.

23. Though the vexed question of how DoWell is defined and redefined is clearly pertinent, it has been entirely eliminated from this discussion.

24. For Piers and his "two infinites" of love, see Anne Middleton, "Two Infinites:
Grammatical Metaphor in *Piers Plowman*," ELH 39 (1972):169-88.

25. For the riddle, see Ben H. Smith, Jr., "Patience's Riddle, Piers Plowman B, XIII,"
Modern Language Notes 76 (1961):675-82, and *Traditional Imagery of Charity in Piers
Plowman* (The Hague: Mouton and Co., 1966); and R. E. Kaske, " '*Ex vi transicionis*' and
Its Passage in *Piers Plowman*" (1963), reprinted with revisions in Blanch, pp. 228-63.

26. The connection with the riddle is underlined by the fact that the word *boiste* (in
which, according to Kane and Donaldson, Patience carries DoWell [B XIII, line 152])
means a special jar or box for carrying such precious or perishable commodities as salve,
ointment, cosmetics, the Host, bread, or letters (*M.E.D.*, s.v. *boiste*, sense 1, a and b). Each
of these meanings, all of which could be pertinent in passūs XIII, is more or less explicitly
evoked in describing the "liflode" Patience unwraps in passūs XIV or the functions he
claims it will perform for Hawkin.

27. See Stella Maguire, "The Significance of Haukyn, *Activa Vita*, in *Piers Plowman*"
(1949), reprinted in Blanch, pp. 194-208—still very suggestive, in spite of being dated in
some respects.

28. See Sister Mary Clemente Davlin, O.P., " 'Petrus, id est, Christus': Piers Plowman as
'The Whole Christ,'" *Chaucer Review* 6 (1972):280-92.

"Festina lente"

Motto of Tiberius Claudius Nero Caesar, Roman Emperor (14–37)

Idcirco haec dicit Dominus Deus:
Ecce ego mittam in fundamentis Sion lapidem,
Lapidem probatum,
Angularem, pretiosum, in fundamento fundatum;
Qui crediderit, non festinet.
Isaias 28:16

"Halt Masz"

Motto of Maximilian I, Holy Roman Emperor (1493–1519)

Patientiae Triumphus
The Iconography of a Set of Eight Engravings

PRISCILLA L. TATE

he *Triumph of Patience* series of engravings, far from being a mere illustration of time-honored concepts, is above all a significant and original theological interpretation of the virtue. Due undoubtedly to Maarten van Heemskerck's collaboration with Dirck Volckertszoon Coornhert, a theologian and man of letters who surely was more than the mere engraver of the set, it is infused with a high degree of artistic and intellectual subtlety. Furthermore, patience in this allegory may well have been intended to be understood as the highest aim of the perfect prince. In this respect, the eight engravings can be considered a Mirror of Princes. On the basis of my study,[1] I suggest that Charles V (d. 1558) was the ruler to whom Van Heemskerck and Coornhert directed their allegory.

Coornhert, the engraver of this set, occupied a pivotal position in the literary and intellectual history of the Netherlands in the late sixteenth century.[2] The first to translate many classical and medieval writers into Dutch, Coornhert later became the state secretary of Holland under William of Orange. Though a foe of Calvinism, Coornhert was nevertheless a black sheep in the Catholic fold. Near the end of his life he engaged in a literary battle with Justus Lipsius (1547–1606) over what he believed to be the intolerance of Neo-Stoicism.[3] Though this allegory of Patience is Stoic in flavor, in the sense of endurance (*Constantia*), it does not by any means propound the Stoic ethic of *Indifferantia*. It is therefore tempting to view Coornhert's hand here as harbinger of his later stand against Neo-Stoicism.

Maarten van Heemskerck (1498–1574), the designer of the prints, is considered to have nourished the seedling of Italian mannerism in the North. After becoming a master in the painter's guild of his native Haarlem, he went to Italy (1532–36), a decision which was to become imperative later in the century among artists in the North. According to Carel van Mander, he was greatly taken with the art of his Italian contemporaries and with the antique, which are immortalized in his Roman sketchbooks.[4] Van Heemskerck's collaboration with Coornhert, begun in 1547, terminated in 1559 when Coornhert occupied himself almost exclusively with literary and political activities.[5]

After returning from a two-year stay in Rome (1546–48), Hieronymous Cock, an artist with a penchant for business, established himself as a publisher and print dealer. His firm became one of the more important in the Netherlands during the years 1550–70, and he was to employ such notables as Pieter Brueghel (1550), Giorgio Ghisi (1550), and, of course, Coornhert (1554).[6] Thus, in all probability, the set was designed and published between 1555 and 1559. Stylistically and thematically, *Patientiae Triumphus* is entirely consistent with the didactic engravings and allegories produced jointly by the three men during these years.[7]

As is apparent from the title *Patientiae Triumphus*, van Heemskerck/Coornhert present a virtue triumphant; and she can be seen in the first engraving seated on a chariot, drawn forward by her helpmates *Spes* (Hope) and *Desiderium* (Spiritual Desire). Following her as booty and "bound in disgrace" is the captive *Fortuna*, testifying to the conquest of the helmeted Patience. This formal pattern of vanquished following victor is maintained throughout the set of eight engravings, so that the allegory can properly be termed the *Trionfi* of Patience.

It has never been observed, I believe, that the *Triumph of Patience* is to be viewed as a continuous triumphal procession. This is suggested by the fact that all eight engravings have the same horizon line in common, so that all the figures exist in one spatial continuum. Numbered from 1 to 8 in the lower right-hand corners, the prints of this set should be read from right to left, so that Christ is at the head of the procession. This can be demonstrated by placing the *Triumph of Isaac* to the left of the *Triumph of Patience*. When the two prints are thus side by side, it becomes clear that the footboard of the cart in engraving no. 2 extends backward into no. 1. Moreover—like the pieces of a jigsaw puzzle—the leaves and branches of a tree, partially visible in the *Triumph of Patience*, perfectly complete those of the tree in the *Triumph of Isaac*. The result is, clearly, that we have a continuous stage setting common to all eight prints.[8]

The stage upon which this triumphal procession takes place may in fact be an altar. This is suggested by what at first seems to be an insignificant idiosyncrasy in the printing of engraving no. 2: In the *Triumph of Isaac* there appears a puzzling cup-like indentation in the horizon line separating foreground and background, just beneath the tassel of the camel's bridle. On close examination of the print, a second notch, identical in shape with the crevice in the pavement, can be seen in the altar (represented in the background) at which Isaac kneels in obliging readiness for the sacrifice. Such indentations in altars—gutters, so to speak—served the necessary function of draining off blood, so that the sacrificial animal might be properly presented for the holocaust. When we recall that all eight prints are in a spatial continuum, with the horizon line of each one corresponding to that of all the others, the conclusion seems to be that Isaac, and possibly all of the figures, were meant to be enacting their respective triumphs on top of an altar. Each in his own way had offered himself as a sacrifice.

A passage in Ezekiel may have inspired such a visual metaphor. The prophet describes eight sacrificial rites, which are to be performed for the inauguration of the New Covenant. Before citing this passage we should recall that Christ, the patient hero in engraving no. 8 of our set, is iconographically presented in the form of a *Majestas Domini*, the elevated and triumphant Christ of the Kingdom of Peace, the Christ of the Second Coming. One of the biblical sources for such representations is chapter 43 in Ezekiel:

4. And the majesty of the Lord went into the temple by the way of the gate that looked to the east.

5. And the spirit lifted me up and brought me into the inner court: and behold the house was filled with the glory of the Lord.

18. And he said to me: Son of man, thus saith the Lord God: these are the ceremonies of the altar, in what day soever it shall be made: that holocausts may be offered upon it and blood poured out.

25. Seven days shalt thou offer a he-goat for sin daily: they shall offer also a calf of the herd and a ram of the flock without blemish.
26. Seven days shall they expiate the altar and shall cleanse it: and they shall consecrate it.
27. And the days being expired, on the eighth day and thenceforward, the priests shall offer your holocausts upon the altar and the peace offerings: and I will be pacified towards you, saith the Lord God.

If this passage indeed contributed to the inspiration of the van Heemskerck/Coornhert *Triumph of Patience*, then each triumphal figure can be regarded as a station along the road leading even closer not only to the sacrifices of Christ on the cross, but also to the fulfillment of the promise that Christ died for the salvation of mankind.

Such an interpretation is consistent with the biblical meaning of patience—suggested, for example, in the following passage from Hebrews: "And therefore we also having so great a cloud of witnesses over our head, laying aside every weight and sin which surrounds us, let us run by patience to the fight proposed to us. Looking on Jesus, the author and the finisher of the faith, who having set joy before him, endured the cross, despising the shame, and now sitteth on the right hand of the throne of God" (12:1–2). The language of Hebrews suggests the visual imagery in our engraving, where Patience and other figures in the set are armed for the fight, clad in the raiment of their virtue, as Christian soldiers obedient and persevering.[9] Moreover, each of the Old and New Testament figures in our set, like Patience, is considered a type for Christ, perhaps constituting "the great cloud of witnesses" mentioned in verse 1.

In regard to the last engraving, *Triumph of Christ*, it should be once again stated that patience is above all the quality demanded of men who fervently await the Last Judgment. Saint James (5:7–11) exhorts:

Be patient therefore brethren, until the coming of the Lord. Behold, the husbandman waiteth for the precious fruit of the earth: patiently bearing till he receive the early and latter rain. Be you therefore also patient and strengthen your hearts: for the coming of the Lord is at hand.

Behold, we account them blessed, who have endured. You have heard of the patience of Job, and you have seen the end of the Lord, that the Lord is merciful and compassionate.

With this passage in mind, it may not be entirely coincidental that Job occupies the center position in our triumphal procession, while the resurrected Christ, who gestures in blessing, leads the procession.

That these *tableaux-vivants* are enacted on top of an altar can be interpreted on yet another level, adding to the rich symbolic harmony of the *Triumph of Patience*. On the one hand, in terms of the passage in Ezek. 43, each of the central figures in the set is to be understood as a sacrificial offering; consequently, each of the eight is displayed on top of the altar, as is prescribed by ritual. We should note, however, that altars are traditionally erected above relics of saints. In these engravings, the order is reversed. The martyred victims are resurrected, so to speak, as is Christ in the last engraving. The *arma Christi*, the instruments of Christ's passion which are represented in his banner, specifically suggest this interpretation; for they were, since the time of Pope Innocent VI (1353), commonly held to be the relics of Christ. The meaning of this inversion is clearly that expressed by the last Latin verse accompanying engraving no. 8, *Triumph of Christ*, which reads: "The uppermost heavens we now behold and every name is elevated and triumphant." I suggest that "every name" refers to the preceding figures, who obediently allowed themselves to be sacrificed in accordance with Divine Will, and who, because of their faith in the Covenant of God, are now vindicated.

This hypothesis gains support from the fact that Christ in the last engraving is represented in the *Majestas Domini*, thus introducing an element of Apocalyptic immediacy. The number of our engravings, eight in total, is appropriately symbolic of the perfection and completion prophesied at the end of time. I mention here only a few of the many subtle and fascinating numerical mysteries: Eight is the number of perfection, the promise of a new life. Christ was resurrected on the eighth day, according to the Jewish calendar, and to such patristic writers as Saint Ambrose and Origin.[10] In Saint Augustine's *Civitas Dei*, and elsewhere, the eighth day of the week is considered the Day of Judgment, the beginning of eternal peace, and the beginning of eternal life.[11] Thus, to present each of the eight figures on top of an altar lends to our allegory of Patience a remarkable degree of theological subtlety which is developed in many of the iconographic details and especially in the recurrent leitmotif of the stone. Particularly I have in mind the square cube upon which *Patientia* is seated, the stones with which David overcame Goliath, the flintstones in the banner of Tobit, the stoning of Saint Stephen, and the large stones under the cross.

In the Old Testament, the stone is a sign of God, or a manifestation of his nearness, and, in particular, the sign of his covenant. The Ten

Commandments, for example, were given to Moses on tablets of stone; and, elsewhere in the Old Testament, the stone is symbolic of God's promise to man.

The stone, as a motif in the allegory, is introduced in the first engraving where *Patientia* is seated upon a weathered cube, calling to mind Isa. 28:16, where Christ is metaphorically the "tried" cornerstone of the Faith: "Therefore thus saith the Lord God: Behold I will lay a stone in the foundations of Sion, a tried stone, a corner stone, a precious stone, founded in the foundations. He that believeth, let him not hasten."[12]

In I Pet. 2:4, this "tried stone" which the builders (i.e., men) had rejected was "chosen and made honorable by God." Christ is then termed the "living stone": "Be you also living stones built up, a spiritual house, a holy priesthood, to offer up spiritual sacrifices, acceptable to God by Jesus Christ." It is noteworthy to find that the subsequent verses focus attention on Patience: "For what glory is it, if, committing sin and being buffeted for it, you endure? But if doing well you suffer patiently: this is thanksworthy before God. For unto this you are called: because Christ also suffered for us, leaving you an example that you should follow his steps" (I Pet. 2:20–21).

In sum, the conventional stone used as the seat of Patience is properly explained in the strictly theological setting of the first print, as a significant and precious attribute of the virtue. In the *Triumph of Patience* (the key engraving, summing up, as it were, like a prelude preceding a set of variations on a theme), *Patientia* and *Fortuna* are placed in eloquent contrast. Patience, whose attribute, the stone, symbolizes solidity, immobility, and impregnable virtue, has vanquished fickle Fortune, who is characterized by her attribute, which here is represented as a broken wheel, indicating irrational mobility. The motif of Patience contrasted to opposing vices is a leitmotif which runs through the iconography of all eight engravings.

The stone appears again in the fifth engraving, *Triumph of David*, as the weapon with which he overcomes Goliath, and in no. 7, *Triumph of St. Stephen*, where he is being stoned. In no. 8, *Triumph of Christ*, uncommonly large stones can be seen under the cross upon which Christ is crucified, most probably to be understood as a reference to the above-mentioned passage in which Christ is described as the "living stone."

In engraving no. 6, *Triumph of Tobit*, there appear in his banner four flintstones, which also compose the chain links of the Order of the Golden Fleece. While flintstones can be understood as a variation of the *Patientia*/stone imagery, their transubstantiation into chain links of the

Order of the Golden Fleece leads one to suspect that a reference to a contemporary member of the Order is intended. This becomes more than a suspicion when we realize that Patience, as she is presented in this allegory, is an imperial virtue. A theme related to the leitmotif of the stone, *Festina lente* ("Make haste slowly"), pervades the *Patientiae Triumphus*. While the adage *Festina lente*, an extremely popular one in the sixteenth century, can be seen as a harmonious addition to an allegory of Patience, it is also, traditionally, the motto of kings. Its ancestry is imperial in origin, appearing first on a medal of the Emperor Tiberius (first century).

In the sixteenth century, a variation of this *adagium*, *Halt Masz*, was adopted by Maximilian I (d. 1519) and appears in Albrecht Dürer's *Triumphal Arch* for this ruler. Maximilian I consciously appropriated the venerable motto, for he—and his successor, Charles V (d. 1558)—considered themselves to be the legitimate successors of the Roman emperors. Thus, the repeated visual and textual reference to this motto in our *Triumph of Patience* leads to the conclusion that the entire concept of Patience as a noble virtue is an important aspect of the qualities prerequisite for the prince. Patience, as the virtue that enables princes nobly to endure, is reflected in many personal mottos of the sixteenth century: Pope Hadrian VI (d. 1523), *Patere et abstine*; Charles Joannes Robertus Heyts, Canon of Bruges, *Patiendo Floresces*; as well as *Patior ut potiar*, *Patientia in spe*, and similar mottos shared by members of several noble families.[13]

If indeed this allegory of Patience, as the mirror of the perfect prince, is directed at a contemporary member of the Order of the Golden Fleece, Charles V seems the most likely candidate. During the years in which the set originated (1555–59), Charles V abdicated his crown as Holy Roman Emperor to retire to a monastery in northern Spain (October 1555). It may be that the chain links of the Order, which appear together in Tobit's banner with a device emblematic of *Ecclesia*, refer to his decision to serve the church.

Moreover, it is known that in 1555–56, van Heemskerck and Coornhert published with Hieronymous Cock another important engraved series, *The Labors of Charles V*. Maarten van Heemskerck had, on more than one occasion, been employed by the Emperor. In 1536, while in Rome, he worked with Francesco Salviati on the solemn entry of Charles V into the city. Again, in 1557, van Heemskerck engraved a parade shield and cabasset for the ruler, depicting his *Victory at Muhlberg*, based on a design in the abovementioned set, *The Labors of Charles V*. Hieronymous Cock also had been of service to the Emperor. In

1549, he took part in the decorations for the triumphal entry of Charles V into Antwerp.

While I have not found documentary evidence that *Patientiae Triumphus* was created with Charles V in mind, only in no. 6—where the chain links of the Order of the Golden Fleece appear—is the designer's autograph so completely and prominently engraved.

The *Patientiae Triumphus*, as the mirror of princes and as a continuation in the tradition of *trionfi*, is tradition-bound in the extreme. Though more research should be done on the theological ideas that determined the thinking of Coornhert, he clearly emerges as the more important of the two men involved in the work. Because of Coornhert's intellectual contribution, our set must be viewed as a highly original theological formulation. The *Triumph of Patience*, which is expressed in specific and time-bound imagery based on sixteenth-century intellectual and theological concepts, endures as a testament to God who controls man's fortune. Didactic and moralistic, the van Heemskerck/Coornhert engravings illustrate a Christian lesson (in eight elegant images), placing Patience in a key position with respect to Grace, which God, through Christ, gave mankind.

The sixteenth century was a century of unsettling theological and social conflicts which spared neither nobleman nor commoner. Solutions had to be found to the all-important problem: how to preserve one's faith in view of such great tribulations. The *Patientiae Triumphus* was, in this sense, a beneficial visual and intellectual guideline. Its tenets were summarized in an ideal manner in the words that the artist and iconographic planner of the triumph found in Rom. 5: ". . . we glory in tribulation, knowing that tribulation worketh patience, and patience trial, and trial hope, and hope confoundeth not. . . ."

DESCRIPTION AND COMMENTARY

What follows is an iconographic description and analysis of the eight signed and numbered engravings, accompanied by Latin poems, entitled *Patientiae Triumphus*, by designer Maarten van Heemskerck (1498–1574) and engraver Dirck Volckertszoon Coornhert (1522–90), published at Antwerp by Hieronymous Cock, c. 1555. This commentary is an abridged version of a 1974 study of original engravings in the Duke University Art Museum, the first of which is alone analyzed here in detail and is reproduced in Figure 5.

PHYSICAL AND ICONOGRAPHIC DESCRIPTION

Size: 20.6 × 25.7 cm.
Technique: Engraving (Duke Art Museum accession No. 1972.40.1-8,
Elizabeth van Canon Funds).
Condition and Appearance: Watermarks; in good condition with broad
margins (but see remarks for no. 7).
The eight items are represented on eight separate sheets in the follow-
ing (numbered) sequence, which reads from right (no. 1) to left (no. 8):

1. *Triumph of Patience*
2. *Triumph of Isaac*
3. *Triumph of Joseph*
4. *Triumph of David*
5. *Triumph of Job*
6. *Triumph of Tobit*
7. *Triumph of Stephen*
8. *Triumph of Christ*

1. *Triumph of Patience*

Condition and appearance: Inscribed "PATIENTIAE TRIVMPHVS" in
the lower center portion of the print.[14] In the lower left corner is the
monogram of the designer, Maarten van Heemskerck, " *M* [aarten
Heemskerck] Inue [nit]," followed by "H. Cock excud[it]," identifying
Hieronymous Cock as publisher and bookseller.[15] In the lower right
corner is "·1· *DC* ƒ [ecit]," signifying that this print is the first
in the series and that Dirck Volckertszoon Coornhert engraved [i.e.,
" ƒ "] them.[16]
In the center of the print is a three-wheeled cart bearing a draped and
helmeted female figure who is seated on a cube. The stone is inscribed
" *M* [aarten Heemskerck] Inu[enit]/ *DC* oornhert/fecit."[17] While
the body of the female is slightly turned toward the viewer, she looks
directly ahead, showing her face in right profile. To the right of her helmet is the inscription "PAT • ENTIAE" [*sic*]. Her right hand steadies
a staff, topped by a cross, to which a fluttering banner, the so-called
pennon, is attached. On the pennon is a rose between two thorny plants
identified by Kerrich[18] and suggested by the Latin epigram accompanying
this print. Visible behind her right shoulder is a large scalloped shield
which extends to her knees. In her left hand she carries a five-faceted

FIGURE 5. *Patientiae Triumphus*, engraving by Maarten van Heemskerck and Dirck Volckertszoon Coornhert (c. 1555). Courtesy of the Duke University Art Museum, Durham, N.C.

anvil upon which rests a burning heart underneath a three-headed hammer. A lamb kneels at *Patientia*'s feet just to the left of the cube and looks up at her.

Another draped female figure, identified by an inscription above her head as "FORTVNA," follows *Patientia*, attached to the cart by a cord which loops around her waist. Fortune is blindfolded, her head turned away from *Patientia* and cast down over her left shoulder. She shares significant characteristics with *Occasio*: the two long forelocks of her hair stream out on either side of her shoulders, and the top of her head is bald. In her right hand there is a large razor-like blade; in her left hand she grasps a broken wheel (emblem of *Fortuna*), which rests on the rear of the cart.[19]

Two additional figures, harnessed in front of the chariot, propel *Patientia* and *Fortuna* forward. The lead position is occupied by a female figure, also draped, who shoulders an anchor, holding it upside down. She holds the top part in both hands and balances the stem on her left shoulder so that the bottom of the anchor curves over her head. "SPES" is inscribed beneath the visible fluke of the anchor just above her head. Her head carried high, she strides forward with her left foot, thrusting her right shoulder into the harness.

Her companion is a curly-haired male, dressed in a short tunic, in a bold *contrapposto*-pose, who moves at her side, closer to the beholder and slightly behind. "DESIDERIVM" is inscribed just above his head. With his right foot forward and the harness passed around the middle part of his body, he looks dramatically back over his left shoulder. His left arm swings back toward *Patientia* in an uplifted gesture, and his hand with open palm is illuminated by three concentric rings of radiation. *Desiderium* has four wings, one on each shoulder and ankle. In his right hand he carries a bow, and a bundle of arrows is partially visible between the wings on his back.

Visible in the background between *Desiderium* and *Patientia* is a stormy seascape where a ship with a broken mast sinks into the waves. A smaller storm-tossed boat with four occupants seems to have escaped the disaster.

In the lower foreground of the engraving, just to the left of the feet of *Spes*, the corner of a plank of wood or a slab of stone is visible, cut off by the frame of the engraving. When this print is placed alongside and to the right of the second in the series, *Triumph of Isaac*, it becomes clear that this plank is part of the cart in the second engraving. The tree continuing from the first into the second print is clearly shared by the two. The fact that the first and second engravings are compositionally in a spatial continuum suggests that the entire set—beginning with no. 1, *Triumph of Patience*, and ending with no. 8, *Triumph of Christ*, on the far left—is to be read from right to left. Apart from the cart in no. 2 jutting out into no. 1, and the tree shared by 1 and 2, it is also obvious that all eight engravings share the same horizon line. Clearly, we may speak of a continuous stage setting common to all of the prints.

Beneath the picture and separated from it by an engraved frame is the following Latin text:

> Ac velut angustas rosa candida pullulat inter
> Spinas, nec premitur: florent & lilia Vere:
> Sic iam magnifico vehitur PATIENTIA curru.
> Cui FORTVNA potens, fractis concessit honorem
> Viribus, & inclis sequitur constricta, pudore:
> Hunc SPES alma trahit, volucri STVDIO comitata.

And just as amidst tight thorns the white rose blossoms without being crushed: and the lilies flourish in Spring, thus is Patience now conveyed on her magnificent chariot, to whom mighty Fortune, her powers having been broken, concedes honor and, contained by fetters, follows her in disgrace: This chariot all-nourishing Hope pulls forth, accompanied by winged Desire.

Patience is personified as a woman clad in armor in keeping with one of the oldest traditions of triumphant virtues, the *Psychomachia* of Prudentius. There *Patientia* personified appears as a helmeted female figure who vanquishes the vice, *Ira*. *Ira* commits suicide out of furious chagrin that her arrows slide harmlessly off *Patientia's* armor and helmet (v. 109 ff.). In van Heemskerck/Coornhert's conception, *Patientia* is indebted to yet another and even older triumphal tradition. With *Fortuna* securely bound behind, *Patientia* is borne forward on a cart, in a ceremonial fashion characteristic of triumphal entries of rulers since antiquity.

Her attributes, however, give her triumph a decidedly Christian character. *Patientia* carries a banner with a device referring to one aspect of her virtue, that she bears up under suffering. This interpretation is suggested by Ripa: ". . . the white rose amidst tight thorns blooms without being crushed, as the lilies flourish in spring."[20] This metaphorical combination of the rose amid thorns with the lily echoes Marianic symbolism (Canticle of Canticles 2:1–5), suggesting that *Patientia*, the *rosa sine spinis*, might be equated with the Madonna. This is a logical connection when we recall that in many paintings of Mary under the cross, she is to be understood as the embodiment of suffering. This symbolism, medieval in origin, is presented with particular force in the *Revelations* of Saint Birgitta of Sweden, who records that the Virgin appeared to her in a vision and said: "The sufferings of Jesus were my sufferings, his heart was my heart."[21] It is interesting that both Brueghel and Michelangelo (in the *Last Judgment* in the Sistine Chapel, unveiled in 1541), van Heemskerck's contemporaries in the broadest sense of the word, portray the Madonna sitting on a stone, with folded hands and downcast eyes. This is one of the characteristic elements in representations of *Patienza*, later codified by Cesare Ripa in his *Iconologia*, which further substantiates the link between the Madonna and the virtue *Patientia* (pp. 379–81). Ripa also tells us that Patience places her naked feet on thorns to indicate that she endures the wounds to her honor, possessions, and life.

In her other hand, *Patientia* holds an anvil upon which a heart appears in flames with a hammer poised dangerously above it. A burning heart usually signifies love and is an attribute of both Venus, as goddess of love, and of *Caritas*, the theological virtue of Christian love. Carel van Mander's *Het Schilderboeck*, the first comprehensive art history produced north of the Alps, contains a chapter emphasizing that a burning heart signifies love.[22] Virgil Solis (1514–62), in an engraved set of the Seven Planets, shows Venus with a burning heart.[23] These visual and textual examples are fairly representative of the iconographic tradition, which found expression also in sixteenth- and seventeenth-century emblem books. For example, in Gabriel Rollenhagen's *Nucleus Emblemata* (ed. prin., 1611 [Arnhem], no. 39) we find a giant burning heart set on a hill overlooking a forested valley. It is flanked on the left by an anchor and on the right by an arrow drawn-in-bow, aimed at the center of the heart. The accompanying epigram explains: "Speque metvque pavet calido cor amore perustum/Spes est solicito plena timore venus" ("In hope and fear trembles the heart burning with hot love/Love is hope full of dreadful awe").

The anvil, traditionally the attribute of *Fortitudo*, and the hammer, when combined in sixteenth-century engravings and emblem books, conventionally suggest the idea of steadfastness or endurance. An engraving by Hendrik Goltzius represents *Fortitudo* and *Patientia* (identified by inscriptions). The virtues, personified as two nude females, are shown reclining in intimate proximity against a wooded landscape. *Fortitudo* clutches her attribute, the column, and places her right foot on an anvil upon which lies a two-headed hammer. She looks tenderly down into the eyes of *Patientia*, who holds a press containing, it seems, a human heart. The engraving is accompanied by an inscription: "Grandia robusto faciunt in corpore vires,/Si Patiens aderit mens grauiora ferent ur" ("Strength is made eminent in a robust body,/If a Patient mind is added, Strength increases manifold").[24] Anvil and hammer appear in Juan de Boria's *Empresas Morales* with the motto *In utruque paratus* ("Ready for both functions").[25] We can now see that *Patientia*'s love (the burning heart) in van Heemskerck endures suffering and hardship, the blows of the hammer, yet remains steadfast like the anvil.

In Guillaume de la Perrière's *Le Théâtre des bons engins*, a hammer and anvil are accompanied by the following epigram:

L'Homme constant est semblable a l'enclume,
Qui des marteaulx ne crainct la uiolence.
Cueur uertueulx est de telle coustume,
Que de malheur ne doubte l'insolence:
Ne craint fureur, yre, maleuolence,
Contre tous maulx est prompt à resister,
Pour quelque effort ne se ueult desister,
De paruenir en honneur et prouesse.
Constance fait le saige persister
En son entier, et conquester noblesse.

A steadfast man is like the anvil, which does not fear the power of the hammer. A virtuous heart is thus fortified and fears not the hardness of misfortune. Of fury, anger and malevolence it has no fear, and promptly resists all evil. No opposition can direct it from honorous and virtuous deeds. Steadfastness enables the wise man to reach the fulfillment of his being and attain nobility.[26]

This emblem may in fact have inspired the device in our engraving. Van Heemskerck and Coornhert could have been familiar with this book, the second important emblem book after Alciati's (1531), for it enjoyed a wide circulation and went through many editions. A Dutch translation by Frans Fraet de Vries was published in Antwerp in 1554, and was reprinted in 1556 and again in 1564.[27]

That *Patientia* sits on a cube is another reference to her steadfastness and is a fairly common way of representing the virtue among van Heemskerck's contemporaries in the North. Pieter Brueghel, in his engraving *Patientia* (1554), seats her on a cube, and in an engraving by Cornelius Metsys, *Patientia* is chained to one (Bartsch, IX:111, par. 42). The cube almost universally connotes steadfastness and constancy, and

Cesare Ripa writes that sitting on a stone indicates that *Patientia* endures hardships with a calm spirit.[28]

In Isa. 28:16, the cube, or cornerstone, also symbolizes Christ: "Therefore thus saith the Lord God: Behold I will lay a stone in the foundations of Sion, a tried stone, a corner stone, a precious stone, founded in the foundation. He that believeth, Let him not hasten." A similar passage in Psalms 117:22 is of particular interest in connection with the stone in our engraving: "The stone which the builders rejected: the same is become the head of the corner." This reference to the "rejected stone" and the "tried stone" may explain why the cube in our engraving is nicked and chipped around the edges. In medieval works, such as the *Speculum humane salvationis* (1324), a builder throwing out a stone is represented as a type for the resurrection of Christ. We find in I Pet. 2 that Christ is described as a "living stone" and man is exhorted to "suffer patiently" as Christ suffered and not let his word become a "stone of stumbling." This New Testament chapter embodies many of the leitmotifs in our engraving and may well have inspired many of the idiosyncrasies in van Heemskerck/Coornhert's representation of the *Triumph of Patience.*

The lamb (as *agnus* an attribute of Saint Agnes) is another conventional attribute of *Patientia*. It is the sacrificial animal *par excellence,* associated in Acts 8:32 with the obedient sacrifice of Christ: "He was led as a sheep to slaughter: and like a lamb without a voice before his shearer, so openeth not his mouth." The biblical connotations of the lamb and of the sheep as obedient, sacrificial beasts were continued and greatly embroidered upon in the Middle Ages in commentaries such as the influential *Etymologies* of Isidore of Seville (d. 636).

Patientia is followed "in disgrace" by *Fortuna,* who is represented with the attributes commonly assigned to her and her sister *Occasio,* as a glance at Ripa's *Iconologia* confirms.[29] One of the more important textual sources for representations of *Fortuna/Occasio* is an epigram in the *Greek Anthology.* Here it is explained that *Fortuna's* hair grows only in front because when she arrives she is easy to seize, but once she has passed, there is no way of detaining her.[30] This early work, well known to sixteenth-century humanists, also gives her a razor and a globe as attributes. In the sixth century, Boethius in his *Consolatio Philosophiae* changed the globe into a wheel, arguing that man's fate was fixed to *Fortuna's* wheel, which, as it turned, could bring man up, but would inevitably put him down again. One of the oldest representations of *Fortuna's* wheel is found in the twelfth-century illuminated manuscript of Herrad of Landsberg, the *Hortus Deliciarum,* and the motive appears in the twelfth-century rose windows of St. Etienne of Beauvais and in the Munster in Basel.[31] In the sixteenth century *Fortuna* is represented with many of the attributes she bears in this engraving, and is frequently portrayed against a stormy seascape. An emblem showing *Fortuna* with Mercury in the 1550 edition of Andrea Alciati provides us with a representative example of the marine *Fortuna*.[32]

Fortuna wearing a blindfold may derive from an essay on Chance in Plutarch's *Moralia*, in which he describes *Fortuna* as being blind, and exhorts man to let *Ratio* be his guide.[33] According to Boethius' classical formula, *Fortuna* operated in relative independence of God; however, she nevertheless was subject to Divine Providence. Man, once he committed himself to the world, stood under the sway of *Fortuna* with all her uncertainties.[34] To counter *Fortuna*, man should exercise Virtue and Reason, a theme similar to that of Prudentius. Boethius explicitly states that the virtue accompanying Reason is Patience: "She (Divine Providence) mixeth for others sour and sweet according to the disposition of their souls; she troubles some lest they should fall to dissolution by long prosperity, others are vexed with hardships, that they may confirm the forces of their mind with the use and exercise of patience."[35]

Continuing in the tradition of Boethius' *Fortuna*, we find a fifteenth-century German engraving showing *Fortuna* with her wheel, blindfolded, and bound by a rope held by Christ. This seems also to be the moral of the van Heemskerck/Coornhert allegory of *Patientia*. *Fortuna* brings suffering and hardship to man as directed by Divine Providence. As Christ suffered yet remained virtuous, so should man seek to patiently endure earthly life. For as Christ triumphed over death and was victorious over *Fortuna*, so shall the virtuous man have everlasting life. It is almost apocalyptic that *Fortuna*'s wheel should be broken, signifying that her powers to control man's fate have been broken. Her blindfold, indicating her inability to reason, may also refer to her inability to perceive divine wisdom. That she is the only non-Christian allegorical figure in this engraving strengthens the assumption that she is included not only to demonstrate the triumph of Patience over hardship and misfortune, but also to affirm the triumph of divine wisdom over more naively held beliefs in chance.[36]

To represent *Spes* with the anchor as her attribute is in keeping with one of the earliest Christian traditions and is derived from the words of Heb. 6:18-19: "That by two immutable things in which it is impossible for God to lie, we may have the strongest comfort, we who have fled for refuge to hold fast the hope set before us, which we have as an anchor of the soul, sure and firm, and which entereth even within the veil." One of the Fathers of the early church, Saint John Chrysostom, used the same image: "Just as to be sure he that hopes in man is damned, thus verily that one is blessed who hopes in God. Severing yourself of all (earthly) things, hold on to that anchor."[37] Toward the end of the Middle Ages, the anchor or the spade become the tools most frequently given the virtue, and in Renaissance and Baroque art the anchor predominates, to which Ripa's *Iconologia* bears witness.[38] A late fifteenth-century engraving of Hope shows her sitting on a cube, holding a spade in her right hand and an anchor in her left. She triumphantly places her feet on Judas, who crouches beneath her clutching his bag of money.[39]

In our engraving the anchor as the attribute of *Spes* gains additional significance in conjunction with the other three figures, *Fortuna*, *Patientia*, and *Desiderium*. The anchor of Hope can be understood as the visual antidote for the stormy sea caused by *Fortuna*, which is represented in the background. And, too, she bears her anchor in an unusual fashion, over her shoulder—much as Christ carries his cross in representations of the Passion, evoking the imagery embodied in *Patientia*'s attributes, that she bears up under suffering. In comparison with *Desiderium*, who according to the epigram is winged because he is swift, *Spes* must move more slowly because she carries the weight of the anchor. In a sense, the two figures guiding *Patientia* compose a mini-emblem, illustrating the imperial adage *Festina lente* ("Hurry slowly").

The *Hypnerotomachia Poliphili* (Venice, 1499), one of the cornerstones of subsequent sixteenth-century emblematic inventions, illustrates *Semper festina tarde* with a circle next to an anchor with a dolphin entwined about it.[40] This hieroglyph, which became the personal *impresa* of the publisher of the work, Aldus Manutius, was given further prominence by Erasmus, when he included it in his *Adagia*. This collection of adages became a source of wisdom for Renaissance humanists such as the emblematist Andrea Alciati. In the 1534 edition of his *Emblemata*, the dolphin and anchor accompany a motto which demonstrates his knowledge of its imperial ancestry: *Princeps subditorum icolumitatem procurans* ("The Prince safeguarding the rights of his subjects").

It is possibly not accidental that van Heemskerck's *Desiderium* was made to echo a dichotomy in the gesture of Alciati's *paupertas*: where the latter's *putto* is held down by a stone, *Desiderium* carries his bow; corresponding to the *putto*'s winged uplift, *Desiderium*'s open palm appears framed by a celestial aureole. The anchor of *Spes* and the rings around

Desiderium's hand suggest elements of the hieroglyph in the *Hypnero-tomachia*. It seems that, in our engraving, the iconographic remnants of the *Festina lente* tradition have been given a *Patientia* cast, indicating the subtlety of van Heemskerck's and Coornhert's allegorical inventions.

Desiderium personified by a male figure accompanies *Spes* physically and spiritually. Ripa defines him as hope for things not of this world, and tells us that he burns with spiritual longing for God.[41] That *Desiderium* is given such prominence in this engraving may have been inspired by the Canticle of Canticles, whose imagery concerns a spiritual longing for God. This biblical book, we recall, seems also to have been the source for the imagery in *Patientia*'s banner. Jacobus à Bruck, in his *Emblemata moralia et bellica*, under the motto *Non est mortale quod opto* ("That which I desire is not of this world"), shows a male figure seated on a cube, holding up a ring in his right hand which is illuminated by the sun, very much like the raised hand of van Heemskerck's *Desiderium*.[42] The fact that he carries arrows and a bow, the traditional attributes of *Amor*, possibly suggests that *Desiderium* personifies not only a more etherealized form of Hope, but also is meant to express love for God, the idea conveyed by *Patientia*'s burning heart. Such a fusion of the secular *Amor* with the Christian *Desiderium* corresponds to the moral theology embodied in the two cupid reliefs on the west facade of the Modena Cathedral (c. 1170). Erwin Panofsky suggests that the cupid with the *Ibis* (*hommo carnalis*) is to be contrasted with his counterpart, who has no such animal as its attribute, signifying that he has been baptized and reborn in the new faith.[43]

For the self-assured and inspired figure of *Desiderium*, van Heemskerck has, interestingly, used the pose which originally carried a diametrically opposed meaning: that of a classical warrior fleeing, as it occurs in a statue Heemskerck might well have seen while in Italy, where he assiduously sketched both contemporary and classical art.[44] Thus, van Heemskerck's *Desiderium* is cast in a *Pathosformel* of fear which he has turned into one of fervent striving. This phenomenon of rhetorical economy, in which the same hieroglyph was used to express an opposite meaning, was called an "energetic inversion" by Aby Warburg, who was the first to notice the significance of this by no means uncommon phenomenon.[45]

Space does not permit a detailed examination of the other seven engravings, which are only briefly described in the following *catalogue raisonnée*.

2. *Triumph of Isaac*

Condition and appearance: Van Heemskerck's monogram is inscribed in the lower left-hand corner and Coornhert's in the lower right. A male figure seated sidesaddle on a camel occupies the center of the print. His right heel rests on the neckward slope of the camel's hump, and the ball of his left foot touches a platform-shaped stirrup. He wears a short-skirted garment fringed at the arms and a cloak which streams out behind him. His upper torso is slightly turned toward the viewer and he is looking out. "ISAAC" is inscribed just to the left of his head. He grips the staff of his banner in his right hand, supporting its weight on his right shoulder. Attached to the cross-shaped end of the staff is a banner emblazoned with a representation of foot-cuffs. Kerrich calls it a "fetter-lock"—essentially, a device used to hobble the feet of men or animals.[46] In his left hand he holds the reins of the camel. The bridle of the animal consists of a simple nose band, from which dangles a large tassel, a cone-shaped headpiece. The camel's body is hidden beneath a large blanket. The hump of the beast is bedecked with an additional scalloped trapping.

He pulls a two-wheeled cart which bears a round pedestal, festooned with garlands and two nude figures in relief, which Kerrich calls a "small round Altar."[47] A ram is lying on top of the pedestal with only his fore-quarters visible. From underneath his body project two rod-shaped pieces of wood and a scourge. Along with these objects there are a sword and a smoking urn embossed with an ox head.

There is a small indentation in the horizon line separating foreground and background, just beneath the tassel of the camel's bridle. In the background to the left, two men saddle a mule, and two other figures and a mule move toward a city set against a mountain. On the right a blindfolded youth kneels in profile on a bundle of wood, with his hands held before him crossed at the wrists. In front of him is a square altar bearing a smoking urn and more wood. There is a notch-like indentation in the right side of the otherwise cubical altar, identical with the indentation described in the foreground. Behind him a bearded man, posed in a vigorous *contrapposto*, holds an upraised sword with both hands. The downward momentum of his swing is interrupted by a winged airborne figure who has grasped the blade of the weapon. A ram caught in a thicket is visible in the distant background to the right of these figures.

On the *bas-de-page* and separated from the representation by an engraved frame is the following Latin text:

Sustinet impositum veluti virtute CAMELVS
Pondus, onusque sibi, mitem facilemque oneranti
Se praebet, nec non flectit sua terga retorta:
Vnica sic ISAC soboles fide patris AMRAMI
Dictis audit, obediuit, capitisque pericla
pectore non dubio manifesta subire paratus.

The Camel supports the weight and the burden placed on it as if
motivated by virtue, and offers itself humble and ready to him that
burdens it, and especially accommodates him with its humped back.
Thus, Isaac, the offspring, pays attention moved by singular trust in
the decrees of his father Abraham, and he obeyed without showing
doubt in his soul, ready to face the risks even to life.

3. *Triumph of Joseph*

Condition and appearance: Inscribed in the lower left-hand corner is van
Heemskerck's monogram, with the bar missing, numbered "3" in the
lower right, followed by Coornhert's monogram. A young man on an ox
occupies center stage. He straddles the beast with his legs bent at the
knee, drawn up high, pressing his left heel into its flank. Maintaining
his erect riding form, he looks back and down somewhat pensively over
his left shoulder at a nude woman who has seized his cloak with both
hands. His other garment is a short-sleeved tunic hemmed with strips
of fur, the so-called miniver. His left hand and disrobed shoulder steady a
staff to which a large pennon is attached with ribbons. "IOSEPH" is
inscribed to the left of the cross-tipped staff close to the upper framed
boundary of the print. The banner shows eleven bees around a beehive,
which is topped by a bird. Kerrich suggests it is a phoenix, but admits his
uncertainty.[48] It is most probably an eagle; what can be discerned of its
features corresponds with the eagle decorating the front right corner of
the cart in the last engraving of the set, *Triumph of Christ*. With the
cloak draped around his right arm, Joseph holds the reins of the bull,
which are looped around the animal's horns.

The bull moves forward with its right front leg gracefully lifted and
looks ahead with large, almost human eyes. The animal is crowned with a
headpiece composed of two pieces of fruit and three ears of corn. From
this arrangement two long, thick garlands hang down on either side of its
head. Attached to its horns is another cord which extends horizontally
the length of the animal's body, disappearing beneath the large rectangular saddle blanket and reemerging to form an elegant harness for the
nude female figure. A thicker piece of material is looped once around her

waist and again around her buttocks and is tied to the harness in a thick knot. The extra material hangs down between her firmly, though awkwardly, spread legs and is slightly torn.

With outstretched arm the woman pulls on Joseph's cloak, her body crouched in a *demi-plié*. She supports her weight with her left leg and braces herself with her right, which is extended forward, echoing the placement of the bull's right hind leg. She looks up at Joseph, and "ZEPHIRACH" is inscribed just to the left of her long, straight profile. She wears a round earring and a snake-like bracelet, which is wrapped three times about her upper left arm. Her hair is short and wavy. She wears, it seems, a headpiece, to which her long braid may be attached. It falls down her back, extending almost to her knees, and ends in a tassel.

Behind her is another female figure, apparently not harnessed to the bull. "INVIDIA" is inscribed above her head, slightly to the left. Three snakes writhe through her hair, forming a macabre headpiece appropriate to her vengeful expresson. Her mouth is open, and she is about to chew a human heart, which she grasps firmly in her left hand. Her right arm is folded across her waist, and her hand is slightly fisted, except for the index finger, which is aimed toward the ground. Her long garment is torn just below the knee.

In the background on the left, six male figures, some with shepherd's crooks, are grouped around a circular pit. Two of them support a naked man who is suspended over the cavity. According to Kerrich, this is Joseph, who is being taken out of the pit.[49] To the right of this group there are sheep grazing and in the distance, on a hill, three additional figures (two with shepherd's crooks) are visible. The sky above the central group is filled by a radiating sun. To the right of the sun is a cluster of twelve stars; the uppermost star appears to be brightest. To the right and slightly below the stars is a moon whose craters—or, as those in the sixteenth century would say, "seas"—suggest eyes, nose, and a mouth. The face of the moon looks away from the hilltop scene in the direction in which Joseph is looking.

Beneath the picture, and separated from it by an engraved frame, is the following Latin text:

Impia facta fratrum. macra Inuidia ista figurans,
Vicit IOSEPHVS fidei virtute, & amorem
Illicitum ZEPHIRACH candore animi superauit:
Illius Omnipotens DEVS almam virginitatem

Seruauit sibi in encensum, pinguis bouis instar,
Tristia fata Chanaam patriae quo exhauriat olim.

The impious deeds of his brethren which lean Envy devises, Joseph
defeated by virtue of his faith, and he overcame the Illicit Love of
Zephirach by sheer purity of mind. His gentle virginity God
Almighty preserved for him against the heat of passion, not unlike
the sluggish ox. Through Joseph he brought to an end the sad events
of his fatherland Canaan.

4. *Triumph of David*

Condition and appearance: Inscribed in the lower left-hand corner is the
monogram of the "inventor," van Heemskerck. " ·4· *DC* " is clearly
legible in the lower right corner, signifying this print as the fourth of the
series and Coornhert as the engraver. A male figure mounted on a lion
leads the triumphal procession. He is bearded, attired in elegant and
elaborate armor, with a cape affixed to his left shoulder with a clasp and
fluttering out behind him, indicative of the dynamic progression of beast
and rider. His helmet, a toupha, is trimmed with a hatband which resembles a Roman imperial crown, and is topped by a plume which appears to
be, in its lower portion, part animal. This diminutive beast's head
resembles that of a horse or dog, and its hindquarters and tail could be
those of a dog or long-haired cat. The plume seems to sprout like wings
from the animal's back. Just to the left of the plume, "DAVID" is
inscribed. From underneath the upturned visor of his helmet he looks
firmly ahead, the eyes thus in almost complete darkness, reminding one
of the *facies nigra* of the *melancholicus*. His torso squarely faces the
viewer. His left leg is perpendicular to the ground; and his right leg,
slightly bent at the knee and completely visible, is raised over the
shoulders of the lion as if he were about to swing his leg over the back of
the lion down to the ground. His right arm extends forward over the
lion's neck, and he controls the beast by a deceptively dainty ribbon which
loops through the animal's mouth. In his left hand he holds the strong
rope, which appears to be coiled around the two men in tow behind him,
and supports the cross-topped staff of his banner by resting the end of
the pole on the lion's back. A bridle is represented on his banner.[50] At his
left side rests a sword, pointing down, attached to his body by a strap
which is draped across his left thigh. It disappears underneath his leg and
reappears, traveling diagonally across his chest toward his right shoulder.

A lyre or harp rests between his legs, not visibly attached to man or beast.

The lion's head, slightly turned toward the viewer, looks ferociously out from the corner of its eye. The animal's elaborate trappings consist of an oval-shaped saddle blanket patterned with a fish-scale design, over which is draped a rectangular embroidered piece of material. Additional cloth, apparently between or beneath the decorative blankets, trails the ground. Two figures are behind David and the lion. The one in closest proximity with his back to the viewer is identified as "SAVL" by an inscription above and to the right of his head. He lunges forward with the weight of his disproportionately large body on his right foot and his left leg thrust out behind. His body is twisted in a vigorous *contrapposto*, and his broad back and shoulders are squarely set horizontal with the picture plane. His left arm, continuing the upward thrust of his body, swings around behind his head and his palm is open. His right arm is drawn back and poised for attack as he holds a spear leveled at David. Saul is also bearded and armored, and his epaulettes have a leonine physiognomy. He wears a crown, and a long sword hangs from a girdle around his waist, attached just to the left of the center of his back in a sheath consisting of two looped straps. The handle of the sword is finished with the head of a large beaked bird. Saul is apparently fastened to the rope held by David with a sash which runs diagonally around his upper torso from his waist to his right shoulder.

The second male figure, slightly behind Saul, also lunges forward on one foot and points with his left index finger in the direction of David. His beardless face is angry and contorted, and he sticks out his tongue. "SEMEI" is inscribed in back of his head toward the far right boundary of the engraving. His garment appears to be rent so that his chest is bared to the waist. David's rope rests on Semei's left shoulder, so that his head and right arm are, as it were, caught in a lasso.

In the background on the right, two male figures, identified by Kerrich as David and Goliath, stand on the edge of a cliff.[51] Tents are visible on either side of them in the valley below. David, on the left with his back to the viewer, holds a sling with a stone in his left hand. His arm is drawn back, and he is prepared to release his missile. His right arm is close to his side, and his hand grips a shepherd's crook. He is dressed in a simple tunic and faces Goliath, who wears armor and a helmet with a prominent bushy plume. His right arm extends out in a sweeping gesture, which we may call an *allocutio* gesture of derisive speech, and he openly presents himself as a target for David's attack. He seems to be relaxed. A shield is strapped to his right arm; and he steadies a lance, the placement of which exactly repeats the position of the staff of David's banner in the foreground.

On the *bas-de-page* and separated from the representation by an engraved frame are the following Latin verses:

DAVID magnanimus fortem virtute Leonem
Vicit, & infandum Goliath, vicitque ferocem
Vrsum: sed regem Saulem ambitione tumentem,
Risoresque suos tulit, & fraeno rationis
Vicit, nec voluit sceleratas sumere poenas:
Verum haecquis dubitat diuino numine facta.

Magnanimous David overcame the powerful Lion by means of virtue, and also the unspeakable Goliath, and he overpowered the ferocious bear. But King Saul, swelling with ambition,
And the mockers, he endured and conquered with the restraint of reason; nor did he wish to endure vicious punishment: in truth he doubts that these are the result of Divine Will.

5. *Triumph of Job*

Condition and appearance: Van Heemskerck's monogram in the lower left is of the same size and quality as in nos. 2 and 4. The number 5 appears printed in reverse in the lower right-hand corner next to Coornhert's monogram. Job, identified by the inscription "IOB" [*sic*] directly above his tousled head of hair, is bearded and naked except for a wicker mat covering his thighs, probably intended to represent a sackcloth. He sits on the back of a large turtle with his bare feet crossed at the ankles almost touching the animal's head. This position, connected with representations of death or inhibition, inadversity, or introversion from classical times on, was prescribed for judges in ancient German law books, to denote a calm and elevated state of mind.[52] His countenance, seen in profile, is stern; and his upper body is twisted so that his muscular torso faces the viewer, causing the veins of his neck to bulge. The staff of Job's banner rests on the ground and is steadied lightly by the right wrist and shoulder. The banner itself is emblazoned with a winged heart which bears a balance, a flaming sword, and an orb with a cross.[53]

Job has in tow behind him four male figures, a woman, and a horned monster with a scourge and a grapple hook. In the background to the left is Job, sitting on a dung heap, surrounded by three of his friends and his wife. Behind him ruined buildings are in conflagration.

At the *bas-de-page* is the following Latin poem:

Omnibus amissis, post mille pericula, rebus:
Post tot difficiles casus, varios cruciatus,
IOB quibus infesto tentatus Daemone, Amicis,
Coniuge fallaci, passus tamen est fide cuncta
Constanter, firmusque nimis testudinis instar,
Mansit, quam poterit tectam confringere nemo.

> Having lost his all, after a thousand dangers: after so many difficult
> incidents, and various sufferings, Job, having been besieged by
> them assailed by the Devil, by friends,
> And a treacherous wife, has yet endured them all by steadfast faith—
> and he remained firm to the most, like the tortoise whom shell-
> protected no one was able to break.

6. *Triumph of Tobit*

Condition and appearance: A bearded TOBIAS [*sic*], wearing a pointed
cap and long cape-like cloak and riding a mule, occupies the center of the
print. Van Heemskerck's monogram is in the lower left, followed by
"Martinus Heemskerck Inuentor," the only plate except no. 1 to be so
thoroughly identified. Coornhert's monogram is in the lower right preceded by the number 6, printed in reverse. In the banner Tobit supports
with his left arm are represented four flintstones, identical with the chain
link of the Order of the Golden Fleece, and a nude woman, who is
perched on the rim of a chalice-like fountain, holding a sheaf of grain
over her head. Her breasts are spouting a liquid. Harnessed to the mule is
an old woman, carrying a basket with spindles and a ram. Slightly behind
her and attached to the mule by a rope knotted around his shabby gar-
ments is a beggar holding a staff in his right hand and the leash of a small
dog in his left. He is identified by an inscription between his legs as
"CAECA PAUPERTAS." In the background can be seen the elder Tobit
lowering a body into a rectangular grave.

At the *bas-de-page* is the following Latin poem:

Quanta seni TOBIAE fuerit patientia, quanta
Asperitas vitae tam longo tempore, rebus
Amissis, oculisque, docent veteris monumenta
Scripturae, sed iniquo animo haud tulit, immo
Cernere quem mundi nescit Sapientia, caecus
Ipse fide agnouit, soli cui fidit in aeuum.

What patience old man TOBIAS possessed, how harsh his life had
been, for so long a time—having lost all of his possessions as well
as his eyesight, the monuments of ancient Scripture reveal.
But he endured with a calm mind. Nay, what[54] the Wisdom of the
world does not know how to discern, the blind man himself
recognized by his faith on which alone he relied forever.

7. *Triumph of Stephen*

Condition and appearance: The seventh engraving of the set is printed on
paper that is lighter in weight than the other prints; it appears much
whiter and is generally not as well preserved. Van Heemskerck's monogram (in the lower left) is also relatively smaller in comparison with
those in the preceding engravings. It is numbered 7 in the lower right,
and the engraver's mark of Coornhert follows. Inscribed at the top center
is "STEPHANVS."

Stephen is mounted on an elephant, looking up, his hands folded in
prayer. He is wearing the robes of a deacon. A woman suckling five children is represented in his banner, which he cradles in his left arm. Two
male figures harnessed behind are poised to stone him, and stones litter
the pavement. There are two buildings in the background on the right,
and to the left of Stephen's head can be seen God, crowned with a triple
crown and holding the orb of divine power, and Christ, who bears the
cross on his right shoulder.

The following Latin verses are engraved at the *bas-de-page*:

En pietate virum insignem, virtute decorum,
Clementem Stephanum, placidumque, hilaremque, beningnum,
Munificum supra quam dici possit in omneis:
Nam moriturus constanter precibus, scleratis
Pro hostibus, orabat Dominum vultuque sereno,
Vno in quo fixit sibi Spem, metamque salutis.

Behold the man distinguished by piety, the adornment of virtue,
the compassionate Stephen who is calm, serene, benign, generous
beyond what can be said of most:
For as he was death-bound, he prayed ceaselessly for his crime-
ridden enemies, addressing the Lord, and did this with a serene
countenance, the only one upon whom he had based his Hope, and
the aim of Redemption.

8. *Triumph of Christ*

Condition and appearance: Van Heemskerck's monogram in the lower left corner is smaller than in the initial engravings, close in size to that of no. 7. The number 8, followed by the engraver's mark of Coornhert, is in the lower right. "CR $\frac{1}{5}$TVS" [*sic*] is inscribed in the upper portion of the print to the left of Christ's head. A monumental Christ is posed in a majestic gesture of blessing, and is seated on a terrestrial globe and rainbow. He wears a crown and only the lower portion of his body is draped, revealing a muscular torso. His chariot is drawn by two minute lambs. He holds in his left hand the staff of his banner and the ropes binding those following him. They are, from right to left, a nude woman balancing a transparent globe on her head, behind her a skeleton with an arrow, and two monsters, one of which holds a grapple hook and a scourge. The other, a combination of animals, has the head of a dog and on its stomach an additional face, perhaps that of a wolf, with six teats. The banner of Christ bears the instruments of his Passion, the *arma Christi*. In the background can be seen Christ carrying the cross with the help of another man, Simon of Cyrene (Matt. 27:32); toward the center is Christ on the cross, beneath which are four large stones, and Christ with a banner, ascending into heaven amidst curling clouds of smoke.

At the *bas-de-page*, and separated from the representation by an engraved frame, are the following Latin verses:

Vnica Cunctipotens hominum Spes, veraque vita
CHRISTVS, morigerus fuit aeterno vsque Parenti
Ad mortem, mortemque crucis scelerosam.
AEthera celsa super iam cernimus, omneque nomen
Euecta, atque triumphantem, post Tartara, Mundum,
Daemona, Peccatum, truculentos, depopulata.

Almighty Christ, unique hope of mankind and true Life, was obedient to his Eternal Father even to the point of dying the execrable death of the cross.

The uppermost heavens we now behold and every name is elevated and triumphant—Hell, the World, the Devil, Sin, the Wrongdoers having been eliminated.

NOTES

1. In the writing of this essay I have benefited greatly from the generous assistance of friends, professors, and associates and would especially like to thank the following: Karla Langedijk, who first suggested that the device in Tobit's banner included chain links from the Order of the Golden Fleece, and to whom I am also indebted in more ways than can here be enumerated; Earl G. Mueller, for generously granting me the use of his private library; and Gerald J. Schiffhorst, for his time-consuming critical editing of the manuscript and for bringing important texts concerning patience to my attention. I thank Virginia W. Callahan and William S. Heckscher for the transcription and translation of the Latin poems. To Dr. Heckscher, my mentor and my muse, I would like to express my deepest gratitude and admiration.

2. For a brief biographical sketch of Coornhert's data and significance, see Ulrich Thieme and Felix Becker, *Allgemeines Lexikon der bildenden Kunstler von der Antike bis zur Gegenwart*, 37 vols. (Leipzig: E. A. Seeman, 1907–50), VII: 367. For his literary and political activities prior to 1567 see Olga Rinck-Wagner, "Dirck Volckertszoon Coornhert 1522–1572," *Historische Studien* XXXVIII (1919). For Coornhert's religious views see B. Becker, *Bronnen tot de kennis van D.V. Coornhert*, Rijks Geschiedkundige Publicatien 25 (The Hague, 1928). His place in the larger scheme of religious controversy is discussed by G. Guldner, *Das Toleranz-Problem in den Niederlanden im Ausgang des 16. Jahrhunderts*, Historische Studien 403 (Lubeck and Hamburg, 1968), pp. 65–147.

3. Supposedly, on his deathbed, Lipsius pointed to a crucifix and ironically pronounced, "Haec vera est patientia" ("That is true patience"): Jason Lewis Saunders, *Justus Lipsius; the Philosophy of Renaissance Neo-Stoicism* (New York: Liberal Arts Press, 1955), p. 30. See also Martin Warnke, *Kommentare zu Rubens* (Berlin: de Gruyter, 1965), for an enlightening discussion of Neo-Stoicism and seventeenth century absolutism, with bibliographical references.

4. Christian Hulsen and Herman Egger, *Die romischen Skizzenbucher von Marten van Heemskerck*, 2 vols. (Berlin: Julius Bard, 1916). For a concise yet thorough account of van Heemskerck's life and *oeuvre*, the reader is again referred to Thieme and Becker, XVI: 227–29.

5. The contract granting Coornhert the exclusive privilege of making engravings and designs by van Heemskerck was published by A. van der Willigen, *Geschiedkundige aantekeningen over Haarlemse schilders en andere beoefenaren ven de beeldende kunsten* (Haarlem, 1866), p. 40. For the van Heemskerck / Coornhert collaboration, see also Ilja Marx-Veldeman, "The idol on the ass; Fortune and the sleeper: Maarten van Heemskerck's use of emblem and proverb books in two prints," *Simiolus, Netherlands Quarterly for the History of Art* VI, no. 1 (1972–73):26, n. 33. Marx-Veldeman also discusses the unequivocal relationship between prints engraved or etched by Coornhert after designs by van Heemskerck and Coornhert's own literary work in "Een serie allegorische preten van Coornhert met een ontwertekening van Maarten van Heemskerck," *Bulletin van het Rijksmuseum* II (1971):70–76. On the confluence of their religious views, see Craig Harbison, "Reformation Iconography: Problems and Attitudes," in *Print Review Number Five: Tribute to Wolfgang Stechow* (New York, 1976), pp. 81–85, and the enlightening study by H. R. Hoetink, "Heemskerck en het zestiende eeuwse spiritualisme," *Bulletin Museum Beymans-van Beuningen* XII (1961):20.

6. A provocative study of Cock's importance is Louis Lebeer's "Propos sur l'importance de l'étude des editeurs d'Estampes," *Revue Belge d'archeologie et d'histoire de l'art* XXXVII (1968). Valuable information has been compiled by Timothy Riggs, "Hieronymous Cock (1510–1570): Printmaker and Publisher in Antwerp at the Sign of the Four Winds" (Ph.D. diss., Yale University, 1971), University Microfilms (Ann Arbor, 1972). See also Lydia De Pauw–De Veen, *Jerome Cock Editeur d'Estampes et Graveur 1507 (?)–1570*. Exhibition Catalogue (Brussels, 1970).

7. Thieme and Becker, VII: 367, mention three major allegorical series produced by the trio: *Circulus vicissitudinis rerum humanorum, Patientiae triumphus elegantissimis imaginibus expressus,* and *Twelve Labors of Charles V* (1st ed., 1556).

8. This kind of stage-sharing is by no means uncommon; it governed, for example, the design of Jan Stephan von Calcar's large-size anatomical woodcuts illustrating Andreas Vesalius' *Humani corporis fabrica* (Basel, 1543). That van Heemskerck was familiar with Vesalius is corroborated by Ilja Marx-Veldeman, "Maarten van Heemskerck and St. Luke's Medical Books," *Simiolus, Netherlands Quarterly for the History of Art* VII, no. 2 (1974): 91–100. A similar principle was followed by Albrecht Dürer in composing his woodcuts for the Triumphal Arch of Maximilian (1519), which were spatially conceived for a coherent architectural arrangement.

9. For this concept, see Erwin Panofsky's discussion of Albrecht Durer's engraving of 1513, *Knight, Death, and the Devil,* whose most likely inspiration was Erasmus of Rotterdam's *Enchridion militis Christiani,* 1504 (Erwin Panofsky, *The Life and Art of Albrecht Durer* [Princeton: Princeton University Press, 1955], p. 151).

10. *De Abraham II,* 11:79, in J. P. Migne, ed., *Patrologia Latina,* 221 vols. (Paris, 1844–90), XIV:518. See also *In Psalmos,* 118:1, in Migne, ed., *Patrologia Graeca* (Paris, 1857–66), XII:1585.

11. Saint Augustine, *Civitas Dei,* Book 22, p. 30, par. 5, in Migne, *Patrologia Latina,* XLI: 864; Saint Augustine, *Epistles,* Book 55, p. 9, par. 17, ibid., XXXIII:212; Saint Ambrose, *Enarratio in psalmos,* Book 37, p. 2, par. 2, ibid., XIV:1057.

12. See also Psalms 117:22. This passage in Isaias is of central importance for an understanding of our engraved set.

13. Ercole II, Duke of Ferrara, whose motto was *Patience,* is a classic case illustrating the political dimensions of the "Patience cult" in courtly circles. For a full discussion of the fate of the Este estate, see Rudolf Wittkower, "Patience and Chance: The Story of a Political Emblem," *Journal of the Warburg Institute* I (July 1937–April 1938):171–75.

14. In Joannes Galle's edition this title is omitted, and a cartouche is engraved in its place with the same title in different lettering, and "ELEGANTISSIMIS IMAGINIBVS EX-PRESSVS" added (Thomas Kerrich, *A Catalogue of the Prints which have been engraved after Maarten van Heemskerck* [London: J. Rodwell, 1829], p. 78).

15. A. J. J. Delen, *Histoire de la Gravure dans les Anciens Pays-bays et dans les Provinces Belges des origines jusqu'à la fin du XVIIIᵉ Siecle,* 2 vols. (Paris: Les Editions d'Art et d'Histoire, 1935), II:94.

16. Coornhert's monogram is identified by Delen, II:87; the spelling of his name given here is the version preferred by the artist himself (Olga Rinck-Wagner, "Dirck Volckertszoon Coornhert, 1522-1572, mit besonderer Berucksichtigung seiner politischen Tatigkeit," *Historische Studien* 138 [1919]; reprint ed., Vaduz: Kraus Reprint Ltd., 1965).

17. According to Kerrich (p. 78), these letters were taken out in the late impressions.

18. Ibid.

19. The notions of *Fortuna* and *Occasio*—kept quite separate in Antiquity—are often fused in the Renaissance, with the result that in the field of art composite figures, such as our *Fortuna,* appear with attributes of both. See Aby Warburg, *Gesammelte Schriften* (Leipzig, 1932), I:358-59.

20. In Cesare Ripa, *Iconologia* (Rome, 1603), p. 449, the lily symbolizes faith. In another useful iconographic handbook (Hubert Korneliszoon Poot, *Het groot Natuur, en zedekundigh Werelttoneel of Woordenboek,* 3 vols. [Delft: Reinier Boitet, 1743-50], I:491, II:110), the thorny bush indicates suffering and pain.

21. Emile Mâle, *Religious Art from the Twelfth to the Eighteenth Century* (New York: Pantheon, 1949), p. 116. Carl Gustaf Stridbeck, *Bruegelstudien* (Stockholm: Almquist and Wiksell, 1956), p. 251, discusses *Patientia's* role in allegories of suffering.

22. 2 vols. (Haarlem: Pieter van Wesbysch, 1604), v. 132. In the wall frescoes of the Spanish Chapel in Santa Maria Novella (Florence, Andrea da Firenze, c. 1365), *Caritas* bears the burning heart as her attribute.

23. Adam von Bartsch, *Le Peintre-graveur*, 21 vols. (Vienna: J. V. Degen, 1803–21), IX: 264, par. 160.

24. Bartsch, III:27, pars. 114–17. According to Ulrich Thieme and Felix Becker (VII:367), Goltzius was not an actual student of Coornhert, but was greatly influenced by him.

25. Juan de Boria, *Empresas Morales* (Prague: Iorge Nigrin, 1581), no. 36. The emblem taken from the original German edition by Georg Friedrich Scharffen, *Moralische Sinnbilder* (Berlin, 1968), is reprinted by Arthur Henkel and Albrecht Schöne, *Emblemata; Handbuch zur Sinnbildkunst des XVI und XVII Jahrhunderts* (Stuttgart: J. B. Metzler, 1967), col. 1410.

26. Guillaume de la Perrière, *Le Théâtre des bons engins* (Paris: Denys Janot, 1539), no. 67 (first illustrated edition); reproduced by Henkel and Schöne, cols. 1409–10.

27. Mario Praz, *Studies in Seventeenth-Century Imagery*, 2 vols. (London: The Warburg Institute, 1939, 1947), p. 394. For another instance in which van Heemskerck is thought to have used *Le Théâtre des bons engins*, see Ilja Marx-Veldeman, "The idol on the ass," *Simiolus, Netherlands Quarterly for the History of Art* VI, no. 1 (1972–73):26.

28. Ripa, pp. 379–81. For a selection of emblems conveying this idea, see Henkel and Schöne, p. 7.

29. Pages 169–71.

30. *Fortuna's* baldness in back probably derives from Callistrates' description (third century) of a bronze Kairos by Lysippus. The epigram is to be found in *Anthologia graeca*, trans. William Roger Paton, 5 vols. (London: W. Heinemann, 1927), V:26, par. 275.

31. The illustration from the *Hortus Deliciarum* is conveniently reproduced by J. J. M. Timmers, *Symboliek en Iconographie der Christelijke Kunst* (Roermond-Maaseik: J. J. Romen and Zone, 1947), plate 103.

32. Published in Lyons, the emblem carries the motto *Ars Naturam Adiuuans*. Other examples of *Fortunas* combined with ships can be found on the coat-of-arms of the Ruccellai family of Florence; Pinturichio's floor mosaics for the Cathedral of Siena; and an engraving of 1541 by Hans Sebald Beham (Bartsch, VIII:170, par. 140).

33. Plutarch, *Moralia*, trans. Frank Cole Babbitt, 14 vols. (Cambridge, Mass.: Harvard University Press, 1936), IV:323.

34. Coornhert translates Boethius into Dutch (Thieme and Becker, VII:367).

35. *The Consolation of Philosophy*, trans. "I. T.," rev. H. F. Stewart (London: William Heinemann, 1926), Book 4, chap. 6, pp. 348–49, lines 147–51.

36. In this respect, *Fortuna's* role in this engraving is consistent with Thomas of Aquinas' position on "chance," in the Second Article of "The Providence of God" under the heading "Whether Everything is subject to the Providence of God?" *Basic Writings of Saint Thomas Aquinas*, ed. Anton C. Pegis (New York: Random House, 1945).

37. Migne, *Patrologia Graeca*, LV:col. 144.

38. Ripa gives Speranza an anchor and a crown of flowers (p. 470).

39. Reproduced by Timmers, plate 92.

40. For a discussion of this work and the revival of the learned hieroglyph and emblem in the sixteenth century, see Ludwig Volkmann, *Bilderschriften der Renaissance, Hieroglyphik und Emblematik in ihren Beziehungen und Fortwirkungen* (Leipzig: Karl W. Hiersemann, 1923). In the *Hypnerotomachia* there is a hieroglyph which conveys a similar message. It shows a woman seated with one foot on the ground, one foot raised; in one hand she holds a tortoise and the other hand is winged. The inscription reads: *Velocitatem sedendo, tarditatem surgendo* ("Temper slowness with speed and speed with slowness"). It is interesting to note that van Heemskerck used the motives of tortoise and wing on the funerary monument he erected to his father in 1570. See Marx-Veldeman, "Het grafmonument te Heemskerck en het gebruik van hiëroglyfen in de kring rondom Maarten van Heemskerck," *Nederlands Kunsthistorisch Jaarboek* XXIV (1973):27–45, for a discussion of the monument and the light it sheds on van Heemskerck's theory of art.

41. Ripa, p. 102.

42. Henkel and Schöne, pp. 1277–78.

43. *Renaissance and Renascences in Western Art* (Stockholm: Almquist and Wiksell, 1960), p. 94.

44. Horst Woldemar Janson and Dora Janson, *The Story of Painting for Young People* (New York: H. N. Abrams, 1952), p. 50.

45. William S. Heckscher, "Shakespeare in His Relationship to the Visual Arts: A Study in Paradox," *Research Opportunities in Renaissance Drama* XIII–XIV (1970–71):69, n. 35.

46. Kerrich, p. 78.

47. Ibid.

48. Ibid.

49. Page 79.

50. This, too, is the conclusion of Kerrich, p. 79.

51. Ibid.

52. Erwin Panofsky, *Tomb Sculpture*, ed. H. W. Janson. (New York: H. N. Abrams, 1967), p. 56; Panofsky, *Dürer*, p. 78.

53. Coornhert's notary stamp, used by him as a signature in 1565 and 1566, bears a striking resemblance to Job's pennon device in print no. 5 of this set. Reproduced in Marx-Veldeman, "Het Grafmonument te Heemskerck en het gebruik van hiëroglyfen in de kring rondom Maarten van Heemskerck," p. 38, Fig. 12.

54. We must assume that *quem* is a misprint for *quae*.

Christus Patiens
The Virtue Patience and *Paradise Lost,* I-II

Albert C. Labriola

hristus Patiens was Milton's title or topic for a
tragedy that he did not write. As the brief
outline in the Trinity manuscript makes clear,
the tragedy would have centered on the New
Testament theme of the suffering of Christ
and Christ's endurance of that suffering—his
patience, in other words. The tragedy was to
have depicted the suffering in Gethsemane
and the betrayal by Judas; finally, Christ's
"agony" was to have received "noble expressions."[1] The topic *Christus
Patiens* is followed by three others: Christ bound, Christ crucified, Christ
risen. Whether these topics were being considered as separate tragedies
or as sequential elements of a single work remains unclear. What is clear,
however, is that dominant ideas in Milton's mind included Christ's
humiliation and exaltation—that is, Christ's heroic manifestation of the
virtue patience and the triumph that followed. *Christus Patiens* becomes,
in short, *Christus Victor.*

Although Milton did not write a tragedy on *Christus Patiens*, the
theme was never far from his mind. It is, in fact, a central theme in much
of his major poetry. Christ's manifestation of patience begins at the

Incarnation and culminates in the ministry of Redemption, especially with the activities of the Paschal triduum. For Milton, Christ's patience was supremely exercised in the humiliation and suffering of the Passion and Death; and as the Suffering Servant, Christ provides the pattern and norm for Christian heroism.[2] In the incomplete poem entitled "The Passion," which was to have celebrated some of the activities of the Paschal triduum, Milton calls Christ the "Most perfect *Hero*" (line 13).[3] In *Paradise Regained*, Christ's exercise of patience in the wilderness is clearly preparatory to the supreme exercise later at the Passion and Death; and in *Paradise Lost*, Adam, having learned from Michael about Christ's ministry of Redemption, asserts "that suffering for Truth's sake / Is fortitude to highest victory" (XII.569-70). He also asserts that he has been "Taught" the heroism of patience by the "example" of the "Redeemer" (XII.572-73). If patience and Christian heroism are stressed in Milton's poetry, they are likewise emphasized in his prose, especially in *De Doctrina Christiana*—where, in the chapter on the ministry of Redemption, Milton develops the view that patience and its reward are best reflected in the humiliation and exaltation of Christ, the pattern to which mankind should conform. To emphasize the paramount importance of mankind's participation in Christ's heroism, Milton cites a number of proof-texts, including Rom. 8:17, 29; II Tim. 2:11-12; Eph. 2: 5-6; and I Pet. 4:13. All these proof-texts, which allude to the Paschal triumph and mankind's participation in it, emphasize that mankind must suffer with Christ in order to be exalted with him.

Mankind's imitation of Christ, especially of the suffering Christ (*Christus Patiens*), is periodically stressed throughout *De Doctrina Christiana*, and many of these very same proof-texts, as well as others closely related, are employed again and again. There is no better example than Milton's discussion of the sacrament of baptism. Milton repeatedly mentions that the sign or ceremony of baptism—namely, immersion in running water—is intended to "signify" ("significandam") the believers' "regeneration by the Holy Spirit, and their union with Christ in his death, burial, and resurrection" (XVI:168-69). Having cited some of Saint Paul's comments on baptism, including I Cor. 12:13, Gal. 3:27, Rom. 6:3, and Col. 2:12, Milton remarks that the sacrament "was intended to represent figuratively ["figurate . . . significat"] the painful life of Christ, his death and burial, in which he was immersed . . . for a season" (XVI: 184-85). Referring again to Saint Paul, Milton continues to highlight the same points: "that baptism is not merely an initiatory rite, but a figurative representation of our death, burial, and resurrection with Christ"

(XVI:190–91). Baptism thereby enables mankind to commemorate and participate in Christ's Paschal triumph. In Milton's view, moreover, the Paschal triumph, mankind's participation in it, and the sign or ceremony of the sacrament that celebrates it also recall certain Old Testament personages and events prefiguring both the Paschal triumph and the rite of baptism. Citing Petrine and Pauline proof-texts (for instance, I Pet. 3: 20–21), Milton observes that "Noah's ark was the type of Baptism" and was "the like figure whereunto even baptism doth also now save us" (XVI:190–91). Echoing Saint Paul (I Cor. 10:2), Milton remarks that "all our fathers were baptized unto Moses in the cloud and in the sea" (XVI: 190–91). In *Paradise Lost*, to be sure, Noah and Moses are included among the "shadowy Types" (XII.303) who prefigure Christ's ministry of Redemption. In Milton's thinking the Paschal triumph is central to an understanding of biblical history, typological correspondence, and sacramental celebration.

The principal events of the Paschal triduum—Christ's Suffering and Death, Descent into Hell, and Resurrection—thereby constitute a frame of reference in which much of the action and characterization of *Paradise Lost* may be interpreted. Using techniques of irony, inversion, and parody, Milton in fact characterizes Satan as the demonic counterpart of *Christus Patiens* and *Christus Victor*. Throughout Books I and II of *Paradise Lost*, for example, Milton highlights the "cunning resemblances" (to borrow a phrase from *Areopagitica*) between Satan's raising of the fallen angels from the burning lake and Christ's achievement of the Paschal triumph. In raising the fallen angels, Satan undertakes the demonic counterpart of Christ's ministry of Redemption; and in seeking to undergo the cycle of humiliation and exaltation, he thus displays parodic or "cunning resemblances" to Christ's heroism. From these ironic comparisons, others necessarily follow. Satan's actions at the burning lake are also compared to certain Old Testament prefigurations of the Paschal triumph, notably Noah and Moses, and to the mimetic and symbolic reenactment of the Paschal triumph in the sacrament of baptism.

In *The Legend of Noah* Don Cameron Allen observes that the account of Noah and the Deluge "was always considered one of the best allegorical adumbrations of the life and ministry of Christ"; it was also traditionally interpreted as "the story of the second creation and the first salvation."[4] As the Redemption has been elaborated by the Church Fathers and depicted in Christian iconography, it too is an act of re-creation, because mankind, spiritually dead since the Fall, is upraised and revived through the Paschal triumph of Christ. In many ways the Church

Fathers typically juxtapose Noah and Christ: as creator-figures, as those delivered from death or the threat of destruction, and as deliverers of others from death. In the art of the catacombs Christ sometimes resembles Noah, so that in scenes of the Resurrection the sarcophagus from which Christ is emerging looks like Noah's ark. In his version of the story of Noah and the Deluge, which runs to more than 200 lines in Books XI and XII of *Paradise Lost*, Milton likewise emphasizes that Noah participated in an act of creation and salvation. The Deluge is described imagistically as a reversion to chaos; the emergence of dry earth from the waters and the description of Noah, who will "raise another World" (XI.877) and from whom "a second stock [will] proceed" (XII.7), closely parallel the account of the Son's actions as creator (in Book VII) and as the Redeemer of mankind, a role which is prefigured periodically throughout the epic. In turn, Milton's account of Noah and the Deluge ironically resembles the earlier description of Satan's raising of the fallen angels, and this description of Satan's participation in a "second creation and first salvation" (to quote D. C. Allen) is thematically enriched when interpreted in relation to the typological framework involving Noah and Christ.

Shortly after he is revived, Satan recognizes that the flood-like tempest in which he has been confined is beginning to subside. He lifts himself and travels "till on dry Land / He lights" (I.227–28). In the description of the Deluge in Book XI, Noah seeks out land on which the "foot may light" (line 858) until finally "dry ground appears" (line 861). When Satan stands upright on the shore to address the fallen angels, his arms are outstretched and spear upraised. The *orans* attitude here assumed is also the posture of Noah after the deliverance from the Flood. "With uplifted hands" (XI.863) Noah offers a prayer of thanksgiving for his participation in this "second creation and first salvation." Whereas Noah relates to God with "eyes devout" (XI.863), Satan's eyes convey "obdurate pride and steadfast hate" (I.59) and the resolve to pursue war. To arouse the fallen angels still "covering the Flood" (I. 312), Satan calls so loud "that all the hollow Deep / Of Hell resounded" (I.314–15). This act of re-creation and Deliverance enables the fallen angels to emerge from the waters of destruction. The gradual appearance of the hellish domain and the revival of the fallen angels—"up they sprung" (I.331)— develop ironic comparisons between Satan and Noah, with whom issuance, rebirth, and repopulation are continually associated in Books XI and XII. Many of the same words—"spring," "raise," "issue," and "proceed"—describe the actions of Noah and Satan.

Other images applied to Noah and Satan include those of light and the sun. After the Deluge, God's creation reappears under "the clear Sun" (XI.844), dispelling clouds and darkness, and an image of light is used to contrast Noah's goodness with the depravity of other men: he was "the only Son of light / In a dark Age" (XI.808–9). This image, of course, pertains to Christ, who is described throughout Milton's poetry and prose as the true bringer of light. Several scriptural texts provide the basis for this image, including the Old Testament prophecies (in Isaiah, Job, and the Psalms attributed to David) that look forward to the Harrowing of Hell. In Isa. 9:2, for instance, people walking in the darkness are described as they see a great light.

In describing Satan's relationship with the fallen angels, Milton uses similar images. In an environment of darkness, the fallen angels view Satan "above the rest" (I.589) and recognize that "his form had yet not lost / All her Original brightness" (I.591–92). Likened to "the sun new ris'n" or the sun dimmed by eclipse (I.594–99), Satan appeared "Dark'n'd so" to the fallen angels while he "shone / Above them all" (I.599–600). Admittedly, Milton is suggesting that Satan's downfall has resulted in a diminution of former brilliance. But this striking juxtaposition of light and darkness also enables Milton to highlight the special nature and fullness of Satan's depravity, the extent to which it is held up for the admiration and emulation of the fallen angels, and the manner by which it is visibly imparted to them while they are virtually re-created under his influence. Indeed, the paradoxical image of "Dark with excessive bright" (III.380) describes the godhead throughout *Paradise Lost*. These and other images are continually applied to Satan, Noah, and the Deity, especially the Son. The essential paradigm of descent and reascent, for instance, describes the immersion and emersion of Noah and the ark, but it pertains also to Satan's claim that the fallen angels, having suffered adversity and loss, will "re-ascend / Self-rais'd, and repossess their native seat" (I.633–34). Where there was darkness, Satan promises light; in place of *tristia*, he brings *gaudium*; for despair, he offers hope. What Satan falsely promises the fallen angels, Christ actually achieves for mankind by his humiliation and exaltation, his Death and Resurrection. In the Descent into Hell, Christ delivers and leads the souls from captivity and extends the offer of salvation to mankind generally. In *Paradise Lost* the Harrowing of Hell is suggested in the account of Noah as one who "preach'd / Conversion and Repentance, as to Souls / In Prison under Judgments imminent" (XI.723–25). This description, which echoes I Pet. 3:19 and II Pet. 2:4, where Noah is described as the "preacher of justice," suggests Christ's preaching (as the Church Fathers explain) to those in Hell whom he will shortly liberate and who will be justified in him. The ironic similarity to Satan's preaching in the hellish underworld is striking, for he too professes to be a deliverer. For him, God is the tyrant, and Satan continues to preach the justice of continuing the war of liberation. Like Noah and especially the Son, who actually experienced the waters of death in order to begin the world anew, Satan provides his followers with the pattern and norm for heroism, whereby humiliation is followed by exaltation, descent by ascent, and patience by victory. For this pattern and norm, he, like Christ, is the teacher, the witness, and the judge. Both, in fact, may be described as Saint Paul describes Christ (Col. 1:18): the "first born of the dead."

Like that of Noah, the conduct of Moses prefigures "Mankind's deliverance" (XII.235), and Moses himself "in figure bears, to introduce / One greater" (lines 241–42). The resemblances between Noah and Moses are well-defined, including the experience of immersion and emersion, which traditionally signifies death to sinners and regeneration to believers. Wood as an image of salvation (*lignum vitae*) is another important resemblance, with Noah's ark having been figuratively transformed into Moses' rod, both of which foreshadow Christ's cross as an instrument of deliverance. Then, too, the *orans* posture with arms outstretched is another crucial resemblance, because Noah and Moses are often visualized in this attitude in order to prefigure Christ outstretched on the cross, a posture signifying patient self-sacrifice and loving embrace. Biblical commentary often stresses the sacrifice of Noah, who, "fearless of reproach and scorn" (XI.811), continued to preach to sinners and endured the darkness and confinement in the ark, prefiguring the entombment of Christ and the Descent into Hell. Similarly, Moses' patience during the many adversities in the wilderness gave the example to the Israelites. The family of Noah in the ark and the followers of Moses are traditionally interpreted as prefigurations of the Visible Church, which Milton in *De Doctrina Christiana* defines as "the assembly of those who are called" (XVI:218–19). When Satan "call'd so loud, that all the hollow Deep / Of Hell resounded" (I.314–15), he too is virtually creating his church. Assembled in the temple of Pandemonium, the fallen angels have been called to view Satan as their prophet, priest, and king. As Milton emphasizes in *De Doctrina Christiana*, these are the roles that Christ performs in his state of humiliation, the very same roles so aptly prefigured by the life and actions of Moses. Stripped of the accouterments of divinity, Christ undertakes the ministry of Redemption and performs his prophetic, sacerdotal, and regal offices. When Satan assumes these offices, however, he proudly seeks to invest himself with the glory of the divinity that Christ has voluntarily forsaken.

Scripture characterizes the Exodus from Egypt as a military march with Moses as general, for whom the upraised staff is the principal sign of authority. In Exod. 13:18 the Israelites leave Egypt in battle array. The preparation for the march, the march itself, and the travel through the wilderness afterwards are described as a military struggle. Protective armor, weapons, the numbering of troops, the use of banners and military standards, and the assembling of each tribe under its own standard are characteristically recounted in Scripture and exegetical commentaries and visualized in iconography. Precisely the same images recur in Books I and II of *Paradise Lost*, when the fallen angels regroup under Satan's generalship, march at his direction, are numbered under his view, and rally to his uplifted staff—"Their surest signal" (I.278). In the Dura Synagogue the Israelites in military array at the Exodus are depicted traveling through an opened doorway (with paneled doors) that stand in the center and at the front face of a crenellated wall that represents Egypt.[5] In Patristic commentary on the Exodus, Egypt typically represents Hell, and the doors through which Moses leads the Israelites can indeed be interpreted as the portals of Hell that Christ is shown to be unlocking or pushing down in literary, dramatic, and iconographic versions of the Descent into Hell.

As the events of the Paschal triumph are traditionally interpreted and visualized, Christ often appears as the victorious warrior-king. In the *Biblia Pauperum*, in books of hours, illustrated Bibles, and missals, depictions of the Descent into Hell and the Resurrection show Christ with the victory cross. With its long upright beam and short transverse beam, the victory cross resembles a lance or spear sometimes thrust by Christ into the dragon opposing him. In other words the cross of suffering borne patiently has been transformed into the *crux invicta*, one of the weapons (*arma Christi*) that Christ employs against Satan. The victory cross, with banner or pennon, becomes the sign or standard around which mankind will rally, under which they will be numbered, and by which they will be liberated. Literature as seemingly diverse, yet fundamentally similar, as Fortunatus' sixth-century Passiontide hymn *Vexilla regis prodeunt* and the Anglo-Saxon *Dream of the Rood* summarize much of what the Church Fathers say and most of what iconography depicts about the victory cross. The "banners of the king go forward" (as the title of Fortunatus' hymn suggests), and this context of military struggle and the promise of victory may be used to interpret the demonic counterpart of the victory cross—namely, Satan's "uplifted Spear" (I.347), "mighty Standard" (I.533), and "glittering Staff" (I.535) by which the fallen angels hope to be liberated.

To commemorate, celebrate, and reenact the Paschal victory, mankind participates in the sacrament of baptism, which assimilates much of the Paschal symbolism into its rite and ritual. Twice in Book XII of *Paradise Lost*, Milton mentions baptism; and, like the Petrine and Pauline proof-texts that he cites in his discussion of baptism in *De Doctrina Christiana*, Milton asserts that "the sign / Of washing" enables mankind to be "in mind prepar'd, if so befall, / For death, like that which the redeemer di'd" (lines 442–45). Tertullian, among others, in his treatise *De Baptismo* enumerates the following symbols of baptism: the Creation of the world when the Spirit of God moved over the Deep, the Deluge of Noah, the Red Sea passage, and certain other events from the Old Testament.[6] Much of this symbolism is conveyed by the celebrant at baptism. The pool or font in which the baptism is performed is sometimes called the "laver of regeneration" (by Saint John Chrysostom, Saint Gregory of Nyssa, and Saint Augustine); and the neophytes, who reenact the Old Testament prefigurations of baptism, as well as the Death and Resurrection of Christ, walk through the pool until they are immersed and continue forward until they emerge. Often in the ritual in the early Christian Church, the celebrant, with arms outstretched and cross uplifted, would lead them. Certainly as the neophytes emerged, the celebrant in the *orans* posture would be facing them. He would, moreover, be well illuminated because the neophytes would be greeted by the appearance of light after temporary darkness. The resemblances between this ceremony and Satan's relationship with the fallen angels at the burning lake are clear-cut. Other resemblances include, for example, the celebrant's prayer at baptism that the Holy Ghost will impregnate—the usual word is "fecundate"—the waters, so that another creation will occur. Satan's brooding over the waters with his arms and wings outstretched is a parody of this act of divine insemination, the act that is called for in the baptismal ritual. The neophytes, as they emerge, are the issuance of a new creation—they are "raised" and they "proceed." The pool becomes the "maternal womb," as it is sometimes called in the baptismal liturgy; and Satan's impregnation of the waters at the burning lake and the issuance and procession of the fallen angels may be seen in the context of baptismal regeneration.

From the interrelated perspectives developed in this presentation, Satan in Books I and II of *Paradise Lost* is variously characterized as the demonic counterpart of Noah and Moses, of the suffering and triumphant Christ, and of a celebrant enacting the baptismal rite and ceremony. In this paper these comparisons were only suggested, not fully delineated; nor were they even suggested in relation to other books of *Paradise Lost*. Central to an understanding of all the comparisons is the virtue patience and the triumph that ensues from suffering heroically. Milton's concept of heroism and the virtue patience as an essential part of it loom large in the characterization of Satan. Not that Satan is Milton's hero. On the contrary, what is evident in these comparisons is Milton's technique of defining the image in relation to the idol, the authentic in relation to the counterfeit, and the hero in relation to the pseudo-hero. It is a technique that suggests definition by logical contraries, a technique that Milton as a logician did know. As importantly, it is a technique that enables Milton to develop his sense of irony to the fullest. The means and manner by which Satan seeks to continue his war against the godhead are likened to the very means and manner by which his defeat will be achieved. In pursuing victory, Satan is made to enact his own defeat, a defeat prefigured by the Old Testament activities of Noah and Moses, accomplished in the New Dispensation by Christ's Death and Resurrection, and celebrated by mankind's participation in the rite of baptism—a defeat that will become final at the Second Coming.

NOTES

1. *The Works of John Milton*, ed. F. A. Patterson et al. (New York: Columbia University Press, 1938), XVIII:240–41. Milton's prose is quoted from this edition, with volume and page numbers cited parenthetically.

2. See Burton O. Kurth, *Milton and Christian Heroism* (Berkeley: University of California Press, 1959), esp. pp. 107–34; John M. Steadman, "The 'Suffering Servant' and Milton's Heroic Norm," *HTR* 54 (1961):29–43; idem, *Milton and the Renaissance Hero* (Oxford: Clarendon Press, 1967), esp. pp. 30–43.

3. Milton's poetry is quoted from *John Milton: Complete Poems and Major Prose*, ed. Merritt Y. Hughes (New York: Odyssey Press, 1957).

4. *The Legend of Noah: Renaissance Rationalism in Art, Science, and Letters* (Urbana: University of Illinois Press, 1949), pp. 154, 176 respectively.

5. Erwin R. Goodenough, *Jewish Symbols in the Greco-Roman Period* (New York: Pantheon Books, 1964), vol. X (part II), chap. 16.

6. In *Baptism: Ancient Liturgies and Patristic Texts*, ed. André Hamman (New York: Alba House, 1967), pp. 30–49. See pp. 7–26 for a concise discussion of baptismal liturgies in the early Latin and Greek Church.